Commercial Insurance

Commercial Insurance

Bernard L. Webb, CPCU, FCAS, MAAA
Professor Emeritus of Actuarial Science and Insurance
Georgia State University

Arthur L. Flitner, CPCU, ARM, AIC
Senior Director of Curriculum Design
Insurance Institute of America

Jerome Trupin, CPCU, CLU, ChFC
Partner
Trupin Insurance Services

Third Edition • 1996

Insurance Institute of America
720 Providence Road, Malvern, Pennsylvania 19355-0770

SCHAUMBURG TOWNSHIP DISTRICT LIBRARY
32 WEST LIBRARY LANE
SCHAUMBURG, ILLINOIS 60194

© 1996

Insurance Institute of America

*All rights reserved. This book or any
part thereof may not be reproduced without
the written permission of the publisher.*

Third Edition • July 1996

Library of Congress Catalog Number 96-75990

International Standard Book Number 0-89462-098-3

 Printed in the United States of America on recycled paper

Foreword

The American Institute for Chartered Property Casualty Underwriters, the Insurance Institute of America, and the Insurance Institute for Applied Ethics are independent, nonprofit, educational organizations serving the needs of the property and liability insurance business. The Institutes develop a wide range of programs—curricula, study materials, and examinations—in response to the educational requirements of various elements of the business.

The American Institute confers the Chartered Property Casualty Underwriter (CPCU®) professional designation on those who meet the Institute's experience, ethics, and examination requirements.

The Insurance Institute of America offers associate designations and certificate programs in the following technical and managerial disciplines:

Accredited Adviser in Insurance (AAI®)
Associate in Claims (AIC)
Associate in Underwriting (AU)
Associate in Risk Management (ARM)
Associate in Loss Control Management (ALCM®)
Associate in Premium Auditing (APA®)
Associate in Management (AIM)
Associate in Research and Planning (ARP®)
Associate in Insurance Accounting and Finance (AIAF)
Associate in Automation Management (AAM®)
Associate in Marine Insurance Management (AMIM®)
Associate in Reinsurance (ARe)
Associate in Fidelity and Surety Bonding (AFSB)
Associate in Personal Insurance (API)
Associate in Insurance Services (AIS)
Associate in Surplus Lines Insurance (ASLI)
Certificate in General Insurance
Certificate in Insurance Regulation

Certificate in Supervisory Management
Certificate in Introduction to Underwriting
Certificate in Introduction to Claims
Certificate in Introduction to Property and Liability Insurance
Certificate in Business Writing

The Insurance Institute for Applied Ethics was established in 1995 to heighten awareness of the pervasiveness of ethical decision making in insurance and to explore ways to raise the level of ethical behavior among parties to the insurance contract. The Ethics Institute sponsors seminars and workshops on the role of ethics in the insurance transaction. It also identifies and funds practical research projects on ethics-related topics and publishes the findings. In addition, it produces booklets, newsletters, and videotapes on ethics issues.

The Institutes began publishing textbooks in 1976 to help students meet the national examination standards. Since that time, we have produced more than ninety individual textbook volumes. Despite the vast differences in the subjects and purposes of these volumes, they all have much in common. First, each book is specifically designed to increase knowledge and develop skills that can improve job performance and help students achieve the educational objectives of the course for which it is assigned. Second, all of the manuscripts of our texts are widely reviewed before publication, by both insurance business practitioners and members of the academic community. In addition, all of our texts and course guides reflect the work of Institute staff members. These writing or editing duties are seen as an integral part of their professional responsibilities, and no one earns a royalty based on the sale of our texts. We have proceeded in this way to avoid even the appearance of any conflict of interests. Finally, the revisions of our texts often incorporate improvements suggested by students and course leaders.

We welcome criticisms of and suggestions for improving our publications. It is only with such constructive comments that we can hope to improve the quality of our study materials. Please direct any comments you may have on this text to the Curriculum Department of the Institutes.

Norman A. Baglini, Ph.D., CPCU, CLU
President and Chief Executive Officer

Preface

This text was prepared as one of three for the Program in General Insurance of the Insurance Institute of America (IIA). Numerically it represents the third of the three texts. The first text covers principles of property and liability insurance. The second text addresses personal insurance coverages. This text discusses commercial property and liability insurance coverages. It is designed to be used in conjunction with the course guide for INS 23 in preparation for the INS 23 examination. Successful completion of the INS 21, INS 22, and INS 23 examinations earns the IIA Certificate in General Insurance.

Each major commercial insurance coverage addressed by the text is treated in the same logical manner. First, the exposures to loss that create the need for the coverage are considered. Then the relevant commercial insurance coverage is discussed. The text also provides brief explanations of rating for most of the coverages presented.

Many individuals in a variety of jobs within the insurance business have reviewed the manuscript for this edition of the text to verify that the material was correct, complete, and at an appropriate level for INS studies. Although the following list names only the reviewers who participated in the latest edition, we are equally grateful to those who contributed to the first two editions of *Commercial Insurance*.

Patricia M. Arnold, CPCU, ALCM
Staff Associate—Underwriting
State Farm Insurance Companies

Howard E. Candage, CPCU, AMIM, AAI
Regional Marketing Manager
Hanover of Maine

Barbara P. Cobb, CPCU, CPIW
Henderson & Phillips Insurance

Richard Cohen, CPCU, ARM, CIC
Director, Regulatory and External Affairs Division
National Council on Compensation Insurance

Lowery D. Finley III, CPCU, AAI, PFP
Hilb, Rogal and Hamilton Company of Tidewater

Stephen Horn II, CPCU, ARM, AAI
Senior Vice President
Calco Insurance Brokers & Agents, Inc.

Nanette R. Jennings, CPCU
Underwriter
USAA

Larry L. Klein, CPCU, AIM, AAI
Director
Price Waterhouse, L.L.P.

Melissa McBratney, CPCU, GCA
Assistant Vice President—Regional Operations
Farmers Insurance Group

James J. Markham, J.D., CPCU, AIC, AIAF
Senior Vice President
Insurance Institute of America

Kevin M. Quinley, CPCU, ARM, AIC, AIM
Senior Vice President—Risk Services
Hamilton Resources Corporation

Mary Lou Speckheuer, CPCU, AMIM, CPIW
Principal
Richard M. Marshall & Co.

The following employees of Insurance Services Office, Inc., reviewed the chapters of the manuscript dealing with lines of insurance filed by ISO. Their efforts were coordinated by Paul Edgcomb, CPCU, Assistant Vice President—Customer Service, of ISO.

Christina Cronin, CPCU
Senior Analyst—Commercial Property and Package

Lisa Eimbinder, CPCU
Assistant Manager—Commercial Property and Package

Rosemarie Friend, CPCU
Specialist—Commercial Casualty Division

Gary Grasmann
Manager—General Liability

Loretta F. Newman, CPCU
Manager—Commercial Property and Package

Maurice E. Southwell, CPCU, CLU, ChFC, ARM, AMIM, AU
Manager—Commercial Property and Package

We are also grateful to the members of the Institute's Publications Department for their work in editing the manuscript and typesetting the text. We would especially like to recognize Jackie Yost Limongelli, who ably served as copy editor.

We also thank Estelle Collette of the Institute's Curriculum Department, who handled the word processing for several chapters of the manuscript and managed the correspondence with the manuscript reviewers.

Finally, we thank Connie Luthardt, CPCU, AAI, AIM, AIS, CPIW, who is the INS program director. Connie reviewed all chapters of the manuscript and gave us many helpful suggestions during both the planning and execution of the revision.

The constructive comments of course leaders and students on the first two editions of the text were useful in planning this latest edition. We therefore invite you to help shape the next edition of the text by sending us your comments on the current edition. Please address your comments to the Curriculum Department of the Institutes.

Bernard L. Webb
Arthur L. Flitner
Jerome Trupin

Contributing Authors

The Insurance Institute of America and the authors acknowledge, with deep appreciation, the work of the following contributing authors:

Robert J. Gibbons, Ph.D., CPCU, CLU
Technical Advisor
Insurance Institutes of the Caribbean

Stephen Horn II, CPCU, ARM, AAI
Senior Vice President
Calco Insurance Brokers & Agents, Inc.

Anita W. Johnson, CPCU, CLU, ChFC
Director of Curriculum
Insurance Institute of America

W. Jeffrey Woodward, CPCU
Senior Research Analyst
International Risk Management Institute, Inc.

Contents

Chapter 1

Overview of Commercial Insurance

Just as individuals and families buy homeowners insurance and personal auto insurance, businesses and other organizations buy insurance to protect themselves against the adverse financial effects of property and liability losses. Insurance covering for-profit businesses and nonprofit organizations—such as educational, religious, or governmental entities—is called **commercial insurance**, in contrast with the personal insurance that individuals and families buy to cover their generally nonbusiness insurance needs.

The distinction between personal insurance and commercial insurance is fundamental to property and liability insurers. Some insurers provide only commercial insurance, and some provide only personal insurance. Many insurers provide both types of insurance, but typically they do so through separate personal and commercial divisions. In general, the property and liability insurance needs of businesses and other organizations are more complex than those of individuals and families. Accordingly, commercial insurance involves a far greater number of policy forms and endorsements than those used to provide personal insurance.

This chapter provides an overview of commercial insurance by examining the following topics:

- Insurance as a risk management technique
- Commercial lines of business
- Commercial insurance policies

1

Subsequent chapters of the text will focus on the various commercial insurance coverages introduced in this chapter.

Insurance as a Risk Management Technique

Insurance enables a person or an organization (called "the policyholder" or "the insured") to transfer the financial consequences of a loss to an insurer. The insurer, in turn, pays the policyholder for covered losses and distributes the costs of losses among all policyholders. Insurance is just one technique that organizations use as part of an overall process known as risk management. **Risk management** is the process of identifying, analyzing, and managing loss exposures in such a way that an organization can meet its objectives. A **loss exposure** is a possibility of loss. In other words, if an organization could suffer a particular loss, it is exposed to that type of loss. For example, buildings in the Midwest are exposed to tornado damage and thus are said to have a tornado loss exposure. Tornadoes do not occur in most West Coast states; therefore, buildings in those states do not have a tornado loss exposure.

The loss exposures to which commercial insurance responds include both property loss exposures and liability loss exposures.

- A **property loss exposure** is the possibility that a person or an organization will sustain a financial loss as the result of the damaging, destruction, taking, or loss of use of property in which that person or organization has a financial interest. The possibility of tornado damage, noted above, is an example of a property loss exposure.

- A **liability loss exposure** is the possibility that a person or an organization will sustain a financial loss as the result of a claim being made against that person or organization by someone seeking monetary damages or some other legal remedy. An example of a liability loss exposure is the possibility that a restaurant will be sued by one of its customers who has slipped and fallen because of a water spill on the restaurant's floor.

Property and liability loss exposures can be identified and treated through the **risk management process**. The risk management process consists of the following steps:

1. Identifying and analyzing loss exposures
2. Evaluating the various techniques for treating the loss exposures
3. Selecting the most effective technique or techniques

4. Implementing the selected techniques
5. Monitoring the program and making needed corrections or adjustments

Although this text is concerned primarily with insurance, insurance is only one of several risk management techniques, and it is almost always used in combination with other techniques. These noninsurance techniques include the following:

- **Avoidance**. Avoidance occurs when an organization avoids an identified loss exposure by choosing not to own a particular item of property or not to engage in a particular activity. For example, by not manufacturing a new product, a manufacturer can avoid the potential liability for injuries resulting from the new product.

- **Loss control**. Loss control includes any measure to prevent losses from occurring (such as storing gasoline in sealed, approved containers) or to reduce the size of losses that do occur (such as an automatic sprinkler system in a building).

- **Retention**. An organization that pays all or part of its own losses is said to retain or "self-insure" its losses. For example, a business might choose to self-insure certain exposures or to purchase large deductibles on its insurance policies. When an organization has the financial ability to absorb some or all of its own losses, retention may be less costly *in the long run* than buying insurance to cover the same losses.

- **Noninsurance transfer**. Noninsurance transfer occurs when an organization (such as a building owner) obtains the promise of a second, *noninsurance* organization (such as a remodeling contractor) to pay for certain losses that would otherwise fall on the first organization. Also known as hold harmless agreements or indemnity agreements, noninsurance transfers are commonly included in a wide variety of contracts, such as leases, construction contracts, and purchase agreements.

Lines of Business

Commercial insurance can be divided according to particular lines of business. A **line of business**, or simply a line, is an identifiable type of insurance. The divisions used to identify lines of business depend on the purpose for which the lines are being identified. For example, the lines of business listed in the "annual statement" form that insurers use to report financial data to state insurance regulators differ in some ways from the lines of business commonly referred to by insurance companies and practitioners in their everyday operations. The divisions used in this text, listed below, conform generally to those used by insurers in their everyday operations.

- Commercial property insurance
- Business income insurance
- Crime insurance
- Boiler and machinery insurance
- Inland marine and ocean marine insurance
- Commercial general liability insurance
- Commercial automobile insurance
- Businessowners insurance
- Farm insurance
- Workers compensation and employers liability insurance
- Surety bonds
- Miscellaneous coverages

Commercial Property Insurance

As a general term, **commercial property insurance** refers to any type of commercial insurance that covers loss to property. In this general sense, several of the lines of business listed above are commercial property insurance (as opposed to commercial liability insurance). In a narrower sense, the term "commercial property insurance" is used to describe insurance covering commercial buildings and their contents against loss caused by fire, windstorm, and other perils. Commercial property insurance (in its narrower meaning) provides little, if any, coverage for property while in transit or otherwise away from the insured location and omits most crime-related perils as well as steam boiler explosion and mechanical breakdown. Most references to commercial property insurance in this textbook pertain to the narrower concept of the commercial property line of business rather than to the broader concept of all insurance covering property loss exposures.

Business Income Insurance

When property is physically damaged, the owner suffers a financial loss equal to the reduction in the property's value. Damage to property can also result in lost income and increased expenses. Though sometimes called an "indirect" loss, the loss of income or the increased expenses needed to continue operations can have a devastating financial effect. **Business income insurance** provides organizations a way to protect against this possibility. Although generally included within the commercial property line, business income insurance is so different from insurance against physical loss to buildings and contents that it is treated separately in this text.

Crime Insurance

Commercial **crime insurance** covers property and perils that are not covered by most commercial property policies. For example, money and securities are generally excluded types of property, and employee dishonesty is almost always an excluded cause of loss in commercial property policies. Various commercial crime coverages are available to insure (1) money and securities against a wide range of perils (not limited to crime perils) and (2) property other than money and securities against various crime perils, such as employee dishonesty, burglary, robbery, theft, and extortion.

Boiler and Machinery Insurance

Boiler and machinery insurance is another type of insurance that fills a gap in commercial property policies. Steam boiler explosion, electrical injury (other than lightning), and mechanical breakdown are causes of loss that are typically excluded from commercial property policies. Boiler and machinery insurance can be used to cover damage to property resulting from these perils, as well as resulting business income losses. If, for example, a store lost business income because its air conditioning system suffered a mechanical breakdown during the hottest week of the summer, a properly arranged boiler and machinery policy would cover both the physical damage and the resulting loss of business income.

Inland and Ocean Marine Insurance

In most of the world except the United States, marine insurance principally means insurance on vessels and their cargoes. In the United States, **marine insurance** is divided into ocean marine and inland marine insurance. **Ocean marine insurance** conforms to the international meaning of marine insurance, whereas **inland marine insurance** includes a wide variety of risks that in the United States were first insured by marine underwriters. These risks include property in domestic transit, mobile equipment, buildings in the course of construction, property essential to transportation or communication (such as bridges, tunnels, and radio and television towers), and many other classes of property that typically involve an element of transportation.

Commercial General Liability Insurance

Every business, even one that has little or no *property* exposed to loss, faces the threat of claims and lawsuits for damages arising from its acts or omissions. The basic protection for this exposure is **commercial general liability insurance**. Commercial general liability insurance covers the loss exposures arising from an organization's premises and operations, its products, or its work. It also covers various other offenses that may give rise to claims or suits, such as libel, slander, false arrest, and invasion of privacy.

Commercial Automobile Insurance

Commercial property insurance does not cover physical damage to automobiles. Moreover, commercial general liability insurance excludes liability arising out of the ownership, maintenance, or use of automobiles in most circumstances. Both automobile physical damage insurance and automobile liability insurance are available under a **commercial automobile insurance** policy or in the commercial auto coverage part of a package policy. Various coverages can be added to an auto policy by endorsement, such as auto medical payments coverage and uninsured/underinsured motorists coverage. Commercial auto insurance also encompasses specialized forms for trucking firms and "garage businesses" such as auto dealers and repair shops.

Businessowners Insurance

The **businessowners policy** combines, in a simplified manner, most of the coverages, other than auto and workers compensation, needed by small and medium-sized businesses such as stores, offices, and apartment buildings. Smaller organizations can thus avoid the more complex structure of a policy containing many separate forms providing the various coverages described above. The businessowners policy consists basically of a property coverage form, a liability coverage form, and a common policy conditions form. Several optional coverages that are printed in the property coverage form can be activated by the insured's payment of an additional premium, and a limited number of other optional coverages can be added to the policy by endorsement.

Farm Insurance

Because farmers and ranchers usually live and work on their own land, they need a combination of personal insurance and commercial insurance. **Farm insurance** provides this blend of coverages. The personal insurance aspect is similar to a homeowners policy, covering the farmer's home and household property. The commercial insurance aspect is similar to commercial property and inland marine coverage, covering property used in farming operations, including livestock, mobile equipment and machinery, and farm structures such as barns and outbuildings. Farm insurance also covers liability arising out of either personal or farming activities.

Workers Compensation and Employers Liability Insurance

Workers compensation laws, which apply throughout the United States, obligate employers to pay specified medical, disability, rehabilitation, and death benefits for their employees' job-related injuries and diseases. The obligation to pay these benefits exists regardless of whether the employer was in any way at fault. In theory, employees are precluded from suing their employers for injuries or diseases covered by the applicable workers compensation law. However, in some cases employees are permitted to sue their employers for work-related accidents. **Workers compensation and employers liability insurance** provides two coverages: (1) coverage for benefits the insured employer is obligated to pay under workers compensation laws and (2) coverage for employee claims against the insured employer that are not covered by workers compensation laws.

Surety Bonds

In its simplest form, a **surety bond** is an agreement by one person (the surety) to answer for the failure of another person (the principal) to perform as he or she has promised. The surety is thus similar to a cosigner on a loan. If the surety is required to make any payments or perform any duties on behalf of the principal, the surety is entitled to reimbursement from the principal. In that respect, surety bonds differ from most insurance policies; under an insurance policy, the insurance company cannot require its own insured to reimburse it after it pays a covered claim. Most commercial surety bonds are provided by insurance companies, and surety bonding is regulated in the same manner as insurance. Thus, despite some basic differences from most insurance policies, surety bonds are considered to be a part of the insurance business.

Miscellaneous Coverages

Other property and liability insurance policies are available to supplement the more common policies described above. These coverages include, but are not limited to, the following:

- **Flood insurance policies**, which cover buildings and their contents against loss caused by flooding, mudslides, and related perils.

- **Professional liability policies**, which insure physicians, accountants, engineers, attorneys, insurance agents and brokers, and various other professionals against liability arising out of their professional acts or omissions.
- **Directors and officers liability policies**, which cover the directors and officers of a corporation against claims alleging damages resulting from wrongful acts of the directors or officers.
- **Employment practices liability policies**, which cover an employer against claims by employees alleging that they suffered damages as a result of the employer's discrimination, wrongful termination, sexual harassment, or various other employment-related offenses.
- **Umbrella and excess liability policies**, which provide amounts of insurance in addition to the limits provided by the insured's commercial general liability, auto liability, employers liability, and perhaps other primary liability coverages. For example, an organization might have limits of $1 million on its primary liability policies and an additional $10 million limit on its umbrella liability policy.

Although the coverages listed above have been grouped for the sake of convenience in this text, each of the above might be considered a separate line of business by a particular insurer.

Commercial Insurance Policies

This text will focus primarily on the policy forms developed by Insurance Services Office (ISO), an advisory organization serving insurers throughout the United States. Some insurers use similar policy forms developed by the American Association of Insurance Services (AAIS), an advisory organization similar to ISO. For some lines of business, neither ISO nor AAIS offers a standard form. Thus, any insurer wishing to underwrite one of those lines must develop its own policy forms. Even when a standard policy form exists, many insurers develop their own forms, usually to broaden the coverage and thereby gain a competitive advantage over other insurers.

A commercial insurance policy can be either a monoline policy or a package policy. A **monoline policy** includes only one line of business. A **package policy** includes two or more lines of business. In practice, most organizations have a package policy that provides most or all of their needed coverages. In addition to their package policies, many organizations also have one or more monoline policies from other insurers providing coverages that the package insurer either does not write or is unwilling to provide to the insured. For example, a doctor's office might have an insurance program that consists of the following policies:

1. A package policy covering the following lines:
   - Commercial property
   - Commercial crime
   - Commercial inland marine
   - Commercial general liability
2. A monoline workers compensation and employers liability policy
3. A monoline medical malpractice policy

Advantages of Packaging

Although it is often not possible to package all of an organization's coverages, packaging is used to the greatest extent possible because it has distinct advantages to insurers, insureds, and producers. (A producer may be an insurance agent, an insurance broker, or a sales employee of an insurance company.)

Advantages to Insurer

For the insurance company, one advantage of packaging is reduced administrative expenses. It costs the insurer less to underwrite and issue one package policy instead of two or more monoline policies for the same insured. Also, an insurer will increase its premium volume if it can write a package policy covering a number of exposures for an insured instead of writing one monoline policy. Package policies can also help insurers to mitigate severe loss exposures. If an insured has one particularly hazardous exposure, the higher likelihood of a loss resulting from that exposure can be offset to some degree by the insurer's obtaining a premium for other exposures of the insured that are less likely to result in loss.

Advantages to Insured

As explained above, packaging reduces insurer expenses. Because a significant part of an insurance premium must cover the insurer's expenses, a reduction in expenses can be translated into a reduction in policy premiums. Thus, the economy of issuing package policies instead of monoline policies benefits the insured as well as the insurance company.

Another advantage of packaging to insureds is convenience. The insured with a package policy has fewer policies to buy and maintain. Packaging also reduces the chance of delay in loss settlement resulting from disputes between different insurers. For example, losses involving the loading of automobiles sometimes fall in a "gray area" between auto liability and general liability. If one insurer provides both coverages, payment of a claim will not be delayed as it might be if each coverage were written by a separate insurer and each insurer felt the claim was covered under the other's policy.

Advantages to Producer

Packaging is advantageous to producers for several reasons. First, the availability of package policies facilitates "account selling," that is, obtaining a customer's entire account instead of only part of it. Second, some packages are more easily sold and rated than separate monoline policies. Thus, packaging allows the producer to provide quotes more quickly for prospective customers, increases the producer's efficiency, and reduces the producer's expenses. Also, some insurers may offer financial incentives to producers to sell packages, such as higher commissions on package policies than on monoline policies.

ISO Commercial Package Policy Program

Under the rules and forms developed by ISO and used by its member insurance companies, a **commercial package policy (CPP)** includes the following components:

- Common policy declarations
- Common policy conditions
- Two or more coverage parts

These three components are described in more detail below and are illustrated in Exhibit 1-1.

Common Policy Declarations

The **common policy declarations** (often called the common "dec" page) are printed on one or more pages and are usually located at the front of the policy. They show the following information:

- Policy number
- Names of the insurance company and the producer
- Name, address, and business description of the named insured
- Effective date and expiration date of the policy
- Premium for each coverage part included in the policy
- Total premium

The common policy declarations page also includes a general statement, known as the "in consideration" clause. In this clause, the insurance company agrees with the named insured to provide the insurance as stated in the policy in return for the payment of premium and subject to all the terms of the policy.

Exhibit 1-1
Components of the Commercial Package Policy (CPP)

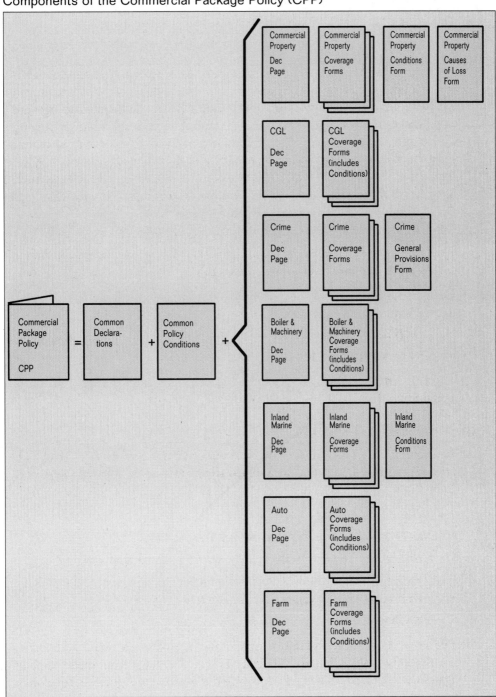

Common Policy Conditions

The **common policy conditions** are usually printed on a separate form that is attached to the policy. The form contains six conditions that apply to all coverage parts in the policy unless a particular coverage part states otherwise. This approach avoids the need to repeat the common policy conditions in each coverage part. The six conditions in the form are titled as follows:

- Cancellation
- Changes
- Examination of your books and records
- Inspections and surveys
- Premiums
- Transfer of your rights and duties under this policy

Cancellation

The insured may cancel the policy at any time by mailing or delivering written notice of cancellation to the insurance company. If two or more insureds are listed in the declarations, only the one listed first (called the **first named insured**) can request cancellation.

The insurance company can cancel the policy by mailing or delivering written notice of cancellation to the first named insured. In order to provide reasonable time for the insured to obtain other insurance, the insurance company is required to give advance notice of cancellation. Notice of cancellation must be mailed or delivered to the insured (1) at least ten days before the date of cancellation if the cancellation is for nonpayment of premium or (2) at least thirty days before the date of cancellation for any other reason.

If the notice of cancellation is mailed, the insurance company is not required to prove that the insured actually received the notice. It is required to prove only that the notice was mailed to the first named insured at the mailing address shown on the policy.

If the cancellation results in a return premium, the refund will be sent to the first named insured. In effect, the first named insured is designated as the agent who can act on behalf of all other insureds for all transactions related to cancellation of the policy.

In almost every state the cancellation provision is superseded by state law, in which case an endorsement is added to the policy. That endorsement modifies the cancellation provisions to conform with the applicable law. The state laws commonly address permissible reasons for cancellation and the advance notification period.

Changes

The common policy conditions include a clause concerning changes in the policy. This clause states that the policy constitutes the entire contract between the parties. The policy can be changed only by a written endorsement issued by the insurance company. Such changes may be made, with the insurance company's consent, upon the request of the first named insured. Only the first named insured has the authority to request policy changes, and the insurance company is authorized to make changes upon the request of the first named insured without specific permission of any other insured.

Examination of Books and Records

The insurance company reserves the right to examine and audit the insured's books and records related to the policy at any time during the policy period and for up to three years after the termination of the policy. This provision is included because many commercial insurance policies are issued with estimated premiums. The final premium is determined after the policy expires, based on reported values of the insured property, the amount of the insured's sales or payrolls, or some other variable premium base.

The insured is required to report the final figures to the insurance company, and the insurance company may accept the insured's reports without verification. However, this provision permits the insurance company to make an on-site verification as it deems necessary. The insurer's rights under this provision may also be exercised during the loss adjustment process.

Inspections and Surveys

The insurance company has the right to inspect the insured's premises and operations at any reasonable time during the policy period. The inspections may be made by the insurer's own personnel or by a rating bureau, service bureau, or other organization acting on behalf of the insurer. Such inspections are important in determining the insurability of the insured's property and operations and in setting proper insurance rates.

The insurance company *may* inform the insured of the results of such inspections and *may* recommend changes. However, it does not have a duty to do either.

The inspections and surveys provision makes it clear that the insurer (1) does not make safety inspections, (2) does not guarantee that conditions are safe or healthful, and (3) does not guarantee that the insured is in compliance with safety or health regulations. These disclaimer clauses have been included in the policy in an effort to protect the insurance company against suits (1) by persons who allege that they were injured as a result of the insurer's failure to detect a hazardous condition or (2) by the insured alleging that the insurer failed to detect a violation of laws or regulations, with a resulting fine or other penalty against the insured. Several such suits against insurers have occurred in recent years.

Premiums

The first named insured is responsible for paying the premium under the policy. Also, as previously mentioned, the insurer must pay any return premium under the policy to the first named insured.

Transfer of Rights and Duties Under the Policy

The insured cannot transfer any rights or duties under the policy to any other person or organization without the written consent of the insurance company. For example, if the insured sells the property covered by the policy, the coverage cannot be transferred to the new owner of the property without the written consent of the insurer. Such a transfer of coverage is generally referred to as an *assignment* of the policy, but that terminology is not used in the common policy conditions.

The transfer of rights and duties condition also provides specifically for the automatic transfer of coverage upon the death of an individual named insured. Upon death, the insured's rights and duties under the policy are automatically transferred to the insured's legal representatives, or, if the insured's legal representatives have not yet been appointed, to any person having proper temporary custody of the insured property.

Coverage Parts

A **coverage part** consists of the following components:

- A declarations page that pertains only to that coverage part
- One or more coverage forms, which contain insuring agreements, exclusions, and other policy provisions
- Applicable endorsements, which modify the terms of the coverage form(s) to fit the needs of the particular insured
- A conditions form containing general provisions that could apply to any of the coverage forms included in the coverage part

The coverage parts that may be used in an ISO commercial package policy correspond generally to the lines of business discussed earlier in this chapter and include the following:

- Commercial property

- Commercial crime
- Boiler and machinery
- Commercial inland marine
- Commercial general liability
- Commercial auto
- Farm

These coverage parts and their components will be discussed in subsequent chapters of this text. Some insurers add other, non-ISO coverage parts to their commercial package policies.

Package Modification Factors

An important element of the commercial package policy (CPP) program is the package discount the insured may receive. The premium for a CPP is determined using the same rules that would apply if each coverage part were being issued as a monoline policy. If both property and liability coverages are provided in the CPP, the application of **package modification factors** often provides a premium discount for the insured. This discount is justified by the various advantages (previously discussed) to the insurer of issuing a package policy rather than a monoline policy or several monoline policies for an insured.

The package discount is determined by applying the appropriate package modification factors to the premiums for the various coverage parts included in the policy. The package modification factors reflect the type of business (apartment, office, mercantile, and so forth), the particular coverage part being rated, and other eligibility requirements. A package modification factor of .75, for example, means that the premium for that coverage part will be three-fourths of the premium that would apply if the coverage part were issued in a monoline policy. The factors vary from state to state and from insurer to insurer.

Summary

The subject of this text is commercial insurance, which is property and liability insurance for businesses and other organizations such as schools and churches. Commercial insurance is one of several techniques used in risk management, which is the process of identifying, analyzing, and managing loss exposures so that an organization can meet its objectives. Other risk management techniques, often used in combination with insurance, include avoidance, loss control, retention, and noninsurance transfer.

Commercial insurance is divided into several lines of business, or distinct coverages. The material in this text is organized along essentially the same divisions as those used by insurers and insurance practitioners. These divisions include commercial property, business income, commercial crime, boiler and machinery, inland and ocean marine, commercial general liability, commercial auto, businessowners, farm, workers compensation and employers liability, surety bonds, and miscellaneous coverages.

Commercial insurance is often provided in a package policy, which is a policy that covers two or more lines of business. Package policies are widely used because they provide distinct advantages of cost and convenience to insurers, policyholders, and producers. In some cases, a policyholder may need to obtain additional coverages under monoline policies. A monoline policy is a policy that provides only one line of coverage, such as a workers compensation and employers liability policy.

Under the commercial package policy (CPP) program of Insurance Services Office (ISO), a package policy consists of common policy declarations, common policy conditions, and two or more coverage parts.

- The common policy declarations page contains essential information about the policyholder and the coverages being provided.

- The common policy conditions form contains six basic conditions that apply to all coverage parts included in the policy.

- Each coverage part consists of a declarations page for that coverage part, one or more coverage forms, and, for some coverage parts, a special conditions form.

The various coverage parts that can be included in a CPP—especially the coverage forms that spell out the insuring provisions of each coverage part—are the main subjects of several chapters in this text. Some insurers add additional, non-ISO coverage parts to their package policies.

The premium for a CPP is often lower than if the same coverages in the CPP were issued in separate monoline policies. This premium reduction results because some coverage parts in a CPP qualify for a discount based on the various advantages to an insurer of issuing a package policy rather than a monoline policy or policies. The discount is determined by multiplying the monoline premium by a package modification factor (such as .90). Package modification factors vary by state and by insurer.

Chapter 2

Commercial Property Insurance

Whether it is the office furniture, fixtures, equipment, records, and supplies of a small insurance agency or the complex machinery of an automated computer chip manufacturer, all commercial enterprises use at least some tangible property. For almost all of them, property insurance is a necessity.

Even those businesses that feel they could absorb any loss or damage to their property without carrying insurance are often required to carry property insurance when they want to obtain financing. Financial institutions that lend money based on a security interest in property want to be sure that the buyer will be able to repay the loan if the property is destroyed. Therefore, insurance coverage naming the lender as a loss payee is an almost universal requirement for mortgages and many other types of loans. It is hard to envision the construction and financing of our country's homes, offices, factories, and shopping malls without the availability of property insurance.

Many of the most basic property coverages an organization needs are commonly provided under the **commercial property coverage part** of Insurance Services Office (ISO) or under similar forms developed by the American Association of Insurance Services (AAIS). The commercial property coverage part can be issued either as a monoline policy or as part of a package policy. It is used to insure physical damage to buildings and their contents—the major property exposure for most organizations. Commercial property insurance also includes forms for insuring loss of business income resulting from physical damage to buildings and contents, an exposure that will be examined in more detail in Chapter 4.

This text focuses on the ISO commercial property coverage part. The various components of this coverage part are briefly introduced below and then described in more detail in this chapter and the two chapters that follow.

Overview of the Commercial Property Coverage Part

The commercial property coverage part consists of the following documents:

1. Commercial property declarations
2. One or more commercial property coverage forms
3. One or more causes-of-loss forms
4. Commercial property conditions form
5. Any applicable endorsements

Commercial Property Declarations

The **commercial property declarations page** contains the following information pertaining specifically to property insurance:

1. A description of the property insured
2. The kinds and amounts of coverage provided and the covered causes of loss (basic, broad, or special)
3. A list of mortgagees, if any
4. The deductible amount
5. A list of the property coverage forms and endorsements attached to the policy
6. The applicable coinsurance percentage(s)
7. Any optional coverages

Supplemental declarations can be added, as needed, on a separate sheet of paper. For example, if an insured such as a fast-food franchise had too many locations to show on the declarations page, a supplemental schedule could be added to show all locations. Exhibit 2-1 shows a specimen declarations page for a commercial property coverage part.

Exhibit 2-1
Commercial Property Declarations Page

COMMERCIAL PROPERTY COVERAGE PART
DECLARATIONS PAGE

POLICY NO. SP 0001   **EFFECTIVE DATE** 10/1/96   ☒ **"X" IF SUPPLEMENTAL DECLARATIONS IS ATTACHED**

NAMED INSURED

AMR Corporation

DESCRIPTION OF PREMISES

PREM NO	BLDG NO	LOCATION, CONSTRUCTION AND OCCUPANCY
001	001	2000 Industrial Highway, Workingtown, PA 19000
		Joisted Masonry
		Storm Door Manufacturing

COVERAGES PROVIDED INSURANCE AT THE DESCRIBED PREMISES APPLIES ONLY FOR COVERAGES FOR WHICH A LIMIT OF INSURANCE IS SHOWN

PREM NO	BLDG NO	COVERAGE	LIMIT OF INSURANCE	COVERED CAUSES OF LOSS	COINSURANCE*	RATES
001	001	Building	600,000	Special	80%	(See Schedule)
		Your Business Personal Prop.	1,120,000	Special	80%	
		Personal Prop. of Others	50,000	Special	80%	
		Business Income w/o				
		Extra Expense	680,000	Special	80%	

*IF EXTRA EXPENSE COVERAGE LIMITS ON LOSS PAYMENT

OPTIONAL COVERAGES APPLICABLE ONLY WHEN ENTRIES ARE MADE IN THE SCHEDULE BELOW

PREM NO	BLDG NO	AGREED VALUE EXPIRATION DATE	COVERAGE	AMOUNT	REPLACEMENT COST (X) BUILDING	PERSONAL PROPERTY	INCLUDING STOCK
001	001				X		

		INFLATION GUARD (PERCENTAGE) BUILDING	PERSONAL PROPERTY	*MONTHLY LIMIT OF INDEMNITY (FRACTION)	*MAXIMUM PERIOD OF INDEMNITY (X)	*EXTENDED PERIOD OF INDEMNITY (DAYS)
		3%	3%			

*APPLIES TO BUSINESS INCOME ONLY

MORTGAGE HOLDERS

PREM NO	BLDG NO	MORTGAGE HOLDER NAME AND MAILING ADDRESS
001	001	Workingtown Savings and Loan Assn.
		400 Main Street
		Workingtown, PA 19001

DEDUCTIBLE

$1,000

FORMS APPLICABLE

CP 00 10, CP 00 32, CP 00 90, CP 10 30

Commercial Property Coverage Forms

The ISO commercial package policy program includes several different commercial property coverage forms. Each **commercial property coverage form** contains an insuring agreement, describes the property covered and not covered, sets forth the additional coverages and coverage extensions, and includes provisions and definitions that apply only to that coverage form. Commercial property coverage forms do not list the causes of loss for which the described property is covered. That function is performed by the causes-of-loss forms, discussed later.

This chapter describes the building and personal property coverage form, which can be used for most organizations. More specialized coverage forms for insuring buildings under construction, condominium association buildings, and the property of condominium commercial unit owners will be discussed in Chapter 3. Coverage forms for insuring the loss of business income (an exposure to be discussed later) will be examined in Chapter 4. Depending on the nature of the insured's loss exposures, more than one commercial property coverage form may be included in a commercial property coverage part.

Causes-of-Loss Forms

The **causes-of-loss forms** specify the perils covered by the commercial property coverage part. The three forms available—termed "basic," "broad," and "special"—allow the insured to select from a range of covered perils.

A commercial property coverage part may contain more than one causes-of-loss form. One causes-of-loss form (such as the special form) may apply to buildings, and another causes-of-loss form (such as the broad form) may apply to personal property. The commercial property declarations indicate which form applies to each type of property at each location.

The causes-of-loss forms will be examined in more detail in Chapter 3.

Commercial Property Conditions

The **commercial property conditions**, which are printed on a separate sheet, apply to all coverage forms included in a commercial property coverage part, unless a coverage form contains a condition to the contrary. Like the common policy conditions, the commercial property conditions eliminate the need to repeat these conditions in each coverage form. The commercial property conditions will be described in more detail in Chapter 3.

Endorsements

Many endorsements are available to tailor commercial property coverage to meet the specialized needs of particular insureds. Some of these endorsements are noted in the sections that follow.

Building and Personal Property Coverage Form

The **building and personal property coverage form (BPP)** is the most commonly used commercial property coverage form. It includes the nine sections listed below and is designed to provide coverage for physical damage to buildings and personal property used for business purposes. "Personal property" is used in its legal sense to mean any property other than "real property" such as land, buildings, and other property attached to land.

- Covered property
- Property not covered
- Additional coverages
- Coverage extensions
- Limits of insurance
- Deductible
- Loss conditions
- Additional conditions
- Optional coverages

Covered Property

The property that can be covered by the BPP consists of the following categories:

1. Buildings
2. Business personal property of the insured
3. Personal property of others in the custody of the insured

Coverage can be provided on any combination of these categories. The insured's selection of coverages is indicated on the commercial property declarations page by entering a limit of insurance for each chosen category of covered property.

An example of the entries on a declarations page is shown in Exhibit 2-1. If there is no entry for one of the categories of covered property (for example, "Building"), then no coverage applies to that category even if the insured owns property fitting that category.

Covered property is insured against direct loss or damage at the described premises caused by a covered cause of loss. Covered causes of loss are determined in the separate causes-of-loss forms.

Building

The policy covers buildings or structures listed and described in the declarations. The definition of **building** also includes the following property:

1. Completed additions to covered buildings
2. Fixtures including outdoor fixtures
3. Permanently installed machinery and equipment
4. Personal property owned by the insured and used to maintain or service the building or its premises (for example, fire extinguishing equipment, outdoor furniture, floor coverings, and equipment for refrigeration, ventilation, cooking, dishwashing, or laundering)

In addition, if they are not otherwise insured, the building description covers additions, alterations, or repairs in progress, including materials, equipment, and supplies used in connection therewith. However, such materials, equipment, and supplies are covered only if they are located within 100 feet of the premises.

Fixtures are items attached to a building or to the land. Outdoor fixtures would include items outside the building but attached to the land, such as light poles and flagpoles. The term "fixtures" is broad enough to include fences and outdoor signs, but these items are specifically excluded from coverage for reasons discussed below under "Property Not Covered."

Business Personal Property of the Insured

"**Your business personal property**" covers personal property owned by the insured and used in the insured's business in or on the described building or in the open (or in a vehicle) within 100 feet of the premises. It includes furniture and fixtures, machinery and equipment, stock, and other similar personal property except those items excluded under the property not covered section. The form defines *stock* as "merchandise held in storage or for sale, raw materials and in-process or finished goods, including supplies used in their packing or shipping." Business personal property of the insured also includes labor, materials, or services furnished by the insured on personal property of others.

The insured's interest in improvements and betterments is also insured as business personal property, even though improvements and betterments are actually a part of the building. **Improvements and betterments** are alterations or additions made to the building at the expense of an insured who does not own the building and who cannot legally remove them. For example, a doctor who rents office space in a commercial building might install built-in bookcases that could not be removed when the lease is terminated. This tenant insured could insure the bookcases as improvements and betterments.

The business personal property item also includes leased personal property for which the named insured has a contractual responsibility to procure coverage. An example of such property is phone or computer equipment leased by the insured under an agreement requiring the insured to purchase insurance on them.

Personal Property of Others

This coverage is designed to protect the insured against loss or damage to the **personal property of others** while such property is in the custody of the insured. It is intended for businesses (generally referred to as "bailees") that have customers' property in their custody, such as lawn mower repair shops and furniture reupholstery shops. The BPP covers such property only while it is (1) in the insured's care, custody, or control and (2) in or on the building described in the declarations or within 100 feet of the described premises.

Property Not Covered

All three classes of covered property may be modified by this section of the form. The covered property section and the property not covered section must be read together in order to determine whether a specific kind of property is insured.

There are several reasons for excluding some kinds of property from coverage. First, it may be illegal to insure some kinds of property, such as narcotics being held for sale outside of normal medical channels. Second, some property, such as foundations of buildings, may not be subject to loss by the perils insured against. Finally, some kinds of property are excluded because they can be insured more advantageously under other forms. Automobiles and aircraft are examples of such property. The commercial property forms do not provide satisfactory insurance for automobiles because the coverage would apply only while the insured property (the automobile) was on the described premises or within 100 feet thereof, whereas the most serious loss exposures for automobiles are off premises. The BPP coverage form lists several classes of property or kinds of property loss that are not covered, as shown in Exhibit 2-2.

Exhibit 2-2

Property Not Covered Under BPP

Covered Property does not include:

a. Accounts, bills, currency, deeds, food stamps or other evidences of debt, money, notes or securities. Lottery tickets held for sale are not securities;

b. Animals, unless owned by others and boarded by you, only as "stock" while inside of buildings;

c. Automobiles held for sale;

d. Bridges, roadways, walks, patios or other paved surfaces;

e. Contraband, or property in the course of illegal transportation or trade;

f. The cost of excavations, grading, backfilling or filling;

g. Foundations of buildings, structures, machinery or boilers if their foundations are below:

(1) The lowest basement floor; or

(2) The surface of the ground, if there is no basement;

h. Land (including land on which the property is located), water, growing crops or lawns;

i. Personal property while airborne or waterborne;

j. Bulkheads, pilings, piers, wharves or docks;

k. Property that is covered under another coverage form of this or any other policy in which it is more specifically described, except for the excess of the amount due (whether you can collect on it or not) from that other insurance;

l. Retaining walls that are not part of a building; described in the Declarations;

m. Underground pipes, flues or drains;

n. The cost to research, replace or restore the information on valuable papers and records, including those which exist on electronic or magnetic media, except as provided in the Coverage Extensions;

o. Vehicles or self-propelled machines (including aircraft or watercraft) that:

(1) Are licensed for use on public roads; or

(2) Are operated principally away from the described premises.

This paragraph does not apply to:

(1) Vehicles or self-propelled machines or autos you manufacture, process or warehouse;

(2) Vehicles or self-propelled machines, other than autos, you hold for sale; or

(3) Rowboats or canoes out of water at the described premises;

p. The following property while outside of buildings:

(1) Grain, hay, straw or other crops;

(2) Fences, radio or television antennas (including satellite dishes) and their lead-in wiring, masts or towers, signs (other than signs attached to buildings), trees, shrubs or plants (other than "stock" of trees, shrubs or plants), all except as provided in the Coverage Extensions.

Insurance is available for almost all of the items listed in the property not covered section. Only contraband or property in the course of illegal transportation or trade is totally uninsurable. Limited coverage is provided for some items in the BPP coverage extensions discussed below. Many items can be insured either by an endorsement adding them to the BPP or, as mentioned, in another policy more specifically designed for insuring such property. Policies that cover property excluded by the BPP will be discussed in later chapters of this text.

Item k (see Exhibit 2-2) is not a complete exclusion of property otherwise insured. The BPP will still cover such property, but only in excess of the other insurance. For example, assume that a computer system valued at $150,000 is insured under the general category of business personal property in a BPP issued by Building Fire Insurance Company and is also insured for $100,000 under a separate data processing policy issued by Computer Casualty and Surety. Assume further that the computer system is totally destroyed by fire, a cause of loss insured under both policies. Since the policy of Computer Casualty more specifically describes the computer system, it must pay its limit ($100,000) before Building Fire pays anything. Building Fire Insurance Company would then pay $50,000, the difference between the limit of Computer Casualty and the amount of loss. If Computer Casualty is insolvent and unable to pay its share of the loss, Building Fire will still pay only its normal share of $50,000. The insured's inability to collect from Computer Casualty does not increase the amount that Building Fire must pay.

Item o of the property not covered section (see Exhibit 2-2) does not eliminate coverage for *all* vehicles or self-propelled machines. The BPP *does* cover the following:

1. Vehicles or self-propelled machines or autos that are manufactured, processed, or warehoused by the insured

2. Vehicles or self-propelled machines, other than autos, that are held for sale by the insured

3. Rowboats or canoes that are out of the water at the described premises

Moreover, the exclusion applies only to vehicles or self-propelled machines that are licensed for use on public roads or are operated principally away from the described premises. Consequently, unlicensed vehicles and vehicles operated principally on the described premises are covered. For example, a truck used only to move steel beams in the storage yard of an iron and steel wholesaler would be covered.

Additional Coverages and Coverage Extensions

The building and personal property coverage form provides several supplemental coverages in addition to the basic coverages for buildings, the insured's business personal property, and the property of others described above. These supplemental coverages are set forth under two subheadings: (1) additional coverages and (2) coverage extensions.

Additional Coverages

The four additional coverages are titled as follows:

1. Debris removal
2. Preservation of property
3. Fire department service charge
4. Pollutant cleanup and removal

Debris Removal

Following a major loss, large amounts of debris may remain on the premises, and the cost of removing the debris may be substantial. The **debris removal** additional coverage covers that cost. The coverage pays for the removal of debris of *covered property* only. It would not, for example, pay for the removal of the debris of the insured's licensed automobiles, since they are not covered property.

The debris removal provision in the additional coverages section applies only to the cost of removing debris of covered property resulting from a covered cause of loss during the policy period. The removal expenses will be paid only if they are reported in writing within 180 days of the loss. Under the debris removal provision, the most that will be paid for such debris removal is 25 percent of the sum of the direct loss payment plus the deductible amount. However, this amount may not be sufficient in some cases. Therefore, the limits of insurance section of the BPP coverage form provides an additional $10,000 limit per location if (1) the direct loss plus debris removal expense exceeds the limits of insurance or (2) the debris removal expense exceeds the 25 percent limitation of direct losses.

The cost to clean up pollution caused by an insured peril is covered. For example, if "building" is shown as covered property, the cost to clean up debris from a fire that causes the release of toxic chemicals onto the floor of the insured's building would be covered. However, the debris removal provision does not apply to costs for cleanup or removal of pollutants from land or water. Limited coverage for these costs is available under the provisions of another additional coverage, which is discussed later in this section.

Examples of Debris Removal Losses

Each of the examples that follow involves a BPP with a limit of $100,000 on the insured's building and a $1,000 deductible.

Example 1—Debris removal is less than 25% of the sum of loss payment plus deductible.

Amount of loss: $10,000 damage to building, $2,000 debris removal

Insured collects:

$10,000	for building damage
2,000	for debris removal
$12,000	
– 1,000	deductible
$11,000	

Example 2—Debris removal is greater than 25% of the sum of loss payment plus deductible.

Amount of loss: $36,000 damage to building, $22,000 debris removal

Insured collects:

$36,000	for building damage
19,250	for debris removal*
$55,250	
– 1,000	deductible
$54,250	

*The insured collects only $19,250 for the debris removal because the coverage for debris removal is limited to 25% of the sum of the insurer's payment for physical loss and the deductible ($9,250, calculated as .25 x [$36,000 + $1,000]) plus the $10,000 additional limit of insurance for debris removal.

Example 3—Building loss exceeds the amount of insurance.

Loss: $105,000 damage to building, $20,000 debris removal

Insured collects:

$100,000	for building damage (limit of insurance)
10,000	for debris removal (additional limit of insurance)
$110,000	

The insurer's payment is not reduced by the deductible. The deductible is subtracted from the amount of the loss (not from the limit), and the remainder exceeds the limit of insurance.

Preservation of Property

After a loss, it is frequently necessary to move the covered property to another location to protect it from further loss. The **preservation of property** clause extends the policy to protect the covered property while it is being moved and for up to thirty days at the new location. This coverage is broader than the normal coverage under the policy. It protects against "any direct physical loss or damage" and is not limited to either the covered causes of loss or locations stipulated in the coverage form. The protection provided under this clause is subject to the limits of insurance stated in the declarations. Thus, no protection is provided by this clause if the limits of insurance have been exhausted by payment for the physical loss.

Fire Department Service Charge

In some areas, the fire department may make a charge for its services in controlling or extinguishing a fire. The **fire department service charge** clause covers such charges up to $1,000 if the charges are assumed by contract prior to loss or are required by local ordinance. This coverage limit is payable in addition to the limit of insurance shown in the declarations and is not subject to any deductible.

Pollutant Cleanup and Removal

The **pollutant cleanup and removal** additional coverage provides limited coverage for the cleanup and removal of pollutants from land or water at the described premises. The BPP defines "pollutant" as follows:

> . . .any solid, liquid, gaseous or thermal irritant or contaminant, including smoke, vapor, soot, fumes, acids, alkalis, chemicals and waste. Waste includes materials to be recycled, reconditioned or reclaimed.

This additional coverage pays the insured's expenses to extract pollutants from land or water at the described premises if the release, discharge, dispersal, seepage, migration, or escape of the pollutants is the result of a covered cause of loss that occurs during the policy period. These expenses must be reported in writing within 180 days after the loss. An aggregate limit of $10,000 per location applies to all such expenses that occur during each separate twelve-month period.

Coverage Extensions

The protection provided by the coverage extensions section of the BPP coverage form applies only if at least 80 percent coinsurance or a value reporting period symbol is shown in the declarations. (Coinsurance requirements and value reporting period symbols are described later in this chapter.)

However, the coinsurance requirement does not apply to loss payments made under the extensions. In addition, the amounts that may be paid under the coverage extensions are additional amounts of insurance and are not subject to the limits of insurance stated in the declarations.

The BPP coverage extensions are titled as follows:

1. Newly acquired or constructed property
2. Personal effects and property of others
3. Valuable papers and records—cost of research
4. Property off-premises
5. Outdoor property

Newly Acquired or Constructed Property

This coverage extension provides automatic coverage for a new building being constructed *at the premises described in the declarations*. Automatic coverage is also provided for newly acquired buildings at other locations provided (1) the newly acquired building will be used for a purpose similar to the use of the building described in the declarations or (2) the newly acquired building will be used as a warehouse. The coverage is $250,000 at each building.

The extension also provides automatic coverage for business personal property at newly acquired locations. This automatic coverage does not apply to property at a fair or an exhibition. The limit for this coverage is $100,000 at each building.

The coverage for buildings and business personal property provided by this extension is temporary. It terminates automatically at the earliest of the following dates:

1. On the expiration date of the policy
2. Thirty days after the acquisition of the new location or the start of construction of the new building
3. On the date the insured notifies the insurer of the new location or new building

Premium for the coverage is calculated from the date of acquisition or start of construction, regardless of when the insurer is notified.

Personal Effects and Property of Others

This coverage extension provides a limited amount of coverage for personal effects (such as a personal radio in an office) owned by an individual insured or a partner, an officer, or an employee of the insured while on the premises described in the declarations. Personal effects are not covered for loss by theft.

The extension also covers property of others in the care, custody, or control of the insured. However, the limit on all property covered by this extension (personal effects *and* property of others) is $2,500 at each described location. If the value of property of others is greater, insurance can be purchased on such property by showing a limit of insurance for personal property of others coverage, as described earlier.

Valuable Papers and Records—Cost of Research

The valuation provision of the BPP coverage form limits any payment for loss of valuable papers and records to the sum of (1) the cost of blank materials for reproducing the records and (2) the cost of labor to transcribe or copy the records. If the damage is so severe that the records cannot be copied or transcribed, the use of this valuation formula could result in a gap in coverage. It would not pay for the cost of research to reconstruct the information on the damaged or destroyed records.

Coverage Extension C provides limited protection for the cost of research and reconstruction of the information contained on destroyed records. The limit for this extension is $2,500 at each described location unless a higher limit is shown in the declarations.

Property Off-Premises

This coverage extension provides limited protection for insured property while temporarily at a location not owned, leased, or operated by the insured. For example, the insured's typewriter or computer would be covered while it is being serviced off premises. The coverage does not apply to stock as defined in the form. Also, there is no coverage for property (1) in or on a vehicle, (2) in the care of the insured's sales personnel, or (3) at any fair or exhibition. The coverage is intended primarily for property off-premises for repair or service. The limit for this extension is $10,000.

Outdoor Property

The outdoor property extension covers loss to outdoor fences, radio and television antennas including satellite dishes, signs not attached to buildings, and trees, shrubs, and plants. Unlike the other coverage extensions, the coverage for outdoor property has its own list of covered causes of loss. It covers only loss by fire, lightning, explosion, riot or civil commotion, and aircraft. Some of the more likely causes of loss to outdoor property—windstorm, vehicles, and vandalism—are not covered. The limit of coverage is $1,000, including debris removal expense, but not more than $250 may be applied to any one tree, shrub, or plant. These limits apply regardless of the types or number of items lost or damaged in one occurrence.

Limits of Insurance

The limits of insurance section states that the most the insurer is obligated to pay for loss in any one occurrence is the applicable limit of insurance shown in the declarations. In some loss situations, however, the amount of loss payment may be restricted. In others, payment of amounts in addition to the limit of insurance may be made. Payment for loss to outdoor signs attached to buildings is limited to $1,000 per sign in any one occurrence. Losses are paid in addition to the limit of insurance under all of the coverage extensions and under the additional coverages for fire department service charges and pollutant cleanup and removal. As previously stated, up to an additional $10,000 will be paid for debris removal under certain conditions. Exhibit 2-3 illustrates the coverages for which payments may be made in addition to the limits of insurance.

Under the provisions of other clauses in the form, the insurer may pay less than the applicable limit of insurance. These clauses are discussed in subsequent sections.

Exhibit 2-3
Losses Paid in Addition to Limits

Coverage	Maximum Payable in Addition to Policy Limit
Debris removal	$10,000
Fire department service charge	$1,000
Pollutant cleanup and removal	$10,000
Newly acquired or constructed building (30 days)	$250,000 at each building
Business personal property at new location (30 days)	$100,000 at each building
Personal effects and property of others	$2,500 at each location
Cost of research for papers and records	$2,500 at each location
Property off premises (with restrictions)	$10,000
Certain outdoor property	$1,000—but only $250 for any one tree, shrub, or plant

Deductible

The BPP contains the following deductible provision:

> We will not pay for loss or damage in any one occurrence until the amount of loss or damage exceeds the Deductible shown in the Declarations. We will then pay the amount of loss or damage in excess of the Deductible, up to the applicable Limit of Insurance.

Thus, the insurer is not obligated to pay anything to the insured unless the loss exceeds the deductible; the limit of insurance then applies to the loss in excess of the deductible. In less formal language, the deductible comes off the loss, not off the limit of insurance. For example, payment under a policy with a $100,000 limit on a building and a $1,000 deductible in each of the following losses would be as follows:

- $500 loss: no payment (loss is less than deductible)
- $100,000 loss: $99,000 payment ($100,000 – $1,000 deductible)
- $110,000 loss: $100,000 payment ($110,000 – $1,000 deductible exceeds limit of insurance)

The deductible applies per occurrence, not per item insured. If more than one item is insured, the deductible is applied to only one item if the loss to that item equals or exceeds the deductible. If the loss to one of the items exceeds the deductible, the deductible is applied entirely to that item with no deductible applied to the other item. This method produces the largest recovery for the insured.

To illustrate, assume that a policy provided a limit of $100,000 on the insured's building and $80,000 on the insured's business personal property. If one occurrence caused a $110,000 loss to the building and a $30,000 loss to business personal property, the insurer's loss payment would be as follows:

- Loss to building: $100,000 ($110,000 – $1,000 exceeds limit of insurance)
- Loss to business personal property: $30,000 (no deductible applies, since deductible was applied to the building loss)

Loss Conditions

The **loss conditions** section of the BPP coverage form stipulates the duties of the insured and the insurer after a loss has occurred, explains methods for establishing the value of damaged property, and provides procedures for adjusting claims. These loss conditions apply in addition to the common policy conditions and the commercial property conditions.

Abandonment

Under the **abandonment** condition, the insured cannot abandon damaged property to the insurer. Although the insurer reserves the right to take all or any part of the damaged property after payment of loss, the decision to take it is at the option of the insurer. The insured cannot require the insurer to take any of the property.

Appraisal

The **appraisal** provision sets forth a method for resolving disputes regarding the *value* of the insured property or the amount of loss. It does not apply to disputes regarding policy coverage or lack of coverage.

If the insured and the insurer cannot agree on the value of the property or the amount of loss, either party may demand an appraisal. The demand for appraisal must be written. Each party appoints a competent and impartial appraiser, and the two appraisers appoint an umpire. If the appraisers cannot agree on an umpire, either of them may request the appointment of an umpire by a judge of a court having jurisdiction over the case. Each appraiser then prepares a statement of the property value and the amount of loss. If the appraisers do not agree, they submit to the umpire the items on which they disagree. A decision agreed to by any two of the three will be binding on all parties.

The insured and the insurer each pay their own appraiser. They share equally the fee for the umpire and the other expenses of the appraisal. Submission to appraisal does not preclude the insurer from denying coverage for the claim.

Duties in the Event of Loss or Damage

The BPP imposes several duties on the insured when a loss occurs. Failure to perform any of these duties may relieve the insurer of its obligation to pay for the loss.

The insured must notify the police if the loss appears to have resulted from a violation of law, such as arson or theft. The insured must give the insurer prompt notice of the loss, including a description of the property damaged. The insured must also provide information as to how, when, and where the loss occurred.

The insured must take all reasonable steps to protect the property from further loss and prepare an inventory. Although the policy does not say so specifically, the cost of protecting the property from further loss is covered. The insured is required to keep a record of expenses incurred in protecting the property "for consideration in the settlement of the claim." If feasible, the insured must set the damaged property aside and in the best possible order for examination.

The insured must, at the insurer's request, furnish the insurer with inventories of the damaged and undamaged property and permit the insurer to inspect the property and records and take samples of the property for testing and analysis. The insured must also submit to examination under oath regarding any matter related to the loss and cooperate with the insurer in the adjustment of the loss.

If the insurer requests a proof of loss, the insured must submit it to the insurer within sixty days after the insurer's request. A **proof of loss** is a sworn statement of the facts surrounding the loss. It includes information as to the time, place, and cause of loss; the value of the property before and after loss; any other insurance applicable to the loss; any mortgages or other liens against the property; the interest of the insured in the property; and other pertinent information. The insurer must supply the insured with a proof of loss form.

Loss Payment

If the insured discharges all of the above duties, the insurer must notify the insured of its intent either to pay the claim or to deny payment within thirty days after receipt of a satisfactory proof of loss. Actual payment must be made within thirty days after the parties have agreed on the amount of loss or an appraisal has been completed. Denial of payment may result either from lack of coverage under the policy or from the failure of the insured to comply with one or more of the policy conditions. If the insurer decides to pay the claim, it can exercise any of the following options:

1. Pay the amount of loss or damage
2. Pay the cost of repairing or replacing the damaged property
3. Take over all or any part of the property and pay its agreed or appraised value
4. Repair, rebuild, or replace the damaged property with other property of like kind and quality

The last option is seldom exercised because the insurer might then become a guarantor of the repaired or replaced property. If the repaired or replaced property proves to be unsatisfactory, the insurer might be required to make it satisfactory even if the cost of doing so exceeds the applicable limit of insurance.

The loss payment clause also states that regardless of the value of the loss, the insurer will pay no more than the insured's financial interest in the covered property. In addition, if the damaged property belongs to someone other than the insured, the insurer may adjust the loss with the owner. If the insurer elects to defend the insured against suits made by property owners, the insurer must pay the defense costs.

Recovered Property

If either the insurer or the insured recovers property for which the insurer has paid a loss, the party that makes the recovery is obligated to promptly notify the other party. The insured has the option of taking the recovered property and refunding the loss payment to the insurer. The insurer would then pay the cost of recovering the property and the cost, if any, of repairing it. If the insured elects not to take the recovered property, the insurer may dispose of the property as it sees fit.

Vacancy

If the building where a loss occurs has been **vacant** for more than sixty consecutive days before the loss occurred, the insurer will not pay if the loss is caused by (1) vandalism, (2) sprinkler leakage unless the sprinkler was protected against freezing, (3) breakage of building glass, (4) water damage, (5) theft, or (6) attempted theft. If any other covered peril causes the loss, loss payment will be reduced by 15 percent.

The vacancy provisions apply differently for a tenant than for a building owner. In the case of a tenant, a vacant "building" means the unit or suite rented or leased to the tenant. A building is vacant when it does not contain enough business personal property to conduct customary operations. Thus, a tenant's coverage could be reduced or eliminated even though the remainder of the building is fully occupied. If the policy covers the building owner, "building" means the entire building, and it is considered vacant when 70 percent or more of its square footage is not rented or is not used to conduct customary operations. Buildings under construction or renovation are not considered to be vacant.

Valuation

The valuation clause sets forth rules for establishing the value of insured property. Subject to the exceptions mentioned below (and summarized in Exhibit 2-4), the insured property is valued at its **actual cash value (ACV)**. The form does not include a definition of actual cash value, but ACV is usually considered to be the cost to replace the property with new property of like kind and quality less depreciation. Depreciation includes any reduction in value because of wear and tear or obsolescence of the property. Thus, depending on the property's age, the quality of maintenance, and other factors, the actual cash value of a particular piece of property can be much less than its replacement cost.

If sufficient insurance is carried to satisfy the coinsurance requirement and the total cost to repair or replace the building is $2,500 or less, the insurer will pay the cost of repair or replacement without a deduction for depreciation, except for the following types of property:

1. Awnings or floor coverings

2. Appliances for refrigeration, ventilation, cooking, dishwashing, or laundering

3. Outdoor equipment or furniture

Actual cash value is used for the excepted items. This limited replacement cost coverage applies only to building losses, not to losses of personal property. Actual cash value is not an appropriate measure of loss for some kinds of property, so the form provides special valuation methods for them.

Exhibit 2-4
Valuation of Property—Building and Personal Property Coverage Form

Property Type	Valuation Basis
Property other than that specifically listed	Actual cash value
Building damage of $2,500 or less	Replacement cost except for some personal property items considered part of a building
Stock sold but not delivered	Selling price less discounts and unincurred costs
Glass	Replacement cost for safety glazing if required by law
Improvements and betterments: (a) replaced by other than the insured	Not covered
(b) replaced by insured	Actual cash value
(c) not replaced	Percentage of cost based on remaining life of lease
Valuable papers and records	Cost of blank media plus cost of transaction or copying ($2,500 research cost as coverage extension)

Stock and Glass

Stock sold by the insured but not yet delivered is valued at the selling price less any expenses and discounts that would have been applicable had delivery been completed. Glass is valued at the cost of replacement with safety glazing material if required by law.

Improvements and Betterments

If the insured is a tenant, the valuation of loss to improvements and betterments depends on whether they are repaired or replaced, and, if so, at whose expense. If the improvements and betterments are repaired or replaced at the expense of someone other than the insured, the insurer is not obligated to pay anything. If the improvements and betterments are repaired or replaced at the expense of the insured, the insurer is required to pay the actual cash value of the lost or destroyed property. If the improvements and betterments are not repaired or replaced, the insurer will pay a proportion of the original cost of the improvements and betterments. This proportion is based on the amount of time remaining under the insured's lease, including periods for which the lease can be renewed at the option of the insured.

Valuable Papers and Records

Valuable papers and records are valued at the cost of new blank media plus the cost of copying or transcribing the information from the damaged papers or records. This method of valuation applies not only to paper records but also to those recorded on magnetic discs, tapes, drums, or other magnetic media. It does not apply, however, to prepackaged computer software programs. The coverage extensions section of the form provides limited coverage for research to reconstruct the information stored on valuable papers and records that are damaged too severely to permit copying or transcribing the information.

Additional Conditions

The building and personal property coverage form provides two additional policy conditions to supplement those found in the common policy conditions and the commercial property conditions. These deal with coinsurance and the interests of a mortgageholder (mortgagee).

Coinsurance

The **coinsurance** clause requires the insured to carry insurance equal to at least a specified percentage of the actual cash value of the property insured. The percentage is shown in the declarations. If the amount of insurance carried is equal to or greater than the required percentage, the insurer will pay covered losses in full (subject to any applicable deductible) up to the limit of insurance. If the amount of insurance carried is less than the required percentage, loss payments will be reduced proportionately.

If the amount of insurance carried does not meet the coinsurance requirement, the amount the insurer will pay (subject always to the limit of insurance) is calculated by the following formula:

$$\text{Loss payment} = \left[\frac{\text{Amount of insurance carried}}{\text{Amount of insurance required}} \times \text{Loss} \right] - \text{Deductible}$$

The amount of insurance required is the actual cash value of the property *immediately before the loss occurred* multiplied by the coinsurance percentage. Note that the deductible is subtracted after the coinsurance penalty has been calculated. The example in Exhibit 2-5 will help to clarify the calculation.

Exhibit 2-5
Coinsurance Example

Actual cash value of covered building at time of loss	$200,000
Limit of insurance	$140,000
Coinsurance percentage	80%
Amount of loss	$ 40,000
Deductible	$ 500

Amount of insurance required = .80 x $200,000 = $160,000

$$\text{Loss Payment} = \left[\frac{140,000}{160,000} \times \$40,000 \right] - 500$$

$$= [^7/_8 \times 40,000] - 500$$

$$= 35,000 - 500 = \$34,500$$

If the amount of insurance carried had been $160,000 or more, the insurer would have paid $39,500, the amount of loss less the deductible.

Mortgageholder

If a mortgageholder is shown in the declarations, the insurer is obligated to pay any claim for loss on the mortgaged property to the mortgageholder. If two or more mortgageholders are shown, they are paid in the order of their precedence. That is, the holder of a first mortgage is paid first. If payment to the first mortgageholder does not exhaust the loss payment, the balance is used to pay the holder of a second mortgage, and so on. If the insured loss exceeds the outstanding balance on the mortgages, the balance is paid to the insured.

In practice, the loss payment check or draft is usually made payable jointly to the insured and all mortgageholders so that they can agree on the division of the payment. In most cases, the loss payment is used to repair or rebuild the mortgaged property, and the mortgages continue in force as before.

Any act or default of the insured does not impair the rights of the mortgageholder, providing the mortgageholder pays any premium due that the insured has not paid, submits a proof of loss if requested, and has notified the insurer of any change in ownership, occupancy, or substantial increase in risk of which the mortgageholder is aware. Consequently, the insurer is sometimes obligated to make a loss payment to the mortgageholder even though it has denied coverage to the insured, for example, an insured who has committed arson. In such cases the insurer, at its option, can (1) take over the rights of the mortgageholder to the extent of such payment and collect the amount of payment from the insured or (2) pay off the outstanding balance of the mortgage and take over all of the rights of the mortgageholder.

If the insurer cancels the policy because the insured failed to pay the premium or if the insurer does not renew the policy for any reason, it must notify the mortgageholder ten days before the termination of coverage. If the insurer cancels the policy for any reason other than nonpayment of premium, it must give thirty days' advance notice to the mortgageholder. If the insurer fails to give the required notice to the mortgageholder, the policy remains in force for the protection of the mortgageholder even though it may not provide any protection for the insured.

Optional Coverages

The optional coverages section of the BPP provides for three optional modifications of the coverage form. These three optional modifications were historically provided by endorsements to commercial property insurance. They are now printed in the coverage form itself but are not applicable unless an appropriate notation is made on the declarations page. Selecting any option does not affect whether a loss is covered. Any of the options may be used for the building only, for personal property only, or for both the building and personal property.

Agreed Value

To activate the **agreed value** option, an amount is entered under the agreed value heading in the declarations for each item to which the option applies. This option enables the insured to remove the uncertainty as to whether the amount of insurance carried complies with the coinsurance clause. With the option in force, the insurer and the insured have agreed in advance that the amount stated in the declarations—the agreed value—is adequate for coinsurance purposes.

The BPP coinsurance provision does not apply to property insured under the agreed value option. However, it is replaced by a provision that, while not called coinsurance, is the practical equivalent of 100 percent coinsurance based on the agreed value. The agreed value option provides that if the limit of insurance equals or exceeds the agreed value stated in the declarations, losses will be paid in full up to the limit of insurance. If the limit of insurance is less than the agreed value, the amount of loss payment is calculated by the following formula:

$$\text{Loss payment} = \left[\frac{\text{Limit of insurance}}{\text{Agreed value}} \times \text{Loss} \right] - \text{Deductible}$$

Coverage under this option extends until the agreed value expiration date shown on the declarations or the expiration date of the policy, whichever occurs first. If the coverage option is not renewed, the coinsurance condition is reinstated.

Inflation Guard

The **inflation guard** option provides a means for automatically increasing the limit of insurance. The limit of insurance automatically increases by the percentage of annual increase indicated in the declarations. This percentage is applied on a pro rata basis, from the date the limit of insurance became effective to the date of the loss, before the loss payment is computed. The percentage of annual increase is shown separately for buildings and personal property.

Replacement Cost

This option replaces actual cash value with **replacement cost** in the valuation section of the form. That is, the insurer is obligated to pay the cost to replace the damaged or destroyed property with new property of like kind and quality without any deduction for depreciation or obsolescence.

The insurer is not obligated to pay replacement cost until the property has been repaired or replaced, and then only if such repair or replacement is completed in a reasonable time. If repair or replacement is not completed in a reasonable time, the loss payment will be based on the actual cash value at the time of loss.

The insured may make a claim on the basis of actual cash value, with the difference between actual cash value and replacement cost to be paid upon completion of repair or reconstruction. The insurer must be notified within 180 days after the occurrence of loss that a claim will be made for replacement cost.

If the replacement cost option is activated, the coinsurance provision continues to apply but with one important difference. The amount of insurance required by the coinsurance provision is found by multiplying *replacement cost* by the coinsurance percentage if the claim is made on a replacement cost basis. If the insured makes a claim on an ACV basis, coinsurance is also calculated on an ACV basis.

The replacement cost option does not apply to (1) property of others, (2) contents of a residence, (3) manuscripts, or (4) works of art, antiques, or rare articles. It also does not apply to stock unless indicated in the declarations.

Functional Building and Personal Property Valuation Endorsements

Old or obsolete buildings and personal property can present difficult insurance problems. For example, assume that a four-story building constructed of brick and heavy mill timbers was once used for textile manufacturing but is now occupied as a warehouse with only the lowest floor in use; the upper floors are boarded up and unoccupied. To rebuild the building as originally constructed would be very expensive, far more than the building's market value. A one-story building of lighter construction would be much less expensive to construct and would serve the same function. Even actual cash value, if calculated as replacement cost less depreciation, may be more than the market value of the building.[1]

Insureds are unwilling to purchase amounts of insurance in excess of the market value of their buildings. Insurers, fearing moral and morale hazards, do not want to write the insurance for such amounts. To cope with this problem, two endorsements are available: (1) functional building valuation and (2) functional personal property valuation (other than stock).

These endorsements provide for loss settlement on the basis of functional replacement cost. **Functional replacement cost** is the cost of replacing the damaged property with similar property that will perform the same function but may not be identical to the damaged property. For example, if a very ornate older building is destroyed, it could be replaced by a less ornate but function-ally equivalent building at a cost lower than that for an exact replacement. The amount of insurance required would be less than that needed for replace-ment cost or actual cash value coverage. The functional replacement cost value is agreed upon in advance by the insured and the insurer. If the property is not replaced, recovery is limited to the smallest of the following:

- The limit of insurance
- The market value of the building or personal property
- The functional replacement cost

Coinsurance does not apply to property insured under this endorsement.

Insuring Fluctuating Values

Many business organizations experience wide fluctuations (increases and decreases) in personal property values, especially the value of stocks of goods held for sale. The BPP does not provide satisfactory coverage for fluctuating values. If the insured organization carries high enough limits to cover the maximum value, it is overinsured for much of the year and pays too much in premiums. If it carries less than the maximum value, it is underinsured during its peak inventory period.

The value reporting form and the peak season limit of insurance endorsement provide possible solutions to the problem of fluctuating values. They are used in conjunction with the BPP or the condominium commercial unit owners coverage form.

Value Reporting Form

Under the **value reporting form**, the insured is required to report the value of the insured business personal property to the insurer periodically during the policy period. The frequency of reporting is indicated by a symbol entered in the declarations. For example, "MR", the most common choice, calls for reporting values on hand on the last day of the month, with the report due within thirty days after the end of the month. Daily, weekly, quarterly, and annual periods can also be selected as a basis for reports by entering other codes in the declarations.

As long as the insured reports values accurately and on time, the insurer will pay the full amount of any loss that occurs (subject to the policy limit and deductible), even if the values on hand at the time of the loss are greater than those last reported to the insurer. To illustrate, assume that Tri-State Supply, a wholesaler, insures its business personal property under a value reporting form subject to a limit of $1 million for its single warehouse location. Tri-State's last monthly report of values was made on time and showed the full value of business personal property—$800,000—as of the date of the report. Three weeks later, a fire destroyed the warehouse and its contents. Even though the value of covered personal property had increased to $900,000 since the last report, the loss was covered in full (minus the deductible).

Penalties for Improper Reporting

To encourage accurate and timely reports, the value reporting form provides penalties for failure to comply with the reporting requirements set forth in the form. Separate rules apply when (1) no report is made, (2) one or more reports are past due after the initial report, and (3) reports are inaccurate. The penalties for improper reporting are determined at the time of loss.

No Report Made

If the insured has not made any reports at the time of loss (and one or more should have been made), the insurer will not pay more than 75 percent of the amount it would have been obligated to pay if all reports had been made properly and on time. Also, the insurer will pay only for loss that occurs at locations shown in the declarations. There will be no payment for loss at newly acquired locations.

Report Past Due After at Least One Report Is Made

If at least one report has been made, but one (or more) is past due at the time of loss, the insurer's liability is limited to the value reported on the last report received for the location at which the loss occurred. If the loss occurs at a location for which no value was shown on the last report received, the insurer will not pay anything.

Inaccurate Reports

If the values reported are less than the actual values on hand at the time the report was made, the loss payment will be calculated by the following formula:

$$\text{Loss payment} = \left[\frac{\text{Value reported}}{\substack{\text{Actual value} \\ \text{as of last} \\ \text{report}}} \times \text{Loss} \right] - \text{Deductible}$$

This formula works like 100 percent coinsurance but is based on what should have been reported compared to what was reported. It is sometimes called an "honesty clause." To illustrate, assume that Hobby Shop is insured under a value reporting form with a limit of $300,000 and a $500 deductible. Two weeks after sending its last report of values to the insurer, Hobby Shop suffered a small fire loss that caused $20,000 damage to its personal property. In its investigation of the loss, the insurer found that the personal property value last reported by Hobby Shop was $200,000 but that the actual value as of the date of the report was $250,000. The amount of covered loss would be calculated as follows:

$$\left[\frac{\$200,000}{\$250,000} \times \$20,000 \right] - \$500 = \$15,500$$

The penalties for improper reporting may be substantial. The value reporting form should be used only for those insureds who have adequate accounting records and personnel to prepare timely and accurate reports. However, when an insured does follow all requirements, the value reporting form provides excellent insurance protection for fluctuating values.

Determining Premium

The insured pays an advance premium at the inception of the policy. The advance premium is based on 75 percent of the limit of insurance. The final premium is determined after the policy anniversary, based on the reported values. If the insured reports values in excess of the policy limits, the premium is based on the values reported. However, the insurer is not obligated to pay more than the policy limit in the event of loss, even if the reported values are higher. Thus, care should be taken to set the limit high enough to cover any possible increase in value.

Peak Season Limit of Insurance Endorsement

The **peak season limit of insurance endorsement** provides differing amounts of insurance for certain time periods during the policy term. For example, a toy store may have a policy providing $100,000 coverage on personal property with a peak season endorsement increasing coverage to $200,000 during the period from October 1 to December 31 when it expects to have higher inventory values. This would have exactly the same effect as endorsing the policy on October 1 to increase the coverage and endorsing it again on December 31 to reduce the coverage. The peak season endorsement eliminates the bother of these extra transactions and the possibility that they might be overlooked.

The peak season endorsement is usually attached when the policy is issued (although it may be added mid-term), and a pro-rata premium is charged for the period during which the limit is increased.

The peak season endorsement is suited to smaller businesses that have regular fluctuations in inventory. Although the value reporting form might be more effective at matching coverage to exposures, many smaller firms do not have accounting systems of sufficient sophistication to generate the required reports accurately and on time. Furthermore, many insurers would decline to issue a value reporting policy for a smaller insured since the premium may not be large enough to warrant the added expense of processing the reports and calculating the final premium.

Blanket Insurance

The basic method of insuring buildings and personal property is to schedule a specific amount of insurance in the declarations for each building and a specific amount of insurance for personal property at each location. This approach is called **specific insurance**. An example of how specific insurance might be indicated in the declarations of a commercial property policy is as follows:

- $100,000 on the building at 123 Main St., Des Moines, IA
- $80,000 on your business personal property at 123 Main St., Des Moines, IA

The alternative to specific insurance is blanket insurance. **Blanket insurance** is insurance that covers either of the following with *one* limit of insurance:

1. Two or more types of property
2. One or more types of property at more than one location

No special endorsement is required to effect blanket insurance. The word "blanket" is simply added to the statement of coverage in the declarations. If the property described above was insured on a blanket basis, the statement of coverage in the declarations might read as follows:

- $180,000 blanket on the building and your business personal property at 123 Main St., Des Moines, IA

Property at different locations can also be covered on a blanket basis. In that case, coverage can apply to one or more types of property at more than one location, for example:

- $1,000,000 blanket on buildings and business personal property at:
    123 Main St., Des Moines, IA
    987 Third St., Des Moines, IA
    12 Elm St., Ames, IA
        -or-
- $950,000 blanket on buildings at:
    78 Broadway, Malvern, PA
    971 Tenth St., Philadelphia, PA
    88 Highland Rd., Pottstown, PA

Coinsurance Requirement for Blanket Insurance

Blanket insurance may involve an additional cost. The minimum coinsurance clause is 90 percent, but the rates are the same as for 80 percent coinsurance. The insured with blanket insurance must insure to 90 percent of value to avoid a coinsurance penalty but does not receive the 5 percent discount that applies to specific insurance with a 90 percent coinsurance clause. Thus, to meet coinsurance requirements, the insured with blanket insurance must buy more insurance than otherwise would be required.

Advantages of Blanket Insurance

Why would an insured want to spend the additional premium to obtain blanket insurance? To understand the reasons, consider the example of Mary, who owns and operates furniture stores at two locations. Assume that the value of Mary's business personal property in each store is $100,000 at the inception of the policy. To comply with the 80 percent coinsurance clause, Mary might purchase specific insurance with a limit of $80,000 on her business personal property at each location. In that event, if the loss exceeds $80,000, she will be uninsured for the portion in excess of $80,000. If she purchased a blanket policy with a limit of $180,000 (90 percent of $200,000), she would be fully insured for the loss at any one location up to $180,000 as long as the total amount of insurance satisfied the coinsurance clause.

Or, suppose that at the time of the loss the value of her property at one store has increased to $120,000 and the value of the property at the other store has decreased to $80,000. If she has not adjusted her insurance, a total loss at the first store would leave her with a $40,000 uninsured loss if she had specific insurance even though the total amount of insurance was adequate. With blanket insurance, her $120,000 loss would have been paid in full.

Furthermore, Mary may not be exactly sure of the insurable value at each location. With specific insurance, she would either have to purchase a higher amount of insurance to provide a cushion against error in estimating insurable values or risk an uninsured loss. With blanket insurance, assuming the two locations are not likely to be damaged by the same occurrence (such as a hurricane that devastates a wide area), the minimum amount of insurance needed to comply with coinsurance would be sufficient to protect her property fully.

In general, the greater the number of locations and the smaller the proportion of total value at any one location, the greater is the advantage of obtaining blanket insurance.

Combining the Agreed Value Option With Blanket Insurance

Most risk managers, consultants, and other experienced insurance practitioners regard the combination of the agreed value option with blanket insurance as the preferred method to provide property insurance. The agreed value clause avoids any coinsurance penalty, and if separate locations are involved that are not subject to the same loss, the danger of underinsurance is greatly reduced.

Even if only one location is involved, blanket insurance with the agreed value option is preferable to specific insurance. An example of such a situation is a small retail firm that owns the building in which it operates. Assume that the firm carries specific insurance of $100,000 on the building and $50,000 on the contents with the agreed value clause applicable to both. Assume also that a fire occurs, causing the following loss:

$$\begin{array}{rl} \$\ 80,000 & \text{building damage} \\ \underline{\$\ 60,000} & \text{contents damage} \\ \$140,000 & \text{total damage} \end{array}$$

In this case, the contents were totally destroyed and (immediately before the loss occurred) were worth more than the insured had, in good faith, estimated at inception of the policy. Specific insurance would pay $130,000 ($80,000 for the building plus $50,000, the specific limit of insurance, for the contents). In contrast, blanket insurance with a $150,000 limit would pay the full $140,000 loss. And with the agreed value option in effect, the recovery would not be reduced by failure to conform with the coinsurance requirement.

Summary

Many of the basic property coverages an organization needs are commonly provided under the commercial property coverage part. A commercial property coverage part consists of (1) commercial property declarations, (2) one or more commercial property coverage forms, (3) one or more causes-of-loss forms, (4) commercial property conditions, and (5) any applicable endorsements.

The most commonly used commercial property coverage form is the building and personal property coverage form (BPP). The BPP can be used to insure (1) buildings, (2) business personal property of the named insured, and (3) personal property of others in the named insured's care, custody, or control. With only minor exceptions, property is covered only while located on or within 100 feet of the insured premises. The property not covered section lists the various types of property that are not covered by the BPP. However, most property not covered can be insured by adding optional coverage endorsements to the BPP.

The BPP provides several additional coverages and coverage extensions to supplement its basic coverage for buildings and personal property. The additional coverages apply to (1) debris removal, (2) preservation of property, (3) fire department service charges, and (4) pollutant cleanup and removal. The coverage extensions provide limited coverage for (1) newly acquired or constructed property, (2) personal effects and property of others, (3) the cost to reconstruct information on destroyed records, (4) property while off the insured premises, and (5) certain types of outdoor property.

The BPP contains various conditions that address such matters as the insured's duties after loss, the insurer's loss payment options, valuation of covered property, mortgageholders' rights and duties, and coinsurance requirements. The BPP also contains three optional coverages. The agreed value option suspends the coinsurance requirement. The inflation guard option automatically increases the limits of insurance in accordance with a percentage shown in the declarations. The replacement cost option modifies the BPP valuation condition to apply to most property on a replacement cost basis instead of an actual cash value basis.

The BPP can be supplemented by either of two forms to address the problem of fluctuating (increasing and decreasing) personal property values: the value reporting form and the peak season limit of insurance endorsement.

The value reporting form requires the insured to report the value of covered property periodically (usually monthly) during the policy period. Premiums are then based on the values reported. As long as the insured makes timely and accurate reports, the insurer will pay the full amount of any loss that occurs (subject to the policy limit and deductible), even if the values on hand at the time of the loss are greater than those last reported to the insurer. The penalties for late or inaccurate reporting can be severe, so the value reporting form is not recommended for insureds that would have trouble making the reports.

The peak season limit of insurance endorsement provides differing amounts of insurance for certain time periods during the policy term. Although the value reporting form can do a better job of matching coverage (and premiums) to exposures, the peak season endorsement is often preferred by smaller businesses that do not want to make the reports required by the value reporting form.

The basic approach to insuring buildings and personal property is called specific insurance, whereby a limit is shown for each covered building and for personal property at each building. An alternative to specific insurance is blanket insurance, whereby two or more types of property at one location or one or more types of property at multiple locations are covered under a single limit of insurance.

Blanket insurance is subject to a 90 percent coinsurance requirement instead of the usual 80 percent coinsurance requirement. However, blanket insurance can provide better coverage than specific insurance because the full blanket limit can be applied to any one loss. The blanket approach is often combined with the agreed value option.

Chapter Note

1. In many states, problems with calculating the actual cash value for older, obsolete buildings and equipment have led the courts to adopt the "broad evidence rule." The broad evidence rule states that all indicators of value, such as replacement cost, market value, assessed value, and many others, must be considered in setting actual cash value.

Chapter 3

Commercial Property Insurance, Continued

This chapter continues the discussion of commercial property insurance that began in Chapter 2. The chapter covers the following topics:

1. The commercial property causes-of-loss forms
2. The builders risk coverage form, used for insuring buildings during construction
3. Coverage forms for insuring condominium associations and condominium unit owners
4. The commercial property conditions form, which is included in every commercial property coverage part
5. Commercial property rating

Causes-of-Loss Forms

The first insurance policies covering buildings in colonial America covered loss by fire only. In time, lightning was added as an insured cause of loss, as well as some other perils. In the 1930s several additional perils (windstorm, civil commotion, smoke, hail, aircraft, vehicles, explosion, and riot) were grouped into an endorsement known as "extended coverage." This endorsement was added to fire insurance policies to provide a combination known as "fire and extended coverage." Generations of insurance students have used the memory device "W C SHAVER" to remember the perils included in the extended coverage endorsement. Extended coverage was followed by "broad form" coverage, which added even more perils, and "special form" coverage, which covered all perils except those specifically excluded. Fire and extended coverage has been superseded by "basic form" coverage, which includes the fire and extended coverage perils plus a few others.

The perils covered in a contemporary commercial property policy are specified in any of three causes-of-loss forms:

- Causes of loss—basic form
- Causes of loss—broad form
- Causes of loss—special form

In addition, a causes of loss—earthquake form can be used to add earthquake as a covered peril.

Causes of Loss—Basic Form

The **causes of loss—basic form** (or simply "basic form") consists principally of two sections:

- Section A, a listing of several covered causes of loss (also known as *perils*), which are subject to some definitions and limitations expressed within that listing
- Section B, a set of exclusions that further limit the application of the covered perils

When trying to determine whether a particular cause of loss is covered, one needs to consider those two sections equally. A cause of loss that seems to be covered because it is listed as such in section A may not actually be covered because of a more specific exclusion in section B. For example, assume that a steam boiler exploded in the basement of an apartment building and extensively damaged the boiler and the building. Although "explosion" is listed as a covered cause of loss in section A, section B contains an exclusion of *steam boiler* explosion. Thus, the building owner's commercial property policy would not cover this loss. (Steam boiler explosion is usually insured under separate boiler and machinery forms, discussed in Chapter 6.)

Covered Causes of Loss

The causes of loss covered by the basic form are listed in Exhibit 3-1 and described below.

Exhibit 3-1
Covered Causes of Loss in Basic and Broad Forms

Both Forms Cover:	**Broad Form Also Covers:**
1. Fire	12. Falling objects
2. Lightning	13. Weight of snow, ice, or sleet
3. Explosion	14. Water damage
4. Windstorm or hail	
5. Smoke	
6. Aircraft or vehicles	
7. Riot or civil commotion	
8. Vandalism	
9. Sprinkler leakage	
10. Sinkhole collapse	
11. Volcanic action	

Fire and Lightning

Although the form does not define fire, the courts generally have held that fire insurance covers only damage by *hostile fire* (fire that is not in a place where fire is intended to be). Therefore, the policy would not cover damage caused by a fire in a stove (a *friendly fire*), but it would cover damage caused by a fire that escaped from a stove.

Lightning, also not defined in the form, is a naturally occurring electrical discharge between clouds or between a cloud and the earth. The peril of lightning does not include artificially generated electrical current.

Explosion

The basic form contains no formal definition of explosion. However, the form states that the term includes the explosion of gases in a furnace or flues (called "combustion explosion") but does not include either of the following:

- The rupture of pressure relief valves
- The rupture of a building (such as a grain storage shed) resulting from the expansion or swelling of its contents caused by water absorption

Certain exclusions, discussed later in this chapter, place further limitations on the types of explosions covered.

Windstorm or Hail

Covered wind or hail damage does not include damage caused by frost, cold weather, ice (other than hail), snow, or sleet, even if driven by wind. Also, damage by rain, snow, sand, or dust to the interior of a building or property inside the building is not covered unless the building first sustains exterior damage by wind, and the rain, snow, sand, or dust enters through the damaged part.

Smoke

Covered smoke damage must be sudden and accidental. There is no coverage for damage by smoke from agricultural smudging or industrial operations.

Smoke damage resulting from a *hostile* fire is covered by both the smoke peril and the fire peril. (The fire peril applies because fire was the cause of the damage.) However, smoke damage can result from sources other than a hostile fire, and such smoke damage is covered by the smoke peril unless it originated from agricultural smudging or industrial operations. For example, damage caused by the sudden and accidental discharge of smoke from a defective oil burner in the insured's heating furnace would be covered by the smoke peril but not by the fire peril (because the smoke did not come from a hostile fire).

Aircraft or Vehicles

In order to be covered, damage caused by aircraft must result from actual physical contact with the aircraft or objects falling from it. Spacecraft and self-propelled missiles are considered to be aircraft, but the war exclusion (discussed below) would eliminate coverage for damage by missiles in time of war. To be covered, vehicle damage must result from accidental physical contact with a vehicle or an object thrown by a vehicle. There is no coverage for damage caused by vehicles owned by the insured or operated in the insured's business.

Riot or Civil Commotion

The basic form does not define riot and civil commotion. In most states, a riot is defined by law as a violent public disturbance by three or more persons. However, the policy states that riot or civil commotion includes the acts of striking workers while occupying the insured premises as well as looting occurring at the time and place of a riot or civil commotion.

Vandalism

Vandalism means the willful or malicious damage to or destruction of property. The vandalism peril does not cover breakage of glass (other than glass building blocks) that is part of a building, a structure, or an outside sign. Damage to other property *resulting* from glass breakage is covered. The vandalism peril does not cover loss by theft, but damage to the building caused by the entry or exit of burglars is covered.

Sprinkler Leakage

Sprinkler leakage means the escape of any substance from an automatic fire protection or extinguishing system. The system need not be a water sprinkler system. It could use carbon dioxide, halon, or any other extinguishing agent. The collapse of a tank constituting a part of such a system is covered, as is the cost of repairing damage to the system if the damage results in the sprinkler leakage or if the damage is caused by freezing. Also covered is the cost to tear out and replace any part of the building or structure to repair damage to the automatic sprinkler system.

Sinkholes

Sinkholes result from underground water dissolving limestone and creating an empty space or cavern under the ground. When the roof of the cavern gets too close to the ground surface, the surface collapses, causing damage to buildings or other property located over or near the resulting sinkhole. Damage to buildings or other property is covered, but the cost of filling the sinkhole is not. Collapse into other underground openings, such as mineshafts, is not covered.

Volcanic Action

The volcanic action peril covers damage caused by lava flow, ash, dust, particulate matter, airborne volcanic blast, or airborne shock waves resulting from a volcanic eruption. Since such losses may occur over a relatively long period of time, the basic form stipulates that all eruptions that occur within any 168-hour period are considered a single occurrence and thus subject to only one deductible. The cost to remove ash, dust, or particulate matter is not covered except for the ash, dust, or particulate matter that caused loss to insured property.

Exclusions

Covered causes of loss are further defined or limited by the exclusions applying to the basic causes-of-loss form. The basic form exclusions are described below.

Ordinance or Law

To promote public welfare and safety, municipalities regularly upgrade the building codes that set the standards for new construction or significant remodeling. For example, a building code might require that elevators be provided in multistory buildings or that heavier gauge electric wiring be used. Furthermore, in some cities building codes require that new buildings in certain areas be fire resistive. Old buildings that do not comply with the codes may continue to be used without change. However, if a building that does not comply with the code sustains damage by fire or another peril, the building code may require that the restoration meet the new standards.

Complying with the new code may impose additional losses on the owner in any or all of the following ways:

1. The old structure may have to be totally demolished, for example, if it is a frame building in an area where only fire-resistive construction is permitted. Demolishing the undamaged parts of the building changes what would have been a partial loss to a total loss.

2. If demolition is required, the building owner will also incur the costs of demolishing the undamaged parts of the building and removing the debris of that property.

3. Whether or not the entire building has to be replaced, the restoration will be more expensive if the code requires more costly construction methods or additional facilities. For example, a major added cost in reconstructing buildings substantially damaged by Hurricane Andrew resulted from the requirement that building service equipment that was previously located at or below the grade level had to be relocated above the expected flood level.

The ordinance or law exclusion eliminates coverage for these additional consequential losses. However, they can be covered by endorsement for an additional premium. Insureds and their advisers should carefully examine the need for this additional coverage.

Earth Movement

No coverage is provided for damage caused by earth movement, other than sinkhole collapse. Earth movement includes earthquake, landslide, mine subsidence, and similar movements. Damage by fire or explosion caused by earth movement is covered.

Earthquake coverage can be added for an additional premium. When it is added to the policy, it also covers land shocks and movement resulting from volcanic eruption (which are not covered by the volcanic action peril).

Governmental Action

Seizure or destruction of property by governmental action is not covered. This exclusion does not apply to the destruction of property by governmental order to stop the spread of a covered fire. In that event, the policy provides coverage.

Nuclear Hazard

There is no coverage for loss caused by nuclear reaction, radiation, or radioactive contamination. Loss by fire resulting from these causes is covered. Some coverage for radioactive contamination can be provided by endorsement.

Utility Services

There is no coverage for loss caused by power failure or failure of other utility service if the damage causing such failure occurs away from the described premises. However, loss from a covered peril resulting from power failure is covered. Coverage for off-premises service interruption caused by an insured cause of loss is available by endorsement.

War and Military Action

There is no coverage for loss caused by war, revolution, insurrection, or similar actions.

Water

Loss caused by flooding and related perils is difficult to insure. Depending on their locations, some insureds have a much greater likelihood than others of suffering a flood loss. Moreover, the consequences of a flood can be catastrophic. Insurers therefore exclude flood losses from general property forms such as the BPP. The BPP excludes damage caused by the following:

- Flood, surface water, tides, and tidal waves
- Mudslide or mudflow
- Backing up of sewers, drains, or sumps
- Underground water pressing on, or flowing or seeping through, foundations, walls, doors, windows, or other openings

However, damage by fire, explosion, or sprinkler leakage caused by any of the foregoing is covered.

Other Exclusions

The basic form also excludes loss or damage caused by the following:

1. Artificially generated electric currents. However, if a fire results, the resulting fire damage is covered.
2. Rupture or bursting of water pipes unless caused by a covered cause of loss, but this exclusion does not apply to sprinkler leakage.
3. Leakage of water or steam from any part of an appliance or system containing water or steam (other than an automatic sprinkler system), unless caused by a covered cause of loss.
4. Explosion of steam boilers, steam pipes, steam turbines, or steam engines owned by, leased to, or operated by the insured. However, if such an explosion causes a fire or a combustion explosion, the damage caused by fire or combustion explosion is covered. (For a definition of "combustion explosion," see page 53.)
5. Mechanical breakdown, including rupture or bursting caused by centrifugal force.

The exposures excluded in items 4 and 5 above can be insured under boiler and machinery insurance, which will be discussed in Chapter 6.

Insuring Flood Losses

Because all three commercial property causes-of-loss forms exclude flood losses, insurance against flood, if wanted, must be specially arranged. Three common approaches to insuring flood are as follows:

1. Buying a separate flood insurance policy through the **National Flood Insurance Program (NFIP)**

2. Paying an additional premium for a flood coverage endorsement to the commercial property policy

3. Obtaining a separate "difference in conditions" (DIC) policy

National flood insurance is available through the NFIP either directly from the Federal Insurance Administration or through any of the many private insurance companies that participate in FIA's "Write Your Own" program. In many cases, such as when the property is located on or near a flood plain, the NFIP is the only available source of flood insurance. A drawback of federal flood insurance is that the maximum limits permitted by the National Flood Insurance Program may be insufficient for some insureds.

Some insurers are willing, in return for an additional premium, to add independently filed flood coverage endorsements to their commercial property policies. This approach is more likely to be available when the insured's flood exposure is minimal. In many cases, insurers offer water damage endorsements that only partially modify the flood exclusion. For example, an endorsement may cover loss resulting from seepage or sewer backup but not from flood or surface water.

A DIC policy is a special type of property coverage that supplements a commercial property policy written on a named perils basis. The DIC policy, in effect, converts the insured's named perils coverage to "all-risks." Many DIC policies do not contain a flood exclusion and thus cover that cause of loss (subject, in many cases, to a flood sublimit that is lower than the overall policy limit). A DIC policy can also be structured to cover flood losses that exceed the limits of the insured's federal flood insurance policy. DIC policies will be described in more detail in Chapter 7.

Causes of Loss—Broad Form

The **causes of loss—broad form** (or simply "broad form") covers all of the perils covered under the basic form plus (1) falling objects, (2) weight of snow, ice, or sleet, and (3) water damage (see Exhibit 3-1). Two "additional coverages" are also added: breakage of glass and collapse.

Falling Objects

The coverage for falling objects does not include damage to personal property in the open, such as a glass-topped table. The peril also does not include damage inside a building unless the roof or an outside wall is first damaged by a falling object.

Weight of Snow, Ice, or Sleet

The coverage for damage caused by the weight of snow, ice, or sleet does not cover damage to gutters, downspouts, or personal property in the open.

Water Damage

The water damage peril covers loss from leakage of water or steam resulting from the breaking apart or cracking of a part of an appliance or system containing water or steam. If the building is covered property, the form also covers the cost to tear out and replace any part of the building to repair damage to the appliance or system that leaked. It does not cover the following:

1. The cost to repair any defect that caused the loss or damage.
2. Gradual damage that occurs over a period of fourteen days or more.
3. Discharge or leakage from an automatic sprinkler system. (The sprinkler leakage peril would cover such damage.)
4. Discharge or leakage from a sump, including overflow due to sump pump failure.

The water damage peril also does not cover damage resulting from freezing unless the insured has made a reasonable effort to heat the building or, if the building was not heated, unless the system has been drained and the water supply shut off.

Additional Coverages

The broad form provides two additional coverages, "breakage of glass" and "collapse." In older editions of commercial property forms, both glass breakage and collapse were listed as covered perils. However, glass breakage and collapse are usually not *causes* of loss but rather are *results* of some other causes. For example, breakage of glass could be the result of a fire or vandalism, and collapse could be the result of faulty construction or the buildup of ice or snow on a roof not designed to bear such weight.

Breakage of Glass

The basic and broad forms both cover glass breakage caused by a covered cause of loss. For example, glass breakage caused by fire, windstorm, or explosion is covered under those perils. An important exception to the above statement is that the vandalism peril specifically excludes damage to glass, other than glass building blocks, that is part of a building, a structure, or an outside sign.

The purpose of the additional coverage for breakage of glass is to enhance the broad form to cover glass breakage caused by vandalism or any other unexcluded peril that is not otherwise one of the covered causes of loss in the broad form. However, when glass breakage is covered only by the breakage of glass additional coverage (such as glass breakage caused by vandalism), coverage is limited to $100 for each pane, plate, or multiple-plate insulating unit, subject to a total of $500 for any one occurrence. These special limitations do not apply to glass breakage caused by a covered cause of loss (such as fire, explosion, or windstorm), *other than vandalism.*

The reason for this two-tier treatment of glass breakage is that vandalism is one of the most frequent causes of glass breakage. Under the broad form, insurers are willing to provide only *limited* coverage for glass breakage caused by vandals. If an insured wants more extensive coverage for glass breakage, the coverage can be bought under the glass coverage form (see below).

The breakage of glass additional coverage applies only to glass that is a part of a building. Neon tubing is specifically excluded. In addition to the glass itself, the additional coverage also insures damage *resulting* from glass breakage—such as torn draperies or water damage caused by the entry of rainwater through a window broken by vandals—subject to the $500 per occurrence limit.

Another commercial property coverage form, the **glass coverage form,** is available for covering glass breakage caused by any peril except nuclear hazard, war, or fire. Moreover, the glass coverage form usually applies without any dollar limits. Many insureds with expensive plate glass windows, such as retail stores, purchase the glass coverage form because the $100 per pane limit is inadequate for their needs.

Under the glass coverage form, the insurer agrees to pay the costs of replacing the broken glass, removing debris of covered property, temporarily "boarding up" the openings left by broken glass, and repairing or replacing the frames encasing covered glass. Coverage is subject to a deductible that can be different from the one that applies to the insured's building and personal property coverage.

Collapse

Like glass breakage, collapse was once treated as an insured peril but is now covered as an additional coverage. Under this additional coverage, the insurer agrees to pay for loss resulting from collapse of a building or any part of a building if the collapse is caused by one or more of the following:

- The covered causes of loss under the broad form.
- Hidden decay.
- Hidden insect or vermin damage.
- Weight of people or personal property.
- Weight of rain that collects on a roof.
- Use of defective materials or construction methods if the collapse occurs during the course of construction. (Collapse of a *completed* building caused by defective materials or construction is covered only if it is caused in part by a cause of loss listed above.)

The additional coverage for collapse also covers loss to covered property caused by the collapse of *personal property* inside a building. For example, a free-standing shelving unit in a warehouse might collapse, resulting in damage to merchandise being stored on the shelving. Even though the building or any part of it did not collapse, the collapse coverage would still apply.

Causes of Loss—Special Form

The **causes of loss—special form** (or simply "special form"), instead of listing the perils covered, states that it covers "risks of direct physical loss," subject to the exclusions and limitations expressed in the form. Moreover, use of the term "risks" requires that loss or damage be accidental and unforeseen by the insured in order to be covered.

This type of coverage has long been known as "all-risks." However, the possibility of court decisions making the term "all-risks" broader than intended resulted in a switch to the current terminology, "risks of direct physical loss." The shorthand phrase "all-risks," still widely used by insurance people, will be used in this text to mean "risks of direct physical loss." (For obvious reasons, the term "all-risks" is generally not used when speaking to *insureds*.)

The special form offers the following advantages to the insured:

- Certain causes of loss that are omitted or excluded under the broad form are not excluded—and are therefore covered—under the special form. Most significantly, the special form covers theft of covered property under a wide variety of circumstances, subject to some exclusions and limitations described below. The basic and broad forms cover theft by looting at the time of a riot or civil commotion but in no other circumstances.
- By covering any risk of loss other than those that are specifically excluded, the special form covers losses that the insured might not have anticipated.

- The special form shifts the "burden of proof" from the insured to the insurer. Under a named perils form, such as the basic or broad form, the insured must prove that the loss was caused by a covered cause. Under the special form, an accidental loss is presumed to be covered unless the insurer can prove that it was caused by an excluded peril.

Exclusions and Limitations

The special form contains most of the exclusions of the basic and broad forms, including many (but not all) of the limitations expressed in the descriptions of the basic and broad covered causes of loss. In those instances in which the special form does not contain an exclusion or a limitation equivalent to any of those contained in the basic and broad forms, it provides broader coverage. Two examples are given below:

1. The vehicle peril in both the basic and broad forms excludes loss or damage caused by or resulting from vehicles owned by the named insured or operated in the course of the named insured's business. The special form, in contrast, does not contain a similar exclusion. Thus, the special form covers such loss or damage to covered property.

2. The windstorm peril in both the basic and broad forms excludes damage to the interior of a building by rain, snow, sleet, ice, sand, or dust, unless the roof or walls of the building are first damaged by a covered cause of loss. The special form contains the same exclusion, but with an additional exception: The special form exclusion does not apply if loss results from the melting of ice, sleet, or snow on the building or structure. Thus, unlike the basic and broad forms, the special form covers loss caused by water that enters a covered building because of "ice dam" in the building's gutters.

Exclusions Unique to the Special Form

Although the special form covers more causes of loss than the broad form, it nevertheless contains some exclusions and limitations that have no counterparts in the broad form. The special form, as explained above, covers any risks of loss other than those that are specifically excluded. Thus, many hard-to-insure perils that are not covered under the basic and broad forms (because they are not named as covered causes of loss in those forms) must be specifically excluded in the special form. Examples of perils that the special form specifically excludes are as follows:

- Wear and tear
- Rust, corrosion, fungus, decay, or deterioration
- Smog
- Settling, cracking, shrinking, or expansion

- Infestations and waste products of insects, birds, rodents, or other animals
- Damage to personal property by dampness or dryness of atmosphere, changes or extremes in temperatures, or marring or scratching

However, the insurer will pay losses caused by a "specified cause of loss" that results from the excluded peril. The special form defines **"specified causes of loss"** to include all of the causes of loss insured under the causes of loss—broad form. For example, a basement wall of an insured building might crack because soil has settled beneath the foundation. The special form excludes such cracking damage. However, if the settling and cracking cause a natural gas pipe in the building to rupture, resulting in an explosion (a "specified cause of loss"), the resulting explosion damage will be covered even though the special form excludes the initial cause of loss (settling).

The special form also excludes loss caused by the following:

1. Weather conditions that contribute to other excluded causes of loss. If, for example, covered property is damaged by flood waters that were driven in part by high winds, the flood damage will not be covered even though windstorm is not otherwise excluded.

2. Acts or decisions, including the failure to act or decide, of any person, group, organization, or governmental body. Thus, for example, if flooding occurs because municipal authorities fail to take proper flood control measures, the flood exclusion cannot be overcome by the insured's claim that the municipality's failure to act was the cause of the loss.

3. Faulty or inadequate planning, zoning, surveying, siting, design, specifications, workmanship, repair, construction, renovation, remodeling, grading, compaction, materials, or maintenance.

If one of these excluded causes of loss results in a covered cause of loss, the insurer will pay the loss resulting from the covered cause. For example, the failure of a city's fire department to take necessary measures might allow a fire to spread and burn down several adjoining row houses. Even though the fire department's failure to act contributed to the destruction of the adjoining row houses, they were destroyed by fire, a covered cause of loss. Thus, the loss would be covered.

Another noteworthy exclusion that is unique to the special form eliminates coverage for the release, discharge, or dispersal of pollutants. However, the exclusion does not apply to any release of pollutants caused by any of the "specified causes of loss."

Loss to the following kinds of property is covered only if it is caused by "specified causes of loss":

1. Valuable papers and records
2. Animals, and then only in the event of their death
3. Fragile articles if broken, such as glassware, statuary, marble, chinaware, and porcelain (but not including building glass, containers of property held for sale, and lenses)
4. Builders' machinery and equipment owned or held by the insured unless on or within 100 feet of the described premises

Theft-Related Exclusions

The special form does not contain a general exclusion of theft, and thus it covers any theft of covered property that is not specifically excluded. Since coverage for theft is probably the greatest advantage of the special form over the broad form, the pertinent theft exclusions are described in some detail below.

The special form excludes dishonest acts of the insured or of partners, directors, or employees of the insured. Employee dishonesty (embezzlement) losses can be covered under separate crime coverage forms, discussed in Chapter 5.

The special form also excludes the voluntary surrendering of possession of property as the result of a fraudulent scheme or trickery. If, for example, a thief posing as an honest customer tricks the insured's salesperson into *voluntarily* allowing the thief to remove merchandise from the insured's store, the resulting theft loss will not be covered. Similarly, the special form excludes loss of property transferred outside the described premises on the basis of unauthorized instructions.

Loss by theft of construction materials not attached as part of the building is excluded unless the materials are held for sale by the named insured. Moreover, the special form excludes loss of property that is simply missing without explanation or that is evidenced only by an inventory shortage.

Despite these theft-related exclusions, the special form provides expansive theft coverage. Burglary and robbery, two of the most common types of theft other than employee dishonesty, are covered. *Burglary* is the taking of property by breaking and entering, and *robbery* is the taking of property accompanied by a threat of violence to the person having custody of the property. (These terms will be described in more detail in Chapter 5, which deals with separate crime insurance forms.)

The special form imposes limits on theft loss of certain kinds of property that are especially attractive to thieves. Such property can be insured for higher limits under separate crime or inland marine forms. The special form's theft limits are as follows:

- $2,500 for furs and garments trimmed with fur
- $2,500 for jewelry, watches, and precious metals, but the limit does not apply to jewelry or watches valued at $100 or less per item
- $2,500 for patterns, dies, molds, and forms
- $250 for stamps, tickets, and letters of credit

The special form does not provide any coverage for theft of *money*, which is the type of property most attractive to thieves. This is because money is not covered property under any of the commercial property coverage forms (such as the building and personal property form) to which the causes-of-loss forms are attached. Separate crime coverage forms are available to cover theft of money.

Additional Coverages

The special form contains an additional coverage for collapse that is essentially the same as the additional coverage for collapse under the broad form. The special form, unlike the broad form, does not contain an additional coverage for breakage of glass. However, the special form, like the broad form, imposes a $100 per pane limit and a $500 per occurrence limit on glass breakage caused by vandalism or any nonexcluded peril other than the "specified causes of loss."

Additional Coverage Extensions

Two additional coverage extensions extend the policy to cover two kinds of losses that would not otherwise be covered: loss to property in transit and certain repair costs related to damage caused by water or other specified substances.

Property in Transit

The property in transit extension provides up to $1,000 of additional protection for loss to the insured's property in transit. The property must be in or on a motor vehicle owned, leased, or operated by the insured and cannot be in the custody of the insured's sales personnel. It covers only those losses that occur within the coverage territory. (The builders risk form, discussed later in this chapter, increases this sublimit to $5,000.)

The transit extension does not provide "all-risks" coverage. The perils insured against are fire, lightning, explosion, windstorm, hail, riot, civil commotion, vandalism, upset or overturn of the conveying vehicle, collision of the conveying vehicle with another vehicle or an object other than the roadbed, and theft. The coverage for theft is limited to theft of an entire bale, case, or package by forced entry into a securely locked body or compartment of the vehicle, evidenced by marks of the forced entry.

Since the property in transit coverage extension is limited in terms of both the limit of coverage provided and the perils covered, insureds who regularly (or even occasionally) have property in transit should consider covering such property under an inland marine or ocean marine policy, which will be discussed in Chapter 7.

Cost of Tearing Out and Replacing

A clause titled "water damage, other liquids, powder or molten material damage" extends coverage to pay for the cost of tearing out and replacing any part of a building necessary to repair an appliance or a system from which water or another liquid—or even powder extinguishing agents or molten materials—escaped. The extension does not pay for the repair of any defect that resulted in the leakage. It will pay for repairs to fire extinguishing equipment if the damage results in the discharge of any substance from an automatic fire protection system or is directly caused by freezing.

Causes of Loss—Earthquake Form

All three causes-of-loss forms exclude loss by earthquake and volcanic eruption, other than volcanic action as defined in the forms. Coverage for earthquake and volcanic eruption can be added by using the **causes of loss—earthquake form**. The earthquake form can be used in conjunction with any of the three causes-of-loss forms or on a stand-alone basis.

Under the earthquake form, all earthquake shocks that occur within a 168-hour period (seven days) are considered to be a single occurrence. Similarly, all volcanic eruptions that occur within a 168-hour period are considered to be one occurrence. Consequently, the policy limit and deductible would apply only once to all losses incurred during a 168-hour period.

The deductible is stated as a percentage of the limit of insurance or, in the case of blanket insurance, of the value shown in the insured's statement of values.

Other Commercial Property Coverage Forms

The building and personal property coverage form (BPP), which was described in Chapter 2, is intended to meet the needs of the vast majority of organizations that wish to insure their buildings and business personal property. More specialized commercial property coverage forms for insuring buildings or business personal property or both are available for those that need them. Three such forms, described below, are the builders risk coverage form, the condominium association coverage form, and the condominium commercial unit-owners coverage form.

Builders Risk Coverage Form

The BPP provides some protection for new buildings while under construction. However, that coverage is limited and is intended only as incidental protection. Buildings under construction are insured more appropriately under the **builders risk coverage form**. The discussion that follows describes the ISO builders risk coverage form in terms of its notable *differences* from the BPP.

Eligible Property and Insureds

The builders risk coverage form may be used to insure any building in the course of construction, including buildings (such as farm buildings and dwellings) that will not be eligible for coverage under the BPP when construction is completed. By using special endorsements, the builders risk form can also be adapted for covering additions or alterations to existing buildings. The parties that can be insured by a builders risk policy include the building owner and the building contractor.

Covered Property

The property covered by the builders risk coverage form is the building described in the declarations while in the course of construction, including the following:

- Foundations
- If not covered by other insurance, temporary structures built or assembled on site, such as scaffolding or concrete forms
- Property intended to become part of the building—such as lumber, uninstalled windows, doors, sinks, and furnaces—while located within 100 feet of the described premises

The builders risk form does *not* cover land or water; outside lawns, trees, shrubs, or plants; outside radio or television antennas, including satellite dishes; or outdoor signs not attached to the building.

Coverage Extensions

The builders risk form contains the same four additional coverages as the BPP but provides only two coverage extensions. The first builders risk coverage extension provides up to $5,000 at each covered location for damage to building materials or supplies owned by others, such as a plumbing or roofing subcontractor. In order to be covered, the materials must be in the insured's care, custody, or control; must be located in or on the building or within 100 feet of its premises; and must be intended to become a permanent part of the building. The $5,000 limit can be increased by showing a higher limit in the declarations.

The second extension covers loss of or damage to sod, trees, shrubs, and plants outside of buildings on the described premises, but only if the loss or damage is caused by fire, lightning, explosion, riot, civil commotion, or aircraft. The most the insurer will pay under the extension is $1,000 per occurrence, subject to a sublimit of $250 for any one tree, shrub, or plant.

Causes of Loss

Like the BPP, the builders risk form must be combined with a basic, broad, or special causes-of-loss form. Some especially important points about the causes-of-loss forms, as they apply to builders risks, are described below.

Collapse During Construction

The broad and special causes-of-loss forms cover collapse of a building caused by certain named perils, including defective materials or faulty construction, if the collapse occurs during construction. However, the builders risk coverage form specifically excludes collapse occurring during construction. For an additional premium, collapse coverage can be added to the builders risk policy by using the "builders risk—collapse during construction" endorsement.

Theft of Building Materials

Uninstalled building materials at construction sites are a target for thieves. Thus, owners and contractors usually want theft coverage, but insurers are understandably cautious in providing that coverage.

As discussed earlier in this chapter, the basic and broad causes-of-loss forms do not cover theft. Although the special form covers theft, it excludes theft of building materials and supplies not attached as part of the building or structure. Thus, even with the special form, the builders risk coverage form does not cover theft of uninstalled building materials. However, the excluded exposure can be insured by adding an optional endorsement, titled "builders risk—theft of building materials, fixtures, machinery, equipment." This approach allows the insurer to provide coverage for an additional premium that is appropriate for the exposure.

Property in Transit

The special causes-of-loss form contains an extension that provides up to $1,000 coverage for property in transit. If the special form is attached to the builders risk coverage form, a provision in the builders risk form increases the limit from $1,000 to $5,000. When a higher limit of transit insurance is needed, or if the insured wants property in transit to be covered against a broader scope of perils, a separate transit insurance policy can be obtained. Transit insurance will be described in Chapter 7.

Need for Adequate Insurance

A condition in the builders risk form titled "need for adequate insurance" replaces the coinsurance provision found in the building and personal property form but is, in effect, a 100 percent coinsurance clause, with one exception. The clause requires the insured to carry insurance in an amount that is at least equal to the actual cash value of the building *on completion*. In contrast, a 100 percent coinsurance clause would require insurance equal to 100 percent of the value of the building *on the date of loss*. The difference can be substantial.

The amount of loss payment under the builders risk form is calculated by the following formula:

$$\text{Loss payment} = \left[\frac{\text{Limit of insurance}}{\substack{\text{Actual cash value of building} \\ \text{on completion}}} \times \text{Loss} \right] - \text{Deductible}$$

Builders risk insurance can also be provided on a reporting basis; policy premiums are determined on the basis of periodic reports of value rather than on an estimate of the completed value. The reporting approach is seldom used because of the difficulty of making timely and accurate reports of value.

When Coverage Ceases

Coverage under the builders risk form terminates upon the earliest of the following:

1. The expiration date shown in the declarations
2. The date of cancellation
3. The date when the property is accepted by the purchaser
4. When the insured's interest in the property ceases
5. When the insured abandons construction with no intention to complete it

6. Unless the insurer indicates otherwise in writing:
    (a) Ninety days after the construction is completed or
    (b) Sixty days after the building is occupied in whole or in part or is put to its intended use

Other Provisions

In addition to the provisions discussed above, the builders risk form includes provisions relating to the limits of insurance, deductible, abandonment, appraisal, duties in the event of loss or damage, loss payment, recovered property, and mortgageholders. These provisions are essentially the same as the corresponding clauses in the BPP. The valuation clause is much shorter than that of the BPP. It merely says that the covered property will be valued at actual cash value at the time of loss. There is little difference between actual cash value and replacement cost for most buildings under construction since they experience little, if any, depreciation.

Farm Property Insurance

Neither the BPP nor any of the commercial property forms described in this chapter are suitable for insuring farms (or ranches). Typically, farmers live on the land they work and, like any other homeowner, need insurance covering their residential property. In addition, farmers face commercial loss exposures that arise out of their farming operations. Specialized **farm insurance policies** are available to cover both the residential exposures and the commercial exposures faced by farmers.

Farm insurance is usually provided by insurers who use their own, independently developed forms. AAIS and ISO also file farm coverage forms on behalf of their member insurers. The ISO farm property coverage form is highlighted below as an example of the various farm policies on the market. (Farm *liability* coverage will be described briefly in Chapter 8.) The ISO farm property form contains provisions for the following coverages:

Coverage A—Dwellings

Coverage B—Other Private Structures Appurtenant to Dwellings

Coverage C—Household Personal Property

Coverage D—Loss of Use

Coverage E—Scheduled Farm Personal Property

Coverage F—Unscheduled Farm Personal Property

Coverage G—Other Farm Structures

Coverages A through D, like a homeowners policy, cover the farmer's *residential* property. Coverages E and F provide different ways to cover personal property used in farming operations:

- With *scheduled* coverage, separate limits apply to each specifically described item or class of property.
- With *unscheduled* coverage, a single limit applies to all "farm personal property" as defined.

Coverage G insures barns, silos, and additional farm structures other than the dwelling and structures pertaining to the dwelling, such as a detached garage.

The options for covered causes of loss are similar to those of the commercial property causes-of-loss forms. However, the farm form covers some additional livestock perils, such as drowning, electrocution, accidental shooting, and so on.

The farm property form does not cover growing crops. Farmers can insure growing crops under (1) crop insurance provided by private insurers or (2) multiple peril crop insurance provided by the U.S. government.

Condominium Coverage Forms

Condominiums involve the separate ownership of individual units in a multiple-unit building or buildings. In a condominium, each unit owner is the owner of that condominium unit and has an undivided interest with all other unit owners in the jointly owned "common elements" of the building. A condominium association is formed by unit owners to manage the condominium and to own the common elements.

The precise dividing line between the condominium unit (owned by the unit owner) and the common elements (owned by the association) depends on the terms of the particular condominium association agreement, also referred to as the master deed, declarations, or bylaws. State laws can also specify the division of property ownership. Whenever insurance is arranged for a condominium unit owner or association, the pertinent documents and laws must be reviewed carefully in order to ascertain insurance needs.

The unique legal characteristics of condominiums make it necessary to use specialized forms for insuring the respective interests of condominium associations and unit owners. There are two commercial property condominium forms: one for condominium associations and another for owners of *commercial* condominium units.

Two other forms of community ownership, the cooperative corporation and the planned unit development (also called a "homeowners association"), are in many respects similar to condominiums. In each case there is joint ownership of some property. Insurers often use condominium forms to insure cooperative corporations and planned unit developments.

Condominium Association Coverage Form

Like the BPP, the **condominium association coverage form** provides coverage for property in three categories:

1. Building
2. Business personal property of the named insured (which is the association of unit owners)
3. Personal property of others

The discussion that follows highlights the fundamental differences between the condominium association coverage form and the BPP. These differences, which principally concern the building and business personal property items, are due to the unique nature of condominium property ownership.

Building Coverage

The building coverage of the condominium association coverage form closely resembles the building coverage of the BPP. However, a significant difference relates to the following types of property contained within individual units of a condominium building:

- Fixtures, improvements, and alterations
- Appliances, including (but not limited to) those used for refrigerating, ventilating, cooking, dishwashing, laundering, or housekeeping

The condominium building coverage applies to the above items only if the condominium association agreement requires the association to insure them. Otherwise, such property items are not included in the association's building coverage. As will be explained in more detail below, the unit owner's coverage picks up where the association's coverage leaves off, and vice versa.

Business Personal Property

Many condominiums have community clubhouses, health clubs, and the like. The furnishings and equipment of these facilities can be covered as business personal property. As in the case of building coverage, the condominium association coverage form clarifies the dividing line between personal property insured by the association and that insured by individual unit owners:

- Business personal property is covered if it is owned by the association or if it is indivisibly owned by all unit owners.
- Business personal property is not covered if it is owned only by a unit owner.

Other Provisions

Most of the conditions of the condominium association form are the same as those of the BPP. Some of the more notable variations from the BPP are described below.

The condominium association form provides that it is primary as to any loss covered by both that form and the condominium commercial unit owners form. The unit owners form is excess in such situations.

The condominium association form also includes a provision waiving the insurer's right to recover from a unit owner for any loss the insurer has paid to the condominium association. If, for example, the condominium building burned down because of a fire that resulted from a unit owner's negligence, the insurer, after paying the loss, would not be able to exercise its usual right to recover damages from the unit owner.

If the division of ownership between the association and the unit owners (as determined by the condominium association agreement or by state law) differs from the division indicated in the policy form, an endorsement can be used to adapt the policy to meet such requirements. Standard endorsements are provided by ISO to comply with most applicable state laws, but manuscript endorsements may be needed to comply with some condominium association agreements.

Condominium Commercial Unit-Owners Coverage Form

Commercial condominium units are used for offices, stores, and other business activities. The **condominium commercial unit-owners coverage form** is used for insuring owners of such *commercial* condominium units only. Owners of *residential* condominium units should purchase coverage under homeowners policies designed for unit owners.

Covered Property

The condominium commercial unit-owners coverage form covers only "your business personal property" and personal property of others. These coverages are basically the same as in the BPP. Fixtures, improvements, and alterations that are part of the building and owned by the unit owner are included in the definition of "your business personal property" in the unit-owners form.

An exclusion in the unit-owners form coordinates that coverage with the condominium association's coverage. Fixtures, improvements, alterations, and appliances (such as those used for refrigerating, cooking, and so on) are not covered by the unit owner's policy if the condominium association agreement requires the association to insure them. If the agreement requires the association to insure such property but the association fails to do so, the unit owner's policy still does not apply. Another policy provision makes unit-owners coverage excess over the coverage of any association insurance covering the same property.

Optional Coverages

Two optional coverages that are often needed by condominium unit owners are available in a single endorsement that can be attached to the unit-owners coverage form.

One of these optional coverages is **loss assessment coverage**, which covers the unit owner's share of any assessment made by the association against all unit owners because of physical loss or damage to condominium property caused by a covered cause of loss. Typically, a condominium association has the right to assess all unit owners for uninsured losses that the association incurs. These uninsured losses can result, for example, from a large deductible on the association's property policy.

The other optional coverage is **miscellaneous real property coverage**, which extends the unit-owners form to cover real property items that pertain only to the named insured's condominium unit or that the named insured has a duty to insure according to the condominium association agreement. An example of property insurable under this endorsement is a storage or garage building owned by the association but used solely by the unit owner.

Commercial Property Conditions

One of the documents required to make up a commercial property coverage part is the **commercial property conditions form**. The nine conditions expressed in this form apply in addition to the common policy conditions, described in Chapter 1. The commercial property conditions are listed below:

- Concealment, misrepresentation, or fraud
- Control of property
- Insurance under two or more coverage parts
- Legal action against the insurance company

Insurance for Highly Protected Risks

Insurance for **highly protected risks,** commonly known as **HPR insurance,** is used to insure large, well-protected properties. HPR insurance originated with New England textile manufacturers who, in the early 1830s, formed mutual insurance companies, known as factory mutuals, to obtain lower insurance rates for their mills. They felt that lower rates were justified by the heavy-timber construction of their mills and the extensive fire protection equipment that they had installed.

So successful was the concept that the estimated rate of $.84 per $100 insurance for a typical mill in 1830 was reduced to $.30 by 1875. In 1910, with the introduction of the first automatic sprinkler systems, the rate was further reduced to $.10 and by 1935 had dropped to approximately $.03 per $100 of insurance.* Today, HPR rates as low as $.01 per $100 of insurance are not unheard of.

HPR coverages are broader in many respects than standard forms, and HPR rates are often considerably lower than most insurers' standard commercial property rates. But not every insured can qualify for HPR insurance, and not every insurer is able to provide it. The insured must have a proactive management determined to control the risk of property loss. The insurer must be able to provide the specialized engineering services needed to implement a highly effective loss prevention plan for the insured's property. Most HPR insurance is written by pools of insurance companies and by a few large insurers.

Properties qualifying for HPR insurance generally have the following characteristics:

- Fire-resistive, noncombustible, or heavy timber (mill) construction
- Automatic sprinkler systems and other loss prevention equipment
- Adequate water supply and water pressure
- Adequate public or private fire protection

There is no one standard HPR policy; each pool or individual insurer offering HPR insurance develops its own policy forms. Generally speaking, HPR policies contain a broader definition of property covered, cover more perils, and provide more supplementary coverages than the ISO commercial property forms. ISO forms are sometimes amended to provide coverage similar to that of HPR policies.

*"HPR—It Pays," a speech by Wolfgang F. Friedel, Vice President, International Operations, Arkwright Mutual Insurance Company, at Nordic Risk Management Conference, Oslo, Norway, October 1960.

- Liberalization
- No benefit to bailee
- Other insurance
- Policy period, coverage territory
- Transfer of rights of recovery against others

Concealment, Misrepresentation, or Fraud

The commercial property coverage part is *void* if the insured commits any fraudulent act related to the coverage. (A **void contract** is one that never legally existed.) Submission of a fraudulent claim, for example, would void the coverage part.

The coverage part is also void if the insured conceals or misrepresents any material fact pertaining to (1) the coverage part, (2) the covered property, or (3) the insured's interest in the covered property. A **misrepresentation** is an active misstatement of a fact. For example, assume that John Doe, who has previously been convicted of arson, applies for fire insurance. If the application specifically asks whether the applicant has ever been convicted of arson and Doe responds that he has not, his answer would be a misrepresentation.

Concealment does not involve an active misstatement of fact. A **concealment** is a passive failure to disclose a material fact. In the example, if the application does not ask about past convictions for arson and Doe simply remains silent about his conviction, this could be considered concealment.

Misrepresentation or concealment does not always void coverage. Only *material* misrepresentation or concealment voids coverage. A fact is material if knowledge of it would cause the insurer to charge a higher premium or decline to write the coverage. For example, an insured might state that his or her building is painted red when in fact it is painted yellow. This misstatement would have no bearing on the insurance and would therefore not be material.

Control of Property

The control of property condition consists of two parts. The first part states that coverage under the policy will not be affected by acts or omissions of persons other than the insured if the others are not acting under the direction or control of the insured. The second part of the condition says that a violation of a policy condition at one location will not affect coverage at any other location.

To illustrate how this clause might apply, assume that a liquor store's policy is endorsed to require that its burglar alarm system be maintained in working order at all insured locations. Assume also that the insured leases these locations from other parties. The first part of the clause would protect the insured if the system was disconnected by a building owner, providing the owner was not under the insured's control.

The second part of the control of property condition can be important to the insured if the policy provides coverage at more than one location. In the absence of this part of the control clause, the insured's failure to maintain the alarm system at one location might suspend coverage at all locations, even though the alarm systems are properly maintained at the other locations. Under this provision, only the coverage at the location with the deficient alarm system would be affected.

Insurance Under Two or More Coverage Parts

This policy condition is necessary because several coverage parts can be included in a single commercial package policy. When that is the case, some property might be covered under two or more of the coverage parts. This clause prevents double recovery by the insured in such instances. The total payment under all applicable coverage parts is limited to the actual amount of the loss. Duplication, or "stacking," of the limits is avoided.

Legal Action Against the Insurance Company

This condition spells out two requirements the insured must meet before legal action can be brought against the insurance company to enforce the policy. First, the insured must have complied with all conditions of the policy, including those in the coverage part and the common policy conditions, as well as the applicable loss conditions. Second, the action must be brought within two years after the date on which the direct physical loss occurred.

Liberalization

If the insurance company adopts any revision that would broaden the coverage under the commercial property coverage part and for which there is no additional premium charge, the broader coverage is extended automatically to outstanding policies. This automatic coverage applies only if the broadening amendment is adopted during the policy term or within forty-five days before the effective date of the policy. Liberalization applies only to amendments that broaden coverage and not to those that restrict coverage.

The liberalization clause is beneficial to insureds because it provides them with the broadened coverage automatically and immediately upon adoption, even if they are not aware of the broadening amendment. However, it applies only to broadening amendments for which there is no additional premium charge.

The liberalization clause is beneficial to producers because it relieves them from having to search their client files to find insureds who would benefit from adding the amendments. In addition, insurance companies are relieved of the cost of issuing numerous individual endorsements to add the broader coverage to outstanding policies.

No Benefit to Bailee

A *bailee* is a person or business organization that has temporary custody of the property of another. Examples are dry cleaners, television repair shops, laundries, and fur storage firms. Bailees may be liable to *bailors* (the owners of the property) for damage to the property they hold. Bailees sometimes try to limit their liability by contractual provisions stating that the bailee is not liable for damage if the damage is recoverable under insurance carried by the bailor. The "no benefit to bailee" clause is intended to defeat such provisions in the bailment contract and to reinforce the insurance company's right of subrogation against the bailee. (The "Transfer of Rights of Recovery Against Others" section that appears below explains subrogation.)

Other Insurance

An insured may have more than one policy covering a given loss. In keeping with the principle of indemnity, the other insurance condition limits the total recovery from all applicable insurance to an amount not in excess of the actual loss sustained.

If the other insurance is provided by another policy subject to the same plan, terms, and conditions, then each policy pays in the proportion its policy limit bears to the total policy limits of all applicable policies. For example, assume that a building is insured with two policies (as shown in Exhibit 3-2), both using the ISO commercial property coverage part. If a covered loss of $50,000 occurs, 40 percent ($20,000) would be paid by Insurance Company A and 60 percent ($30,000) by Insurance Company B.

If the other insurance is not subject to all of the conditions of the ISO commercial property coverage part, then the policy subject to the commercial property coverage part is excess coverage and pays only to the extent the covered loss exceeds that amount due from the other policy.

In the example, if Company B's policy included the commercial property coverage part, but Company A's policy did not, Company A would pay the entire $50,000 loss (assuming no other limiting provision, such as coinsur-

Exhibit 3-2
Application of the Other Insurance Clause

Insurance on Building
- Insurance Company A $100,000
- Insurance Company B $150,000

Total insurance $250,000

Company A's share of insurance $= \dfrac{\$100,000}{\$250,000} = .40 = 40\%$

Company B's share of insurance $= \dfrac{\$150,000}{\$250,000} = .60 = 60\%$

Covered Loss of $50,000

If both policies are subject to the same plan, terms, and conditions:
- Insurance Company A pays 40 percent of loss = $20,000
- Insurance Company B pays 60 percent of loss = $30,000

If Insurance Company B used ISO Commercial Property
Coverage Part and Insurance Company A did not:
- A. Covered loss $50,000
  - Insurance Company A pays as primary — payment of $50,000
  - Insurance Company B pays as excess — payment of $0
- B. Covered loss $200,000
  - Insurance Company A pays as primary — $100,000
  - Insurance Company B pays as excess — $100,000

Note: These examples ignore any coinsurance, deductible, or other clauses that might otherwise apply.

ance, applied) since the amount of loss was less than Company A's policy limit. Company B would pay nothing. If the loss had been $200,000, Company A would pay its policy limit ($100,000), and Company B would pay the excess ($100,000).

The proration of coverage between dissimilar policies is often complicated by the presence of an excess provision in the other policy or policies. When each policy provides that it is excess, the courts generally disregard the excess provisions and require each company to share in the loss.

Policy Period, Coverage Territory

The commercial property conditions state that coverage begins on the effective date and ends on the expiration date shown in the common declarations. The declarations state that the beginning and ending time is 12:01 A.M., determined by standard time at the insured's mailing address as shown in the common declarations, even though some or all of the insured property may be located in a different time zone. The insured property is covered only while it is located within the United States of America (including its territories and possessions), Puerto Rico, or Canada.

Transfer of Rights of Recovery Against Others

This policy condition enables the insurance company, after it has paid a loss under the policy, to recover the amount paid from any party (other than the insured) who caused the loss or is otherwise legally liable for the loss. This process is known as **subrogation**, though that term is not used in the policy. For example, the owner of a building might enter into a contract to have the building renovated by a contractor. If the building is damaged by a fire caused by the negligence of the contractor, the building owner would have a right to recover from the contractor for the fire damage. If the owner collects instead from his or her insurance policy, the owner's insurance company, after payment of the fire loss, would take over the right of recovery from the contractor, and the insured would be obligated to assist the insurance company in its efforts to recover the amount paid.

If the insured takes any action that eliminates the insurer's right of recovery (other than those actions specifically authorized by the policy), the insurer may not be required to pay the loss. The policy specifically permits the insured to waive the right of recovery against any other party, provided the waiver is made in writing and before the loss occurs. In the example above, the property owner could have included in the written agreement with the contractor a clause waiving the owner's right of recovery from the contractor for fire damage to the building. Such a clause would have precluded the insurer from seeking recovery from the contractor, but it would not have impaired the owner's right to collect from the insurer, since the "waiver" was in writing and given before the loss occurred.

Waiver of recovery may be given by the insured *after* loss only to (1) another party insured under the same policy, (2) a parent or subsidiary company, or (3) a tenant of the insured property. Any other waiver given by the insured after loss has occurred may impair the insured's right to collect from the insurer for the loss.

Rating Commercial Property Coverage

A **rate** is the price per exposure unit for insurance coverage—for example, $1.00 per $100 of insurance coverage. **Rating** is the process of applying a rate to a particular exposure and performing any other necessary calculations to determine the policy premium for that exposure.

Thus, as a simplified example, if the applicable rate for a particular coverage is $.50 per $100 of insurance and the limit of the coverage is $100,000, the premium for the coverage would be calculated as follows:

$$\frac{\$.50}{\$100} \times \$100,000 = \$500$$

In reality, rating is usually more complicated. Rates are seldom round numbers like $1.00 or $.50, and neither are property insurance limits. Moreover, additional calculations are often needed. For example, the rate or the premium must often be multiplied by additional factors to account for territorial differences in theft losses (if theft is a covered cause of loss), to reduce the premium when the insured has selected a high deductible, to increase the premium when a coverage option has been added, and so on.

In most insurance organizations, rating is performed by employees called *raters*. In some cases, raters perform their work using a calculator and a rate manual. In other cases, the rater keys the necessary rating information into a computer, and a computer-rating program processes the information and calculates the premium. Computerized rating has become increasingly common in recent years.

The primary source of information for rating ISO coverages is the **Commercial Lines Manual (CLM)** published by ISO. (Similar information is provided by the American Association of Insurance Services on behalf of its member companies for rating AAIS coverage forms.) The CLM contains nine divisions, as follows:

1. Automobile
2. Boiler and machinery
3. Crime
4. Farm
5. Fire and allied lines
6. General liability
7. Professional liability

8.   Inland marine

9.   Multiple line

Division 5 (fire and allied lines) contains rating procedures and loss costs for the ISO commercial property coverages. **Loss costs** are the portion of the rate that covers projected claim payments and loss adjusting expenses. To convert these loss costs to complete rates that can be used to rate a policy, each insurer must increase the loss costs to cover other predicted expenses that the insurer will incur (such as underwriting, marketing, and taxes). In addition, a charge is usually added to allow for possible errors in the insurer's predictions. An allowance for insurer profit may also be added.

Most insurers that provide commercial property insurance follow the CLM rating procedures in applying their own rates. Because these rating procedures are many and detailed, the discussion that follows does not attempt to describe the actual mechanics of rating. Rather, the discussion focuses on the **rating factors** that principally affect the premium for commercial property coverage on buildings and business personal property. The factors that affect the premium are information that the producer often needs to transmit to the underwriter and the rater. Understanding those factors is also fundamental to reducing the cost of insurance, since many of the factors are within the insured's control.

Some of the factors affecting commercial property premiums are various aspects of coverage expressed in the commercial property coverage part. Other factors—such as the type of building construction and the type of business occupying the building—exist independently of the coverage being provided.

Aspects of Coverage

The aspects of coverage that affect the premium are the limit of insurance being provided, the causes-of-loss form that applies, the applicable coinsurance requirement, the amount of the deductible, and any optional coverages that apply to the commercial property coverage part. Builders risk policies also receive special treatment for rating.

Limit of Insurance

The limit of insurance applicable to the coverage is an important component of the final premium since that is the "exposure" against which the applicable rate is multiplied to calculate the premium. Given the same rate, doubling the limit of insurance doubles the premium.

Causes of Loss

The premium for the causes of loss—basic form consists of a Group I premium (for fire, lightning, explosion, vandalism, and sprinkler leakage) and a Group II premium (for all other causes of loss covered under the basic form). The broad form premium consists of the basic form (Group I and Group II) premium plus a premium for the cost of covering the additional perils covered by the broad form. The same approach is used with the special form except that the additional premium is higher than the additional premium that applies to the broad form.

Coinsurance

The rates ordinarily used for insuring buildings and personal property are calculated with the assumption that they will be used with an 80 percent coinsurance clause in the policy. These rates are therefore called the "80 percent coinsurance rates." When a policy contains a higher coinsurance percentage, the 80 percent coinsurance rate is reduced in order to encourage the purchase of higher limits. For 90 percent coinsurance, the 80 percent coinsurance rate is multiplied by .95, and for 100 percent coinsurance, the 80 percent coinsurance rate is multiplied by .90. Thus, with 90 or 100 percent coinsurance, the insured must buy a greater amount of insurance to comply with the coinsurance requirement, but the rate is reduced. (Exhibit 3-3 illustrates this concept.) When the coinsurance requirement is less than 80 percent, the rate is increased.

Deductibles

Commercial property rates are developed with the assumption that the policy will be subject to a base deductible of $250 or $500, depending on the state. Many policyholders are willing and able to retain a larger deductible. Because raising the deductible reduces the insurer's loss payments, rates are reduced accordingly in return for the insured's acceptance of a higher deductible.

Optional Coverages

Adding optional coverages to the building and personal property coverage form or another coverage form ordinarily increases the policy premium.

In many cases, the optional coverage increases the premium only because the limit of insurance must be increased to cover the additional property values being insured. For example, replacement cost insurance does not involve a higher rate, but the amount of insurance needed to meet the coinsurance requirement on a replacement cost basis may be considerably higher than the amount needed on an actual cash value basis.

Exhibit 3-3
80 Percent Coinsurance Versus 100 Percent Coinsurance

> Jeff owns an apartment building worth $100,000. Jeff could insure this building for $80,000 with 80 percent coinsurance, or he could insure it for $100,000 with 100 percent coinsurance. Assuming an 80 percent coinsurance building rate of $1.00 per $100 of coverage, here is how the premiums would compare.
>
> **With 80 percent coinsurance**
>
> $$\frac{\$1.00}{\$100} \times \$80,000 = \$800 \text{ premium}$$
>
> **With 100 percent coinsurance**
>
> The rate would be discounted as follows:
>
> $1.00 × .90 = $.90 rate for 100 percent coinsurance
>
> However, Jeff needs a $100,000 limit to comply with 100 percent coinsurance. Thus, the premium would be calculated as follows:
>
> $$\frac{\$.90}{\$100} \times \$100,000 = \$900 \text{ premium}$$
>
> Jeff would pay an extra $100 premium but would receive an additional $20,000 of protection. Thus, the rate Jeff would pay for this $20,000 extra protection is only $.50 per $100—one-half the rate that applies to the first $80,000.

In other cases, the charge for a coverage option is a separate rate applied to the amount of insurance. For example, a greenhouse that wishes to buy optional spoilage coverage under its BPP will pay an additional premium equal to the applicable spoilage rate times the limit of insurance on the insured's business personal property.

Builders Risks

The rates for builders risk insurance are set at a fraction of the 80 percent coinsurance building rate. As discussed earlier, the limit of insurance under the builders risk coverage form is the full completed value of the building. However, the actual value of the building is considerably less than the completed value until the project nears completion. Builders risk rates are therefore reduced in order to reflect the lower values at risk during the initial part of the policy period.

Other Factors

Apart from the terms of coverage, factors that affect commercial property premiums are the building's construction, its location, its occupancy, and its protection. To a large extent, these factors relate to fire, which is often the most significant cause of loss in a commercial property policy.

Construction

Some types of buildings resist fire better than others, thus lessening the fire risk for both the buildings and their contents. Although buildings can be classified in many ways, the system used to classify buildings for purposes of rating commercial property insurance is based on resistance to fire.

The six construction classes used for purposes of rating commercial property insurance are (1) frame, (2) joisted masonry, (3) noncombustible, (4) masonry noncombustible, (5) modified fire resistive, and (6) fire resistive. Frame construction, which uses wood or other combustible material in the exterior walls of a building (even if covered by brick veneer or stucco), is the most susceptible to fire damage. Fire-resistive construction uses materials with a fire-resistance rating of at least two hours and is the least susceptible to fire damage.

Location

The risk of fire, windstorm, theft, earthquake, and other perils varies depending on the location of the insured property. For example, buildings along the coastline of the southeastern United States are more exposed to hurricane damage than buildings in other areas. Thus, different rates apply to different areas, or the rates are modified by "territorial multipliers" that account for the differences.

Occupancy

Occupancy refers to the type of activity conducted inside the building. Some occupancies are riskier than others. To cite an extreme example, a building, if used for manufacturing fireworks, will face a greater explosion and fire risk than if the same building were used for storing bottled water. Accordingly, commercial property rates are higher for buildings with more hazardous occupancies.

Protection

Fire protection can be either internal (such as a sprinkler system) or external (the local fire department). For purposes of rating commercial property insurance, external protection is graded on a scale of 1 (the best protection) to 10 (the worst), with the assigned number indicating the availability of firefighting personnel and equipment. For internal protection, buildings classified as "sprinklered" receive rate reductions. In contrast, buildings that have certain fire hazards (such as unsafe heating or cooking devices or inadequate electrical wiring) are charged higher premiums than if these hazards did not exist.

Class Rates and Specific Rates

At one time, commercial buildings were inspected individually by rating bureau representatives, and rates reflecting the exposure to loss of a particular business were published. This approach to developing rates is known as **specific rating**.

As the gathering of loss statistics became more sophisticated, insurance companies were better able to generalize about the probabilities of loss within large groups of similar risks and to formulate rates that reflected the average probability of loss for businesses within these groups. With this approach, known as **class rating**, a building and its contents can be rated without inspecting the building and developing a specific rate.

Large businesses, along with certain other businesses with operations involving unusual or increased exposures to loss, are still specifically rated. However, class rating has become possible for the majority of commercial insureds.

Summary

Three causes-of-loss forms are available for expressing the perils covered in a commercial property policy: the basic form, the broad form, and the special form.

The basic form covers fire, lightning, explosion, windstorm, hail, smoke, aircraft, vehicles, riot, civil commotion, vandalism, sprinkler leakage, sinkhole collapse, and volcanic action.

The broad form covers the same causes of loss as the basic form plus falling objects; weight of snow, ice, or sleet; and water damage. Glass breakage and collapse are covered as "additional coverages."

The special form provides so-called "all-risks" insurance, covering risks of loss except those specifically excluded. This approach encompasses the broad form perils plus theft and other perils not specifically excluded.

All three causes-of-loss forms exclude building ordinance or law requirements, earth movement, governmental action, interruption of off-premises utility services, war, flood, electrical disturbances, steam boiler explosion, and mechanical breakdown. The special form contains several additional exclusions.

In addition to the BPP, several other commercial property forms are available for insuring special exposures.

The condominium association coverage form can be used to insure a condominium association against loss to its buildings, its personal property, and the personal property of others. The form covers fixtures, improvements, alterations, and appliances within condominium units only if the condominium association agreement requires the association to insure them.

The condominium commercial unit-owners coverage form provides business personal property coverage for commercial (not residential) unit owners. The form provides essentially the same coverage for the insured's business personal property as the BPP. To dovetail with the condominium association form, the unit-owners form covers fixtures, improvements, alterations, and appliances owned by the insured unless the condominium association agreement requires the association to insure them.

The builders risk coverage form is designed to insure the interests of owners or contractors (or both) in buildings or other structures during construction. The form covers the building under construction and building materials and temporary structures located at the building site. The builders risk form is usually issued with a limit equal to the projected value of the completed building.

The commercial property conditions form must be included in every commercial property coverage part. The commercial property conditions address various matters that could affect any commercial property coverage form.

Commercial property policy premiums are affected by the following factors: the limit of insurance, the causes of loss covered, the applicable coinsurance rate, deductible levels, the presence of optional coverages, and the building's construction, location, occupancy, and protection.

Chapter 4

Business Income Insurance

The purpose of **business income insurance** is demonstrated by the example that follows:

The Country Furniture Store was badly damaged by a fire. Rebuilding the store and replacing its contents took six months. During that time, the store was closed and unable to make any sales. The store's losses consisted of the following:

1. *The decrease in value of the building and its contents*
2. *The loss of income from sales that the store would have made during the six months that the store was closed because of the fire*
3. *The increased costs the store incurred (express delivery of materials and overtime pay for workers) in order to reopen in time for the spring selling season*

Country Furniture Store's building and personal property insurance covered the loss described in item 1 above, and it also covered the cost of removing debris of covered property. The store also had business income insurance, which covered the loss described in items 2 and 3 above. This chapter describes both the business income loss exposure and business income insurance in more detail.

Because the severity of business income loss is directly related to how long it takes to restore the property, business income coverage is called a "time element" coverage. It is also referred to as "business interruption" coverage, because the loss of business income results from the interruption of the insured's business.

Business Income Loss Exposure

For the purposes of discussing the business income loss exposure, the words "business income," "profit," and similar terms are used. Although many kinds of organizations (such as nonprofit organizations and public entities) do not use these accounting labels, they, too, have revenues and expenses that govern their financial existence and make them similar, *for insurance purposes*, to profit-making enterprises. Thus, although this chapter uses terms such as "business income," "business," and "profit," the insurance applies equally to nonprofit and governmental entities.

Net Income

Business income losses can be measured in terms of net income. **Net income**, or profit, is the difference between revenues (assets received, such as money paid for goods or services) and expenses (reductions in net assets, such as money paid for merchandise, rent, and insurance). The definition of net income can be expressed by the following simple formula:

$$\text{Revenues} - \text{Expenses} = \text{Net income}$$

The net income, or profit, a business could have earned will be reduced if the business must close temporarily because of physical damage to its property. When insurance people speak of a "business income" loss, they are referring to this *reduction* in profit.

Changes in Expenses During Business Interruption

When a business is closed temporarily, it must continue to pay most, if not all, of its normal operating expenses. A business can also incur extra expenses during a shutdown. Therefore, both continuing expenses and extra expenses are considered when measuring a business income loss.

Continuing Expenses

Reducing operating expenses is difficult, particularly if business is interrupted for only a short time. Payroll of key employees, debt repayments, taxes, insurance, and many other expenses continue whether or not the business is open. If a longer interruption of business occurs, many expenses can be reduced or eliminated. Production line workers can be laid off, debt can be refinanced, taxes are reduced, and insurance premiums are smaller. It is often difficult to predict which expenses will continue and which will not since there are so many different kinds of loss that might occur. However, the effect of **continuing expenses** on a business income loss can be substantial. In many cases, these expenses are greater than the profit earned by a firm.

Example of a Business Income Loss

Business income losses happen when net income (profit) is reduced by an accidental event. A simplified example would be a record store with annual sales of $1,200,000 and a profit of $240,000 after paying all of the expenses:

Revenues	$1,200,000
Expenses	960,000
Profit	$ 240,000

A fire closes the store for one month, and an estimated $75,000 in revenue is lost from the date of the fire until the store reopens. At the same time, some expenses (payroll, electricity, advertising, and so on) are temporarily reduced or eliminated because the store is closed, saving $40,000. Additional expenses (express freight on replacement merchandise) amounting to $5,000 are required to get the store open as soon as possible. Thus, for the year following the loss, the financial picture would be as follows:

Revenues	$1,125,000
Expenses	925,000
Profit	$ 200,000

The $40,000 business income loss (made up of reduced income, some reduced expenses, and some higher expenses) is the difference between the net income of $240,000 the store had been expected to earn and the $200,000 it did earn despite the fire.

One major difference between business income losses and direct damage losses is that it is much more difficult to agree on the amount of a business income loss because it can only be an estimate based on what might have happened had no loss occurred.

Extra Expenses

Extra expenses are expenses that an organization would not have incurred if the business interruption had not occurred. Examples of extra expenses are as follows:

- In order to reopen an assembly line that had been shut down because of an explosion, the factory owner paid the additional costs of overtime labor and overnight air shipment of needed repair parts.

- After sustaining fire damage to its warehouse, a wholesale distributor rented a similar warehouse and was able to continue its operations within two weeks instead of shutting down entirely for several months.

- A newspaper that suffered a fire in its printing plant was able to rent press time from a competing newspaper in the same city.

Often, extra expense measures pay for themselves. For example, the extra cost of overtime labor and air freight of needed parts might have been considerably less than the income that would have been lost if such measures were not taken. Such measures actually reduce the business income loss, and most organizations will readily undertake measures that reduce loss.

Some organizations will even incur extra expenses that they know will actually *increase* the business income loss. For example, after a property loss occurs, a hospital might incur substantial extra expenses to maintain essential services for its patients even though such expenses will increase the business income loss. The decision to incur such extra expenses depends on the organization's objectives. For some organizations, maintaining continuous service to its customers may be more important than reducing the business income loss.

Property and Perils Involved in Business Income Losses

Business income losses typically result from physical damage to the affected organization's own buildings or personal property. That is not always the case, however. In some cases, a physical loss at one location can cause a business interruption elsewhere.

For example, a business may be shut down because of damage to off-premises property providing utilities, such as electricity, water, or communications. Or one business may depend on another property either as a major customer or as a sole supplier. It is also possible that a business is dependent simply because it is near a key facility or "leader" property, such as a major department store in a shopping mall. If any of these other properties are damaged, the effect could include a business income loss at the location where there was no physical damage.

For business income losses associated with property exposures, the causes of loss are typically the same as those for physical damage losses. Thus, a fire or a windstorm that damages property may also cause a business income loss. However, a business income loss can result when there has been no physical damage to buildings or personal property. The closing of a road or a strike by the firm's employees can cause a business income loss, although such risks are generally not insurable.

Business Income Coverage Form

Insurance for most business income exposures can be provided under either of two versions of the business income coverage form.

- The **business income (and extra expense) coverage form** covers both business income and extra expense losses.
- The **business income (without extra expense) coverage form** covers business income but only covers extra expenses to the extent that they reduce the business income loss.

The business income coverage form (BIC) can be included in a commercial property coverage part, either with or without another commercial property coverage form such as the BPP. The causes of loss covered for business income coverage can be designated by either the same causes-of-loss form that applies to other coverage forms or by a different causes-of-loss form that applies to business income coverage only.

Because the two versions of the BIC are similar in all respects except extra expense coverage, the discussion that follows applies equally to both forms except where specified otherwise.

Coverage

The business income insuring agreement, four additional coverages, and a coverage extension are set forth in the initial section of the BIC entitled "coverage."

Business Income Insuring Agreement

The insurer agrees to pay the actual loss of business income sustained by the named insured because of the necessary suspension of the named insured's "operations" during the "period of restoration." The suspension must result from direct physical loss or damage to real or personal property caused by a covered cause of loss and occurring at the premises described in the declarations. If the insured is a tenant, the definition of "premises" is broadened to include "all routes within the building (used) to gain access to the described premises." Thus, if fire damaged the elevator motors in the basement of a building, a tenant on the tenth floor would be covered for any resulting business income loss even if there was no damage above the first floor. The covered causes of loss are specified in the causes-of-loss form entered in the declarations and attached to the policy.

Business income, for the purposes of this coverage, means the sum of (1) net profit or loss that would have been earned or incurred if the suspension had not occurred and (2) normal operating expenses, including payroll, that continue during the suspension. The amount of profit or loss that would have been earned or incurred if the suspension had not occurred must be estimated based on past and prospective performance of the business. The continuing expenses can be determined precisely during the suspension. Those expenses might include salaries of key employees, property taxes, and interest expenses.

The terms "operations" and "period of restoration" are defined in a separate section of the coverage form. The **operations** of the insured are the business activities of the insured that occur at the premises described in the declarations. **Period of restoration** has a split definition. For business income coverage, it is the period of time that begins seventy-two hours after the time of direct physical loss or damage; for extra expense coverage, it begins immediately after the loss. In both cases, the period of restoration ends when the property should be restored with reasonable speed and similar quality or when the business is resumed at a new, permanent location. Thus, for business income coverage, there is no coverage for the first three days following the loss. This "time deductible" was introduced in the 1995 forms revision; earlier editions of the business income coverage form provided coverage without a deductible. The seventy-two hour deductible can be reduced to twenty-four hours by endorsement for an additional premium.

The period of restoration does not include any additional time that might be required to repair or reconstruct the building in order to comply with any building code or law, unless the policy has been specifically endorsed to cover such additional time. The period of restoration also does not include any increased period required by ordinance or law to respond to or assess the effects of pollutants.

Additional Coverages and Coverage Extension

The business income coverage form provides four additional coverages and a coverage extension to insure some sources of business income loss that would not otherwise be covered by the BIC. These additional coverages and extension consist of the following:

- Extra expense/expenses to reduce loss
- Civil authority

- Alterations and new buildings
- Extended business income
- Newly acquired locations

Extra Expense

The business income *with extra expense* coverage form provides coverage for extra expenses incurred by the named insured to avoid or minimize the suspension of operations. Examples of extra expenses to avoid or minimize the suspension of business are expenses to move to a temporary location, increased rent at the temporary location, rental of substitute equipment (furniture, fixtures, and machinery), and the cost of substitute services such as data processing. The business income with extra expense form covers such expenses in full, subject to the policy limit.

However, extra expenses *to repair or replace property* are treated differently. They are covered only to the extent that they actually reduce the business income loss. For example, a businessowner might pay a contractor at an overtime rate to work around the clock to repair damaged property so that the business can reopen promptly. The additional cost paid to do so would be payable as extra expense, but only to the extent that it actually reduced the business income loss. Thus, if reopening earlier reduced the business income loss by $20,000, the insurer would pay the overtime charges up to that amount (and subject to the limit of insurance).

Expenses To Reduce Loss

Instead of extra expense coverage, the business income *without extra expense* form contains an additional coverage titled "expenses to reduce loss."

Under this coverage, the insurer agrees to pay any necessary expenses incurred by the named insured (except the cost of extinguishing a fire) to reduce the business income loss. Thus, the insured can incur the same types of expenses as covered under the extra expense coverage, but they are covered only to the extent that they reduce the business income loss.

A danger of the business income *without extra expense* form is that the insured can incur more extra expenses than the resulting reduction in the business income loss. A large, uninsured extra expense loss can result. The business income *with extra expense* form greatly reduces that possibility. Since the rate for the business income with extra expense form is close to the rate for the business income without extra expense form, many businesses opt for the broader coverage of the former.

Civil Authority

The typical loss covered under the business income form results from damage to property at the insured's premises. However, limited coverage is provided if access to the insured's premises is prohibited by civil authority because of damage to other property. For example, fire damage to another building may make it unsafe for customers to go to the insured's premises. If the damage to the other premises resulted from a cause of loss covered by the insured's policy, the resulting income loss at the insured's premises would be covered for the period of suspension, beginning seventy-two hours after the time of the action by civil authority, up to a maximum of three consecutive weeks after the time of the action.

Alterations and New Buildings

In most cases, business income losses result from the interruption of operations that are already underway. However, the form also provides coverage for loss of income resulting from a delay in beginning operations if the delay results from damage at the described premises by a covered cause of loss to any of the following:

1. New buildings or structures, either completed or under construction
2. Alterations or additions to existing buildings
3. Machinery, equipment, supplies, or building materials located on or within 100 feet of the described premises (provided they are used in the construction, alterations, or additions or are incidental to the occupancy of new buildings)

The period of restoration for losses to new or altered buildings begins on the date that operations would have begun if the damage had not occurred.

Extended Business Income

Business income coverage ceases when the period of restoration ends, that is, on the date "when the property at the described premises should be repaired, rebuilt or replaced with reasonable speed and similar quality." However, all of the insured's former customers may not return immediately, especially if the interruption has been long. The **extended business income** clause provides coverage for the resulting reduction in earnings. For example, if a restaurant is closed because of fire damage, its regular diners will patronize other restaurants, and it will take time for the restaurant to rebuild its business after the repairs are made. The extended business income coverage begins when the damaged property has been restored and ends when the insured's business returns to normal, subject to a maximum period of thirty days. This period can be extended beyond thirty days for an additional premium.

However, extended business income does not apply to loss of business income as a result of unfavorable business conditions caused by the effect of the covered cause of loss in the insured's area. This limitation would apply, for example, after a severe hurricane, when an insured's hotel has been repaired but still suffers a reduction in income after reopening because of damage to beaches or other recreational facilities in the area.

Concerning loss of rental value, the form specifies that the coverage ends thirty days after the property has been restored or, if earlier than thirty days, on the date on which tenant occupancy could be restored, with reasonable speed, to the level that would have existed had no loss occurred. This makes clear that the thirty-day period does not apply to loss of rental value for property that might, for example, have been unrented even if no loss had occurred. The thirty-day period can be extended for an additional premium. This coverage option, called "extended period of indemnity," is described in more detail later in this chapter.

Newly Acquired Locations

If coinsurance of 50 percent or more is shown in the declarations, the coverage may be extended, at the option of the insured, to property at premises newly acquired during the policy period (other than property at fairs or exhibitions). The coverage at any newly acquired location is limited to $100,000. This coverage is an additional amount of insurance above the limit stated in the declarations and is not subject to the coinsurance clause. An additional premium is charged for the automatic coverage from the date of acquisition of the new property. The coverage terminates on the earliest of (1) the expiration date of the policy, (2) the date on which the insured reports the acquisition to the insurer, or (3) thirty days after the date of acquisition. This extension is intended to be temporary coverage, providing protection until permanent coverage can be obtained.

Exclusions

There are no exclusions stated in the business income coverage form. However, the exclusions in the causes-of-loss form apply to the business income coverage form. There are also six special exclusions in the causes-of-loss forms that apply specifically to business income coverage.

Off-Premises Services Interruption

The first exclusion applies to any loss caused by a power failure or loss of utility service, however caused, *if the failure occurs outside of a covered building.* Thus, loss of business income caused by a fire at an electric generating plant or a windstorm that knocks down telephone lines would not be covered. Power failures can cause severe business income losses. A fire in an electric utility's generating station in Lower Manhattan once shut down electric service to portions of New York City's financial district for up to ten days. The resulting loss of business income for some firms exceeded $1 million. The unendorsed policy excludes such losses.

If, instead, a covered cause of loss occurs at the described premises because of a power or utility service failure (such as freezing of plumbing), causing a reduction in business income, business income coverage applies—but only for loss of business income resulting from the damage caused by the covered peril. Coverage for the excluded exposure, which is significant for some organizations, can be added by endorsement.

Finished Stock Exclusion

The second exclusion provides that the policy does not cover any loss caused by or resulting from damage to or destruction of finished stock or the time required to reproduce finished stock. **Finished stock** is not defined in the causes-of-loss forms, but it is defined in the business income coverage form as stock manufactured by the named insured. Finished stock does not include stock manufactured by the insured and held for sale at a retail location insured under the same coverage part. If a coinsurance percentage is shown in the declarations, finished stock also does not include alcoholic beverages held for aging.

The exclusion of finished stock means that the BIC does not insure any loss of business income resulting from damage to or destruction of finished stock of manufacturers. Loss of profit on finished stock can be covered by insuring such stock for its selling price under the building and personal property coverage form by adding the "manufacturer's selling price (finished stock only)" endorsement. This endorsement amends the valuation basis for finished stock covered by the building and personal property form to selling price less discounts and unincurred expenses.

Antenna Exclusion

The third exclusion eliminates coverage for any income loss resulting from damage to or destruction of radio or television antennas, including satellite dishes, or their lead-in wiring, masts, or towers. Providing coverage for this type of property, as in the case of a television or radio station, may be complex, and the insurer would likely want to consider it separately. However, when the insurer is willing to extend coverage, this exclusion can be eliminated by attaching the appropriate endorsement.

Delay Exclusion

The fourth exclusion has two parts. The first part excludes any increase of loss resulting from a delay in rebuilding, repairing, or replacing property or resuming operations if such a delay is caused by the interference of strikers or others at the location of the rebuilding, repairing, or replacing. The interference must be at the premises where the restoration is in progress. The exclusion would not apply, for example, to a delay in rebuilding a store caused by a strike at a steel mill that prevented the insured from rebuilding because of a lack of steel.

The second part of the exclusion provides that the insurer will not pay for any increase of loss resulting from the suspension, lapse, or cancellation of any license, lease, or contract. However, if the suspension, lapse, or cancellation results from the suspension of operations, the insurer will cover the loss of business income during the period of restoration. For example, if a business loses its exclusive right to sell a product because its operations have been suspended because of a fire at its premises, coverage would apply for income losses arising from cancellation of the exclusive right, but only during the period of restoration. After that, coverage would not apply, despite a continuing loss.

Loss of Privilege

The fifth exclusion applies only to extra expense insurance. It excludes any extra expenses arising from the suspension, lapse, or cancellation of any license, lease, or contract if such expenses are incurred after the end of the period of restoration. For example, if the insured's lease is canceled because fire damage makes the leased premises unusable, any increase in rent at substitute facilities will not be covered after the period of restoration at the damaged premises. The increased rent would be paid under the extra expense coverage *during* the period of restoration. A leasehold interest coverage form can be used to cover the increase in rent to the original expiration date of the canceled lease.

Other Consequential Losses

The final exclusion simply says that the insurer will not pay for "any other consequential loss." The meaning of the quoted phrase is not completely clear. It is not defined in the policy, so it must be given the meaning it would have in ordinary usage. Popular dictionaries do not define "consequential loss," but they do define "consequential." The *American Heritage Dictionary of the English Language* says that "consequential" means "following as an effect, result or conclusion....Consequential sometimes implies an indirect or secondary result."

According to that definition, a consequential loss, as used in the causes-of-loss forms, would be a secondary loss accompanying a business income or an extra expense loss. An example might be the reduction in value of a business resulting from loss of goodwill or market share due to the interruption.

Limits of Insurance

With the exception of coverage for newly acquired locations, the limit stated in the declarations is the maximum amount the insurer will pay for the total of loss and expenses in any one occurrence. The coverage for a newly acquired location is an additional amount of insurance, but the additional coverages for alterations and new buildings, civil authority, extra expense, and extended business income do not increase the limit of insurance.

Loss Conditions

The loss conditions in the business income coverage form are similar to those under the building and personal property coverage form. The BIC loss conditions are entitled "appraisal," "duties in the event of loss," "limitation—electronic media and records," "loss determination," and "loss payment."

Appraisal

The appraisal clause in the business income coverage form allows appraisal of losses in disputes regarding the amount of loss, but not in disputes as to coverage.

Duties in the Event of Loss

The duties of the insured after loss are similar to the duties specified in the building and personal property coverage form. The business income coverage form imposes one additional duty on the insured: to resume operations, in whole or in part, as quickly as possible (if the insured intends to resume operations).

Limitation—Electronic Media and Records

Coverage for a business income loss due *solely* to damage to or destruction of electronic media or records is limited to a maximum of sixty days from the initial date of loss. If other property is also damaged or destroyed, the covered loss is limited to a maximum of (1) sixty days or (2) the period required to restore *the other property* with reasonable speed and similar quality, whichever is longer. This limitation does not apply to an extra expense loss.

Electronic media include tapes, films, discs, drums, or cells used in conjunction with computers to store data and computer programs. Electronic records consist of the data and programs stored on such media. The sixty-day limitation does not apply to damage to the computer, but only to damage to the media and records used with the computer. The period of indemnity for business income loss resulting from damage to the computer continues until the computer is restored with reasonable speed.

Examples of Business Income Coverage for Electronic Media and Records

Example 1:

A covered cause of loss on June 1 damages a computer and the data and media used with it. It takes until September 1 to replace the computer and until October 1 to restore the lost data. The insurer will pay only for business income loss sustained during the period June 1 to September 1. Loss during the period September 1 to October 1 is not covered since loss resulting from damage to electronic media and records is covered only for either sixty days (in this case, until July 31) or the time it takes to restore the other property (in this case, until September 1), whichever is longer.

Example 2:

A covered cause of loss results in the loss of data processing programming records on August 1. The records are replaced on October 15. All other property is restored by September 1. The insurer will pay only for the business income loss sustained during the period August 1 through September 29— sixty consecutive days.

Loss Determination

The amount of a business income loss can never be known precisely, so the form sets forth the items to be considered in estimating it. The business income loss is determined on the basis of the following:

1. The net income of the business before the loss occurred

2. The probable net income of the business if no loss had occurred

3. The operating expenses that must continue during the period of restoration to permit the insured to resume operations with the quality of service that existed prior to loss

4. Other relevant sources of information

Continuing expenses would include payroll and might, depending on the insured's circumstances, include taxes, interest payable on loans, and similar items. "Other relevant sources of information" could include the insured's financial and accounting records, bills, invoices, notes, deeds, liens, and contracts.

The 1995 revision of the business income form states that the amount of loss will not be determined based on the net income that would probably have been earned as a result of an increase in business due to favorable business conditions caused by the effect of the covered cause of loss. This change was motivated by questions that arose following Hurricane Andrew. Insurers felt that the proper measure of damages for a hotel, for example, would be the room rentals that they would normally have earned had Andrew not occurred. Since this was late August, the occupancy rate would normally be about 50 percent. Insured hotel owners, on the other hand, argued that the loss should be based on 100 percent occupancy since their hotels, if they had not been damaged by the storm, would have been filled to capacity. They pointed out that hotels twenty or more miles away from the area were fully occupied by claims adjusters and others involved in estimating or restoring hurricane damage. This change makes it clear that the increase in business resulting from a catastrophe would not be included when estimating net income during the period of restoration.

The loss determination condition also reinforces the insured's obligation to resume operations as soon as practical. If the insured can resume operations in whole or in part and fails to do so, the business income loss payment will be reduced to the amount of loss that would have been incurred if operations had been resumed. The extra expense loss may also be reduced if the insured could have returned to normal operations, without the continuing need for the extra expense, and failed to do so. If the insured does not resume operations, the period of restoration will be based on the time it would have taken to resume operations as quickly as possible.

Loss Payment

The insurer agrees to pay for a covered loss within thirty days after the date on which the amount of loss is agreed to (or an appraisal award is made). The insured must have complied with all policy conditions, including filing a sworn statement of loss.

Coinsurance

The coinsurance provision for business income coverage is expressed as an additional condition. The coinsurance percentage may be 50, 60, 70, 80, 90, 100, or 125 percent. The loss payment is calculated by the same formula used under the coinsurance clause in the building and personal property coverage form. The denominator of the fraction (the amount of insurance required) is found by multiplying the coinsurance percentage by the sum of (1) the insured's net income plus (2) all operating expenses (less certain expenses specified in the form, as shown in Exhibit 4-1) that would have been incurred in the absence of a loss. Both the profit (or loss) and expenses are for the twelve-month period beginning at the inception or latest anniversary date of the policy.

Although the method is similar to that used for the BPP, the coinsurance basis used for business income insurance is significantly different. For other property coverages, the coinsurance basis is the same as the property covered. That is, if a building is the covered property, the coinsurance basis is the value of the building. This is not the case with business income insurance. The item covered in business income insurance is net income plus *continuing* operating expenses; the coinsurance basis is the projected net income and *all* operating expenses except for certain deductible items.

Another difference between the item covered and the coinsurance basis is the period of time used in computing the values. For coverage purposes, the time covered is the period of restoration plus thirty days of extended business income coverage. For coinsurance purposes, it is the estimated net income and expense for one year starting with the policy inception or anniversary. This makes the calculation of the amount of insurance needed to satisfy coinsurance more complicated for business income than for other property coverages. To assist insureds in making the necessary calculations, ISO publishes a business income report/worksheet.[1]

An added complication in selecting a coinsurance percentage is the availability of two endorsements: (1) ordinary payroll limitation and (2) power, heat, and refrigeration deduction. These endorsements reduce both the insured's coverage and coinsurance basis. They are discussed later in the chapter.

The variety of coinsurance percentages that the insured may choose reflects the fact that the maximum probable loss for a given insured seldom equals exactly the projected net income and operating expenses for twelve months. An insured should carry, at a minimum, an amount of insurance equal to its maximum probable loss in order to be properly protected. **Maximum probable loss (MPL)** is the largest loss that an insured is likely to sustain.

For some insureds, MPL may be only a small fraction of the coinsurance basis. For example, a retail store operating in an area where there are numerous empty stores might be able to relocate and be in full operation in three months even if its present location was totally destroyed. In contrast, a manufacturer that uses sophisticated, special-order machinery might be shut down for

Exhibit 4-1
Expenses Excluded When Calculating Operating Expenses for the
BIC Coinsurance Condition

> a. Prepaid freight—outgoing
>
> b. Returns and allowances
>
> c. Discounts
>
> d. Bad debts
>
> e. Collection expenses
>
> f. Cost of raw stock and factory supplies consumed (including transportation charges)
>
> g. Cost of merchandise sold (including transportation charges)
>
> h. Cost of other supplies consumed (including transportation charges)
>
> i. Cost of services purchased from outsiders (not employees) to resell that do not continue under contract
>
> j. Power, heat, and refrigeration expenses that do not continue under contract (if they have been excluded by endorsement)
>
> k. Ordinary payroll expenses excluded by endorsement
>
> l. Special deductions for mining properties

eighteen months waiting for replacement equipment if it sustained extensive physical damage. The retail store might need an amount of insurance equal to less than half its coinsurance basis and could thus choose a 50 percent coinsurance clause; the manufacturer might need an amount of insurance much greater than its coinsurance basis. It could select a 125 percent coinsurance clause, which would lower the rate since higher coinsurance percentages receive lower rates.

An insured must consider other factors in addition to the maximum length of time it will take to restore the property when calculating MPL. These factors include the following:

- The effect of peak seasons. Some retailers do as much as 50 percent of their annual business in December.

- Seasonal variations in construction. Construction work is much slower, if not impossible, during the winter months in many parts of the country.

- Changes in income and expenses during the period of restoration. The period of restoration can begin at the end of the policy year. A rapidly changing business may have a very different profit and loss picture at that time.

- Noncontinuing expenses. Even though they are included in the coinsurance basis, certain expenses, such as rent, might stop and are therefore not part of the MPL.

- Extended business income and extra expense. While not part of the coinsurance basis, these items are part of the MPL.

Once the MPL is determined, the insured can select an appropriate amount of insurance and a coinsurance clause. The following rules of thumb apply:

1. If the MPL is less than 50 percent of the projected annual income and operating expenses, select 50 percent coinsurance and carry an amount of insurance sufficient to satisfy the 50 percent coinsurance clause.

2. If the MPL is between 50 percent and 125 percent of the projected annual income and operating expenses, divide the MPL by the projected annual business income and select the next higher coinsurance percentage.

3. If the MPL is over 125 percent of the projected annual income and operating expenses, select the 125 percent coinsurance clause and carry an amount of insurance equal to the MPL.

For example, if a firm's projected annual business income is $100,000 and its estimated MPL is $68,000, it should select 70 percent coinsurance and carry $70,000 insurance. (68,000/100,000 = 68 percent. The next higher coinsurance percentage is 70 percent. $70,000 insurance is necessary to satisfy the 70 percent coinsurance clause.) Exhibit 4-2 shows a step-by-step method for determining the coinsurance requirement.

To illustrate the selection of an appropriate coinsurance percentage and amount of insurance, assume that Connie's Quilts projects figures for the next twelve months as shown below:

Revenues	$650,000
Excludable items as listed in Exhibit 4-1	$510,000
Estimated MPL during period of restoration, including extra expense and extended business income for 30 days	$110,000

Using the method shown in Exhibit 4-2 and the information shown above, Connie's coinsurance basis is calculated as follows:

$$\$650,000 - \$510,000 = \$140,000$$

The coinsurance percentage can then be determined as follows:

$$\$110,000 \div \$140,000 = .7857$$

Since .7857 is greater than .70, Connie would select the next higher coinsurance percentage, 80 percent. Eighty percent of the coinsurance basis of $140,000 is $112,000. Connie would purchase $112,000 business income insurance with an 80 percent coinsurance clause.

Exhibit 4-2
Step-By-Step Method for Selecting Business Income Amount of Insurance and Coinsurance Percentage for a Mercantile or Nonmanufacturing Firm*

1. Obtain the following figures from the insured:
   A. Estimate of revenues for the twelve-month period beginning with the inception of the policy. (Revenues equal gross sales plus other income, such as gain or loss on sale of equipment. They do not include investment income.)
   B. Estimate of the excludable items for the twelve-month period beginning with the inception of the policy, for the items shown in Exhibit 4-1.
   C. Estimate of the maximum probable business income loss. (Be sure that extra expenses and coverage during the thirty-day period of extended indemnity have been included.)
2. Perform two calculations:
   D. Subtract B from A. (The remainder is the coinsurance basis.)
   E. Divide C by D. (The result is the approximate coinsurance percentage.)
3. You can then select a coinsurance percentage and an amount of business income insurance as follows:
   • If E is not more than .50, select 50 percent coinsurance and an amount of insurance equal to 50 percent of the coinsurance basis.
   • If E is greater than .50 but less than 1.25, select the next higher coinsurance percentage (for example, if E equals .84, select 90 percent coinsurance) and an amount of insurance equal to the selected coinsurance percentage multiplied by the coinsurance basis.
   • If E is 1.25 or more, select 125 percent coinsurance and an amount of insurance equal to the maximum probable loss.

*Selecting the amount of insurance for a manufacturing firm involves converting sales to production, a process that is beyond the scope of this text.

Optional Coverages

The business income coverage form includes four optional modifications of the basic coverage: maximum period of indemnity, monthly limit of indemnity, agreed value, and extended period of indemnity. Each of the options can be activated by an entry in the declarations. No endorsements are necessary to add these coverages.

Maximum Period of Indemnity

The **maximum period of indemnity** option is *not* an additional coverage. It is a restriction of the period of restoration provided by the form, but it has the advantage of voiding the coinsurance clause. If this option is selected, it limits the loss payment to the lesser of (1) the amount of loss sustained during the 120 days immediately following the beginning of the period of restoration or (2) the policy limit. The coinsurance provision does not apply at any location to which the maximum period of indemnity is applicable. This option should be used only when the insured feels certain that any suspension of operations will last no more than four months.

Monthly Limit of Indemnity

The **monthly limit of indemnity** is activated by inserting a fraction in the appropriate space in the declarations. The fraction may be $1/6$, $1/4$, or $1/3$. The fraction is the maximum portion of the policy limit that the insured can recover for any period of thirty consecutive days of interrupted operations. For example, if the fraction shown in the declarations is $1/4$ and the policy limit is $100,000, the maximum amount that the insured would recover for loss during any period of thirty consecutive days would be $25,000. The claim payment would be the lesser of the actual loss sustained or $25,000 for the applicable thirty-day period.

The first period would start with the beginning of the period of restoration. Remember that the period of restoration begins seventy-two hours after the time of direct physical loss. Thus the "three-day deductible" would apply to these optional coverages in the same manner that it applies to the standard business income coverage. As previously mentioned, the seventy-two-hour period can be reduced to twenty-four hours by endorsement.

The coinsurance clause does not apply to any location at which the monthly limit of indemnity is applicable. This option is sometimes chosen because the insured does not want to disclose financial information to prove compliance with the coinsurance clause or because the coinsurance clause requires more insurance than the insured deems necessary.

Agreed Value

The **agreed value** clause is another method of avoiding the possibility of a coinsurance penalty. Two steps are necessary to activate the agreed value clause.

First, the insured must furnish to the insurer a completed business income report/worksheet showing the following:

- The insured's actual financial data for the most recent twelve months' accounting period before the date of the worksheet
- Estimated financial data for the twelve months immediately following the inception of the coverage

Second, the agreed value must be entered in the declarations. The agreed value must be at least equal to the product obtained by multiplying the coinsurance percentage shown in the declarations by the estimated net income and operating expenses shown on the worksheet for the twelve months following the inception of the optional coverage.

The agreed value is effective for a period of twelve months or until the expiration of the policy, whichever comes first. A new worksheet must be filed every twelve months to keep the agreed value clause in force.

The coinsurance clause is suspended while the agreed value clause is in force. However, during this period, the insured must carry an amount of insurance equal to the agreed value if losses are to be paid in full. The coinsurance clause is automatically reinstated if the agreed value clause is permitted to lapse. This could happen, for example, if a policy is renewed but a new worksheet is not submitted by the insured.

To illustrate the operation of this option, assume that ABC Corporation carries a business income policy with an agreed value of $200,000. If ABC carries insurance of $200,000 or more, its covered losses will be paid in full up to the amount of insurance. However, if ABC carries only $150,000 of insurance, only $3/4$ of its covered losses ($150,000/$200,000 = $3/4$) will be paid.

Extended Period of Indemnity

The final option printed in the BIC, **extended period of indemnity**, extends the coverage under the extended business income provision (to allow revenue to return to normal after a business reopens) beyond the standard thirty-day period. The period of indemnity may be extended to 60, 90, 120, 150, 180, 270, or 360 days. The actual number of days selected depends on the insured's estimate of the amount of time it will take for revenues to return to normal after the property is restored. Because many insureds who depend on a steady flow of customers, such as restaurants or clothing stores, would have a hard time returning to normal income levels after a severe loss, this option can be very attractive.

Other Forms and Endorsements

The business income coverage form meets the needs of most organizations. Several more specialized forms and endorsements are available for organizations that have unusual needs.

Extra Expense Coverage Form

Service businesses and organizations such as banks, hospitals, newspapers, and insurance agencies must continue to operate after a property loss, even if the cost of continuing operations is very high. Although such organizations can (and many do) cover *both* their extra expense exposure and their business income exposure under the business income *with extra expense* coverage form, some of these organizations have a minimal business income exposure and therefore wish to buy only extra expense insurance. In such cases, the **extra expense coverage form** is available.

The coverage provided by this form is essentially the same as the extra expense coverage under the business income coverage form, with one major exception. The extra expense coverage form restricts the amount that can be recovered for a relatively short period of restoration. For example, recovery may be limited as follows:

Period of Restoration	*Maximum Recovery as Percent of Insurance*
30 days or less	40 percent
31-60 days	80 percent
over 60 days	100 percent

The following example illustrates the use of these percentage limitations.

County Bank has an extra expense coverage form with the above limitations and a $100,000 limit of insurance. Following a direct damage loss, County Bank paid extra expenses of $90,000 to remain in operation during a period of restoration of forty-five days. Because the period of restoration was more than thirty days and less than sixty days, only 80 percent of the limit of insurance ($80,000) will be paid. The remaining $10,000 will not be covered.

The limitations shown above are used frequently, but other percentages and other periods of restoration can be used to meet the needs of the insured. For most businesses, the extra expense coverage provided with the business income coverage form is a better alternative. The extra expense coverage in the business income with extra expense coverage form is (except for the absence of percentage limitations) identical to that provided by the extra expense coverage form. However, businesses that are primarily concerned with continuing operations may realize a premium savings by purchasing the extra expense coverage form, since it does not contain a coinsurance provision.

Business Income From Dependent Properties

An insured may be so dependent on a single supplier or single customer that damage to the operations of the supplier or customer may interrupt the insured's operations. For example, a manufacturer may use a raw material that is available from only one supplier. If the supplier's factory is destroyed, the manufacturer cannot continue to make its products. The unendorsed business income coverage form does not cover this loss exposure because the loss of business income must result from direct damage to the insured's property.

Two endorsements are available to provide coverage. They are the business income from dependent properties—broad form and the business income from dependent properties—limited form. These endorsements cover the insured's loss of income resulting from direct damage to property at *other* locations. The *broad form* endorsement extends the BIC to include loss from damage to dependent properties, subject to the BIC's regular limit of insurance. The *limited form* is used to provide different limits for dependent property exposures.

Dependent property exposures usually result when the insured has a business relationship with one of the following:

- A *contributing* location, which furnishes materials or services to the insured
- A *recipient* location, which purchases materials or services from the insured
- A *manufacturing* location, which manufactures products for delivery to the insured's customers
- A *leader* location, which attracts customers to the insured's location (a major department store at a shopping center, for example)

A similar endorsement can be added to the extra expense coverage form. This endorsement covers extra expenses incurred to avoid or minimize the suspension of operations resulting from direct damage to the premises of a dependent business property.

Ordinary Payroll Limitation or Exclusion

The coinsurance clause in the business income coverage form requires an amount of insurance based on net income plus operating expenses, including payroll. Some insureds have unskilled workers who can be laid off during a prolonged interruption of operations and recalled when operations are resumed. For these insureds, the coinsurance clause may require an amount of insurance substantially greater than they need to cover their income and continuing expenses. The **ordinary payroll limitation or exclusion endorsement** provides a solution to their problem. The endorsement identifies the job classes considered to be *ordinary payroll* and either limits coverage for such payroll expenses to a specified number of days following direct property loss or excludes such expenses from coverage. The amount of payroll thus limited or excluded from coverage can be deducted from operating expenses in calculating the amount of insurance needed to comply with the coinsurance clause.

Power, Heat, and Refrigeration Deduction

Many manufacturers incur large expenses for power, heat, and refrigeration. These expenses do not continue when operations are shut down. The **power, heat, and refrigeration endorsement** enables manufacturers to adjust their insurance accordingly. It eliminates these expenses from both the definition of business income and the coinsurance computation.

Care must be exercised in selecting this endorsement. Some firms are subject to minimum "energy" charges even if they are shut down. Moreover, there may be no savings in premium unless the excluded energy expenses are a substantial portion of the insured's operating expenses, because the rate for business income coverage is increased when this endorsement is added.

Ordinance or Law Coverage

The business income coverage form does not cover any increase in the period of restoration resulting from compliance with building ordinances or laws. For example, a store might be located in a frame building in an area where all new buildings must be fire resistive. If the frame building is severely damaged, the law may require that it be demolished and replaced with a fire-resistive building. The business income policy would cover only the lost income and the continuing expenses during the period required to repair the frame building with reasonable speed and like quality. It would not cover lost income and continuing expenses during the additional time required to demolish the frame building and build a fire-resistive building. For example, sixty days might be enough time to repair the frame building, but ninety days would be needed to demolish the remains of the frame building and to build a fire-resistive building. The business income form would cover loss of business income for only sixty days. The **ordinance or law—increased period of restoration endorsement** can be used to cover business income loss during the additional time required to reconstruct the building.

Other Endorsements

Several other endorsements are available to meet the specialized needs of some insureds.

- The *business income premium adjustment endorsement* (like the value reporting form described in Chapter 2) allows the insured to carry a limit of insurance set high enough to cover the highest anticipated fluctuation in business income values while paying premium based on the amount of insurance actually required.

- The *business income changes—educational institutions endorsement* adapts the policy to meet the needs of schools.

- The *utility services—time element endorsement* extends the policy to cover loss of earnings resulting from off-premises interruptions of utilities and communications services.

Several other, more specialized endorsements are available for special classes of insureds, such as mining companies and smelters.

Rating Business Income Coverage

Rating business income coverage is closely related to rating property coverage, because the same perils that damage covered property also cause the business income loss. Rating business income coverage begins with the base rate for building coverage written at 80 percent coinsurance. This base rate is multiplied by rating factors that reflect the type of coverage provided. The three aspects of coverage that modify the base rate are as follows:

1. The type of business being insured
2. The coinsurance percentage at which the business income coverage is being written
3. The coverage options the insured has chosen

The final premium for business income coverage can be calculated after the business income rate, including all modifications for optional coverages, has been determined. The rate is applied to the desired limit of insurance to arrive at the final premium.

Summary

A business income loss is measured by the amount of lost profit as well as by continuing operating expenses and extra expenses to stay in business. The causes of loss are often the same as for direct property losses. A business income loss can sometimes be more devastating for an insured than the associated property loss.

The business income coverage form can be included in a commercial property coverage part. The business income coverage form pays the actual loss of business income because of a suspension of "operations" during a "period of restoration."

The period of restoration begins seventy-two hours after the start of the direct physical loss—in effect, a "three-day deductible." This waiting period can be reduced to twenty-four hours by endorsement. The suspension must have resulted from direct physical loss or damage to real or personal property caused by a covered cause of loss and occurring at the insured premises.

Business income, as defined in the form, is the net profit or loss that would have been earned or incurred if the suspension had not happened plus any normal operating expenses that must continue. Certain extra expenses may also be covered. The period of recovery is automatically extended to up to thirty days after the end of the period of restoration.

A business income loss is determined based on (1) the net income of the business before the loss, (2) the probable net income if no loss had occurred, (3) continuing operating expenses, and (4) other relevant sources of information that may be developed.

Four optional coverages are contained within the form and can be activated by an entry on the declarations page. The four coverages are maximum period of indemnity, monthly limit of indemnity, agreed value, and extended period of indemnity. The first three options allow the insured to avoid the coinsurance provisions of the form. In addition to the coverage options, many endorsements are available to modify the coverage to suit the exposures of the insured.

Rating business income coverage is similar to rating direct damage property insurance. The 80 percent coinsurance building rate is modified by business income rating factors that reflect (1) the type of business insured, (2) the coinsurance percentage chosen, and (3) any options or endorsements selected.

Chapter Note

1. The business income report/worksheet is discussed in detail in Chapter 7 of the text for CPCU 3, James S. Trieschmann, et al. *Commercial Property Insurance and Risk Management*, 4th ed. (Malvern, PA: American Institute for CPCU, 1994).

Chapter 5

Commercial Crime Insurance

A *crime* is a violation of law punishable by some governmental authority. In many cases, criminal acts (such as vandalism or theft) are directed against property. The possibility of property damage resulting from such acts is generally an insurable loss exposure.

Many different types of commercial insurance provide some coverage against property losses resulting from criminal acts. Some examples are as follows:

- The basic and broad causes-of-loss forms cover vandalism, riot, and civil commotion.
- The special causes-of-loss form covers theft.
- Automobile insurance policies cover vehicle theft.
- Various forms of inland marine insurance cover theft.

In many situations, however, insurance companies prefer to insure certain types of crime-related property loss under separate crime insurance forms. The reason for this separate treatment is that crime loss exposures can vary significantly among different policyholders. Insurers often prefer to under-write (and rate) these crime exposures separately from other property exposures. From the insured's perspective, **commercial crime insurance** allows an organization to cover crime exposures that are not insured under its other insurance policies.

Overview of Crime Insurance

Some of the most basic features of crime insurance are the covered property, the covered causes of loss, and the extent to which crime insurance covers the financial consequences of crime losses. Another important aspect of commercial crime insurance is the format of the crime coverage part in which it is typically provided.

Property Covered

In commercial crime insurance, covered property is divided into three categories: (1) money, (2) securities, and (3) property other than money and securities. Some crime coverage forms insure all three categories, and other crime forms cover only money and securities or only property other than money and securities.

As defined in crime coverage forms, **money** consists of (1) currency, coins, and bank notes that are in use and have a face value and (2) travelers' checks, register checks, and money orders held for sale to the public.

Securities, as defined in crime policies, are negotiable instruments, nonnegotiable instruments, or contracts representing either money or other property. Also included in the definition of securities are (1) tokens, tickets, and stamps in use and (2) charge slips issued in connection with charge cards, provided the charge cards were not issued by the named insured. The term "securities" does not include "money."

In crime insurance, **property other than money and securities** is tangible property that has intrinsic value. Thus, intangible property (for example, a patent or a copyright) is not covered. "Property other than money and securities" obviously does not include money or securities as defined above. It also does not include property listed in any crime coverage form as property not covered. For example, certain types of property, such as motor vehicles, are excluded by crime coverage forms because such property is covered under other forms of insurance.

Covered Causes of Loss

Various causes of loss can be covered under the ISO commercial crime coverage forms. The definitions of these causes of loss as used in crime insurance may differ somewhat from the usual definitions of these terms. The insurance definitions are summarized below.

Employee Dishonesty

Employee dishonesty, commonly called "embezzlement," is a criminal act committed by an employee acting alone or in collusion with others. The employee must intend to cause the employer a loss and to obtain a financial benefit for the employee or someone else. An intent to cause a loss merely because the employee is angry with the employer is not enough. Although employee dishonesty usually involves taking money, it can also involve taking property such as equipment or stock or even giving unauthorized discounts on merchandise to friends.

Forgery and Alteration

Forgery is generating a document or signature that is not genuine. **Alteration** is changing a document in a manner that is neither authorized nor intended by the insured. "Boosting" a check by increasing its value is an example of alteration.

Robbery

Robbery is the taking of property from a person by one who has caused or threatened to cause that person harm or who has committed an unlawful act witnessed by that person.

Burglary

Burglary is the taking of property from inside a building by unlawful entry or departure from the building. Marks of forcible entry or exit must be evident. Burglary usually occurs when a business is closed, whereas robbery most often occurs when a business is open.

Safe Burglary

Safe burglary is a specific type of burglary in which property is taken from a locked safe or vault, as evidenced by visible signs of forcible entry into the safe. Safe burglary includes removing a locked safe or vault from inside a building.

Theft

Theft means any act of stealing. It includes robbery and burglary and other forms of stealing. For example, unobserved shoplifting is a form of theft. It is not robbery because there is no threat of personal harm, and it is not burglary because there is no forcible entry or exit.

Disappearance and Destruction

Disappearance can include not only a crime but also unknown causes of loss. Theft, burglary, and robbery tend to involve losses from a known location at a known time; disappearance may lack these elements.

Destruction, like disappearance, can result from either criminal or noncriminal acts. Because commercial property forms exclude loss to money and securities by any peril, crime insurance provides an option for covering money and securities against theft, disappearance, and destruction.

Computer Fraud

Computer fraud is a specialized kind of theft in which a thief uses a computer to steal property from its rightful owner. For example, a thief might put directions in an insured's computer to send a check to a fictitious payee at a particular address.

Extortion

Extortion is the surrender of property away from the premises as a result of a threat of bodily harm to someone who is (or allegedly is) being held captive.

Some independently developed crime coverages provide broader coverage for some of the "crime perils." For example, several insurers offer kidnap and ransom coverage that is similar to ISO extortion coverage but also includes threats to destroy property and to injure persons.

Financial Consequences of Crime Losses

As the result of a crime loss, the owner is deprived of the property (as with theft or disappearance), or the value of the property is reduced (as with a safe that has been damaged by a burglar's cutting torch). Crime insurance responds to both of these financial consequences.

Damage to property by crime perils can also result in business income and extra expense losses. For example, theft of a computer system could leave a business totally disabled until the hardware and software could be replaced. Commercial crime insurance does not have any option for covering such business interruption losses. However, such losses can be covered under the business income coverage form by attaching the causes of loss—special form, which covers theft. Business income loss resulting from theft of property eligible for inland marine insurance (such as property in transit or a computer) can be insured under an inland marine form. Inland marine coverages will be discussed in Chapter 7.

Crime Coverage Part

The components of the commercial crime coverage part are comparable to those of the commercial property coverage part, consisting of crime declarations (containing the same types of information as the commercial property declarations), one or more of several crime coverage forms, and a crime general provisions form. The commercial crime coverage part can be written as either a monoline policy or part of a commercial package policy. The discussion that follows describes the various crime coverage forms and the crime general provisions.

Crime Coverage Forms

The crime coverage forms are identified by letters A through R. Forms A, B, O, and P were developed by the Surety Association of America. The other coverage forms were developed by Insurance Services Office. Exhibit 5-1 lists the crime coverage forms by letter and name.

Exhibit 5-1
Crime Coverage Forms

Form A	Employee Dishonesty (Blanket)
Form A	Employee Dishonesty (Schedule)
Form B	Forgery or Alteration
Form C	Theft, Disappearance, and Destruction
Form D	Robbery and Safe Burglary—Property Other Than Money and Securities
Form E	Premises Burglary
Form F	Computer Fraud
Form G	Extortion
Form H	Premises Theft and Robbery Outside the Premises—Property Other Than Money and Securities
Form I	Lessees of Safe Deposit Boxes
Form J	Securities Deposited with Others
Form K	Liability for Guests' Property—Safe Deposit Box
Form L	Liability for Guests' Property—Premises
Form M	Safe Depository Liability
Form N	Safe Depository Direct Loss
Form O	Public Employee Dishonesty (Per Loss)
Form P	Public Employee Dishonesty (Per Employee)
Form Q	Robbery and Safe Burglary—Money and Securities
Form R	Money Orders and Counterfeit Paper Currency

Common Features of Coverage Forms

Although each coverage form insures against different types of crime losses, many of the additional conditions, exclusions, and definitions are the same in most or all forms. These similar provisions are described below.

The limit of insurance applicable to a coverage form is the most that will be paid for an "occurrence," which is an act or a series of related acts.

All of the crime coverage forms exclude losses caused by the named insured or a director, a trustee, or an authorized representative of the named insured. Forms A, O, and P cover only losses caused by employees of the named insured; the other forms exclude such losses.

Most of the coverage forms require the insured to notify the police if there is reason to believe the loss involves a violation of law. One exception is employee dishonesty. Forms A, O, and P do not include such a requirement.

If coverage is provided for property other than money and securities, such property does not include motor vehicles, trailers, or semitrailers, or equipment and accessories attached to them.

Several of the more commonly used crime coverage forms are described below. The remaining forms are summarized in Exhibit 5-9, presented later in this chapter.

Form A—Employee Dishonesty

The employee dishonesty coverage form insures against loss of money, securities, and property other than money and securities resulting from "employee dishonesty" as defined in the form. The definition of "employee dishonesty" has two components:

1. The employee's act must be dishonest.
2. The employee must have intended to cause a loss to the insured and to obtain financial benefit for the employee or someone else.

Employee dishonesty coverage can be provided on either a blanket basis or a schedule basis. A separate version of Form A is available for each coverage basis:

- The *blanket* employee dishonesty form provides coverage for the dishonest acts of all employees.
- The *schedule* employee dishonesty form provides coverage only for the dishonest acts of those employees specifically listed, either by name or by position, in the policy.

The applicable definition of **employee** is essential to defining coverage under the employee dishonesty coverage form. (The same definition is also important to crime forms other than the employee dishonesty forms, because such forms *exclude* the dishonest acts of any "employee.")

In the *blanket* employee dishonesty form, "employee" takes the definition that is provided by the crime general provisions form. By this definition, an employee is someone who is (1) currently employed by the insured or an ex-employee who was terminated in the past thirty days, (2) compensated by the insured by salary, wages, or commissions, and (3) subject to the control and direction of the insured. All three of these criteria must be met in order for a person to be considered an employee for purposes of the blanket form.

This definition also states that temporary personnel provided by employment contractors are included as employees while performing services and subject to the insured's direction and control. However, such temporary personnel are excluded while having care and custody of property outside the insured premises. Agents, brokers, independent contractors, and similar representatives of the insured are excluded from the definition.

The *schedule* employee dishonesty coverage form contains its own definition of "employee." By this definition, an "employee" is either (1) any person named in the schedule or (2) any person engaged by the named insured to perform the duties of a position shown in the schedule. This definition is more limiting than the definition of "employee" that applies to blanket coverage and is the main difference between the two coverages.

Another difference between the blanket and the schedule forms is that the blanket form contains an extension covering loss caused by an employee while temporarily outside the specified coverage territory for not more than ninety days. The specified coverage territory, as defined in the general provisions, is the United States, the U.S. Virgin Islands, Puerto Rico, the Canal Zone, and Canada.

Both versions of the employee dishonesty form exclude coverage on any employee for whom employee dishonesty coverage has previously been canceled and not reinstated. There is also no coverage if the only proof of a loss is an inventory computation or a profit and loss computation. Coverage is automatically canceled on any employee as soon as a dishonest act by the employee is discovered by the insured or any partner, officer, or director of the insured not in collusion with the employee. The dishonest act is not limited to acts committed while working for the insured. It may have occurred before employment by the insured or in connection with other activities. However, the cancellation does not affect coverage for *prior* dishonest acts committed by the employee. The blanket and schedule versions of Form A are summarized in Exhibit 5-2.

Exhibit 5-2
Summary of Coverage Form A—Blanket and Schedule

	Form A—Blanket Employee Dishonesty	Form A—Schedule Employee Dishonesty
Cause of Loss	Employee dishonesty	Same
Property Covered	All "property," including "money" and "securities" owned or held by the insured or for which the insured is legally liable	Same
Culprit	Any "employee"	Any "employee" whose name or position is listed on the schedule
Place Where Effective	U.S., Puerto Rico, Canal Zone, U.S. Virgin Islands, and Canada plus ninety-day travel extension	U.S., Puerto Rico, Canal Zone, U.S. Virgin Islands, and Canada

Exhibits 5-2 through 5-8 are adapted from Dean P. Felton and Keith G. Sears, *Fidelity Bonds* (Malvern, PA: Insurance Institute of America, 1992).

Forms O and P—Public Employee Dishonesty

Forms O and P are used to provide employee dishonesty coverage for governmental entities, such as states, counties, public utilities, and school districts. Forms O and P resemble the blanket version of Form A in that they cover dishonesty of any employee. Forms O and P differ from Form A in a few respects because Forms O and P are designed specifically for public entities.

Under Form O, the limit of insurance applies on a "per loss" basis. Under Form P, the limit applies on a "per employee" basis. To illustrate this difference, assume that four employees were involved in a scheme to steal funds from the insured, and it could be proved that each had stolen $25,000 for a total of $100,000. Form O with a *per loss* limit of $25,000 would pay only $25,000 for this loss, whereas Form P with a $25,000 limit *per employee* would pay the full $100,000 loss. (When it is impossible to prove the amount stolen by each of several employees involved in an employee dishonesty loss, neither form would pay more than $25,000.) Since most employee dishonesty losses involve only one employee, many insureds choose to be covered under Form O with a high limit of insurance.

Form B—Forgery or Alteration

The forgery or alteration coverage form insures against loss caused by the forgery or alteration of a "covered instrument" drawn against the insured's accounts. A covered instrument is a promise, an order, or a direction to pay a certain sum of money that is drawn or purports to be drawn by the insured or against the insured by a person acting as the insured's agent. A covered instrument might be a check, draft, promissory note, bill of exchange, or similar instrument.

The form covers loss sustained anywhere in the world. Coverage applies only if (1) the document is false, (2) a genuine document has been altered to change the payee or the amount payable, or (3) the signature endorsing the document has been forged. A coverage extension provides that reasonable expenses will be paid to defend the insured if the insured is sued for refusing to pay a covered instrument because it has been forged or altered. These legal expenses will be paid in addition to the applicable limit of insurance. Form B is summarized in Exhibit 5-3.

Exhibit 5-3
Coverage Form B—Forgery or Alteration

Cause of Loss	Property Covered	Culprit	Place Where Effective
Forgery or alteration	Checks and drafts issued by the insured	Anyone but an "employee," director, or trustee	Worldwide

Form C—Theft, Disappearance, and Destruction

Form C covers money and securities against loss by "theft," disappearance, or destruction. Section 1 of the form covers money and securities *inside* the "premises" or a "banking premises." Section 2 covers money and securities *outside* the premises while in the care and custody of a "messenger." The form defines the terms in quotation marks above as follows:

- Theft: Any act of stealing
- Premises: The interior of that portion of any building occupied by the insured in conducting its business
- Banking premises: The interior of that portion of any building occupied by a banking institution or similar safe depository
- **Messenger**: The insured or any partner or employee of the insured while having care and custody of the property outside the premises

The form does not define "disappearance" or "destruction." Thus, the form covers any instance of disappearance or destruction unless coverage for the loss is eliminated by one of the applicable exclusions in Form C or the crime general provisions form.

Coverage is extended in Section 1 to loss or damage to a locked safe, cash register, or other container when the damage results from actual or attempted theft of (or from unlawful entry into) such containers. Coverage also applies to damage to the premises resulting from actual or attempted theft of covered property if the insured owns the property or is legally liable for damage to it. Section 2 extends coverage to include the property while it is outside the premises in the care and custody of a messenger or an armored car service.

Form C excludes losses resulting from accounting or arithmetic errors, exchanges or purchases, the unauthorized transfer or surrender of property, or voluntarily parting with title to or possession of any property. Property contained in any money-operated device (such as a vending machine) is not covered unless the amount of money deposited is continuously recorded by an instrument in the device. Damage to the premises by fire or vandalism is also not covered, since these perils are commonly covered by commercial property forms. Form C is summarized in Exhibit 5-4.

Forms D and Q—Robbery and Safe Burglary

Form D covers property *other than money and securities* against actual or attempted robbery and safe burglary, both inside and outside the premises. Form Q covers only money and securities against the same perils. Except for covered property, Forms D and Q provide essentially the same coverage.

Coverage inside the premises is for loss or damage resulting from "robbery" of a "custodian" or from "safe burglary." The terms in quotation marks above are defined as follows:

Exhibit 5-4

Summary of Coverage Form C—Theft, Disappearance, and Destruction

	Causes of Loss	Covered Property	Culprit	Place Where Effective
Section 1	Theft, disappearance, and destruction	Money and securities	Anyone except an insured, partner, employee, director, trustee, or authorized representative	Inside the premises or a banking premises
Section 2	Theft, disappearance, and destruction	Money and securities	Anyone except an insured, partner, employee, director, trustee, or authorized representative	Outside the premises in the care and custody of a messenger
NOTE: Sections 1 and 2 may be written separately or together.				

- Robbery: The taking of property from the care and custody of a person by one who has (1) caused or threatened to cause that person bodily harm or (2) committed an obviously unlawful act witnessed by that person.

- **Custodian**: The named insured or a partner or an employee of the named insured while having care and custody of the property inside the premises, excluding any person while acting as a "watchperson" or janitor. A **watchperson** is a person retained by the insured whose *only duty* is to have care and custody of the property inside the premises. An example of a custodian who is not a watchperson is a cashier in a store.

- Safe burglary: The taking of property from within a locked safe or vault by a person who unlawfully enters the safe or vault, as evidenced by marks of forcible entry. Safe burglary also includes taking a safe or vault from inside the premises.

Damage to the insured's premises or to a locked safe or vault inside the premises is covered if the damage results from actual or attempted robbery or safe burglary. Covered property is covered while outside the premises in the care and custody of a messenger. Through a coverage extension, property is also covered while it is in the care and custody of an armored car service.

Form D contains a special limit for precious metals, precious or semiprecious stones, pearls, or furs. This special limit also applies to manuscripts, drawings, or records. Forms D and Q are summarized in Exhibit 5-5.

Exhibit 5-5

Summary of Coverage Forms D and Q—Robbery and Safe Burglary

	Form D—Robbery & Safe Burglary— Property Other Than Money & Securities		Form Q—Robbery & Safe Burglary— Money & Securities	
	Section 1	Section 2	Section 1	Section 2
Causes of Loss	Actual or attempted robbery of a custodian and/ or safe burglary	Actual or attempted robbery	Same as Section 1 Form D	Same as Section 2 Form D
Covered Property	Property other than money and securities		Money and securities	
Culprit	Anyone except an insured, partner, employee, director, trustee, or authorized representative		Same as Form D	
Place Where Effective	Inside the premises or inside a safe or vault within the premises	Outside the premises in the custody of a messenger	Same as Section 1 Form D	Same as Section 2 Form D

Form E—Premises Burglary

Like Form D, the premises burglary coverage form also does not cover money and securities. Form E covers property other than money and securities inside the premises. It also covers damage to the insured's premises resulting from a covered cause of loss. The covered causes of loss are (1) actual or attempted "robbery" of a "watchperson" and (2) actual or attempted "burglary."

Note that Form E covers robbery only if the robbery is committed against a watchperson. A "watchperson," recall, is a person whose *only duty* is to have care and custody of property inside the premises. Thus, robbery of an employee who had additional duties (such as a salesperson or cashier in a retail store) would not be robbery of a watchperson and therefore would not be covered under Form E.

Form E defines "burglary" as the taking of property from inside the premises by a person unlawfully entering or leaving the premises *as evidenced by marks of forcible entry or exit*. Thus, "burglary" includes either breaking in (the more common mode of burglary) or "breaking out." Breaking out occurs when a thief conceals himself within a store and then, after the store has closed, forcibly exits the store in order to steal property. Whether breaking in or breaking out, the burglar must leave marks of the forcible entry or exit in order for Form E to cover the loss.

If a covered loss occurs, coverage is thereafter suspended until the premises are restored to the same condition of security that existed before the loss occurred. However, if at least one watchperson is on duty while the business is closed, this coverage restriction does not apply.

The special limit for certain property that applies to robbery and safe burglary coverage under Form D also applies to premises burglary coverage under Form E. Form E excludes losses that occur while there is a change in the condition of the risk if that change (1) is within the control of the insured and (2) increases the possibility of loss. Losses resulting from fire are not covered unless the loss is from damage to a safe or vault. Loss that occurs *during* a fire inside the premises is not covered, nor are vandalism losses. Form E is summarized in Exhibit 5-6.

Exhibit 5-6
Summary of Coverage Form E—Premises Burglary

Causes of Loss	Covered Property	Culprit	Place Where Effective
Actual or attempted burglary and robbery of a watchperson	Property other than money and securities	Anyone except an insured, partner, employee, director, trustee, or authorized representative	Inside the premises only

Form F—Computer Fraud

The computer fraud coverage form insures against loss of money, securities, and property other than money and securities by "computer fraud." The form defines "computer fraud" as shown below. (Definitions of the terms in quotation marks are the same as the definitions previously given for Form C.)

> Theft of property following and directly related to the use of any computer to fraudulently cause a transfer of that property from inside the "premises" or "banking premises" to a person (other than a "messenger") outside those "premises" or to a place outside those "premises."

For example, Form F would cover theft resulting from someone (other than an employee) using his or her computer to gain access to the insured's computer system and directing shipments of covered property to unauthorized parties.

Form F does not cover loss caused by acts of employees, directors, trustees, or representatives while acting alone or in collusion with other persons, as well as loss by authorized representatives while performing services for the named insured. Moreover, Form F provides no coverage for loss in which the proof depends on an inventory or a profit and loss computation.

Form F contains a special limit on manuscripts, drawings, or records of any kind, including the cost of reconstructing them. The cost of reproducing data stored on computer media can be insured for higher limits under an electronic data processing floater, discussed in Chapter 7. Form F is summarized in Exhibit 5-7.

Exhibit 5-7
Summary of Coverage Form F—Computer Fraud

Cause of Loss	Covered Property	Culprit	Place Where Effective
Computer fraud	Money, and property other than money and securities	Anyone except an insured, partner, employee, director, trustee, or authorized representative	U.S., Puerto Rico, Canal Zone, U.S. Virgin Islands, and Canada

Form H—Premises Theft and Robbery Outside the Premises—Property Other Than Money and Securities

Form H can be used as an alternative to Form D and Form E. Section 1 of Form H covers property other than money and securities inside the premises for loss caused by actual or attempted theft. Damage to the insured's premises is

Exhibit 5-8
Summary of Coverage Form H—Premises Theft and Robbery Outside the Premises—Property Other Than Money and Securities

	Causes of Loss	Covered Property	Culprit	Place Where Effective
Section 1	Actual or attempted theft	Property other than money and securities	Anyone except an insured, partner, employee, director, trustee, or authorized representative	Inside the premises
Section 2	Actual or attempted robbery	Property other than money and securities	Anyone except an insured, partner, employee, director, trustee, or authorized representative	Outside the premises in the custody of a messenger

NOTE: Sections 1 and 2 may be written separately or together.

covered if the damage results directly from the actual or attempted theft. Because theft is any act of stealing, Form H provides broader coverage than is provided by both Form D and Form E. Form H is summarized in Exhibit 5-8.

Various instances of "theft" (any act of stealing) do not meet the policy definitions of "burglary" or "robbery." For example, a shopper might steal merchandise from a small retail store while the only attendant on duty is in the lavatory. Or a ring of thieves might stage a medical emergency or a quarrel to distract store employees while an accomplice sneaks merchandise out of the store. In neither of these cases is there a forcible entry or exit (thus, no burglary) or a threat of harm or the observation of an "obviously unlawful act" (thus, no robbery). However, both of these losses would qualify as "theft" and would be covered under Form H.

Section 2 of Form H covers property other than money and securities while it is outside the premises in the care and custody of a messenger or an armored car service. The covered cause of loss under Section 2 is actual or attempted *robbery*, not theft.

As in Form E (premises burglary), coverage under Form H is suspended after a loss until the premises are restored to the same condition of security that existed before the loss occurred. This restriction does not apply if at least one watchperson is on duty while the business is closed.

Coverage under Section 1 does not include losses resulting from changes in conditions; fire, unless loss is from damage to a safe or vault; vandalism; or voluntary parting with title to or possession of property. The form also excludes loss resulting from inventory shortage or the transfer or surrender of property.

Other Crime Coverage Forms

In addition to the forms described above, there are some crime coverage forms that see only limited use. These forms are summarized in Exhibit 5-9.

Arranging Crime Coverage To Meet Individual Needs

Almost any combination of forms A through J plus Q and R is possible for most insureds except financial institutions. (Crime insurance for financial institutions is provided under specialized policies called financial institution bonds.) Forms K through P can be added for eligible insureds.

The most usual combination of crime coverage forms is the following:

- Form A (covers money, securities, and all other property against employee dishonesty)
- Form B (covers checks and other orders drawn on the insured against forgery or alteration)
- Form C (covers money and securities against theft, disappearance, and destruction)

This combination covers the exposures common to most businesses. Most businesses have employees, issue checks, and handle money, securities, or both. Some businesses may elect to retain (self-insure) crime exposures. If so, they should be certain that they have not underestimated the potential losses they face. Employees of small businesses have embezzled large sums; check forgery has become common; and even firms that handle only a nominal amount of cash can suffer large losses due to the theft of checks or securities.

For most insureds, theft of property other than money and securities is covered by their commercial property insurance with the causes of loss—special form. However, if an insured desires more limited coverage or, more likely, if the underwriter is unwilling to provide the broader coverage, crime forms providing narrower coverage can be used. For example, Form Q (covering *robbery and safe burglary* of money and securities) could be substituted for Form C (covering *theft, disappearance, or destruction* of money and securities), and Form E

Exhibit 5-9

Summary of Other Crime Coverage Forms

Form	Causes of Loss	Covered Property	Place Where Effective
Form G—Extortion	Extortion	Money, securities, property other than money and securities	U.S., U.S. Virgin Islands, Puerto Rico, Canal Zone, Canada
Form I—Lessees of Safe Deposit Boxes	• Theft, disappearance and destruction • Burglary, robbery, vandalism	• Securities • Property other than money and securities	Inside a safe deposit box or inside a depository premises
Form J—Securities Deposited with Others	Theft, disappearance, and destruction	Securities	Inside custodian's premises; while being conveyed by custodian or employee; while on deposit by custodian
Form K—Liability for Guests Property—Safe Deposit Box*	Legal liability	Property of guests	Safe deposit box in insured's premises
Form L—Liability for Guests Property—Premises*	Legal liability	Property of guests	Inside premises or in insured's possession
Form M—Safe Depository Liability**	Legal liability	Property of customers	Inside customers' safe deposit boxes, inside premises
Form N—Safe Depository Direct Loss**	Robbery, burglary, destruction, damage	Property of customers	Inside customers' safe deposit boxes, inside premises
Form R—Money Orders and Counterfeit Paper Currrency	Good faith acceptance of: (1) money orders not paid by issuer or (2) counterfeit currency	Money orders and counterfeit paper currency	U.S., U.S. Virgin Islands, Puerto Rico, Canal Zone, Canada

*Forms K and L (formerly known as innkeepers liability) are used for hotels, motels, and similar businesses.

**Financial institutions, such as banks, are not eligible for Forms M and N. Safe depository coverage for financial institutions is provided by a financial institution bond form.

(covering *burglary* of property other than money and securities) could be used in place of Form H (covering *theft* of property other than money and securities).

Crime coverage forms can be modified through the use of endorsements. Some endorsements add covered causes of loss or extend coverage to additional types of property. Other endorsements can be used to restrict coverage.

The modular approach to commercial crime insurance allows businesses another way to match coverage to their particular needs: by selecting different limits for each form of coverage. For example, a fast-food restaurant in a mall might select a relatively low limit for forgery or alteration coverage (or eliminate the coverage altogether) and a higher limit for theft, disappearance, or destruction coverage on money and securities. A business organization providing temporary employees to other organizations might reverse the selection and buy higher limits for forgery or alteration coverage because its exposure is greater for forgery or alteration of checks than it is for theft of money.

Crime Coverage for Financial Institutions

Few industries have crime loss exposures equal to those faced by financial institutions. Insurance for those exposures is provided by **financial institution bonds** developed by the Surety Association of America. These insurance policies are called "bonds" because one of the principal coverages they provide is employee dishonesty insurance, which was traditionally a form of "fidelity bond."

While banks and savings and loan associations readily come to mind as examples of financial institutions, other entities, such as stockbrokers, finance companies, and even insurance companies, can also be insured under financial institution bonds. Entities eligible for financial institution bonds are not eligible for the ISO coverages discussed in this chapter.

The most widely used financial institution bond is Standard Form No. 24, used to insure banks and savings and loan associations. For many years, this form was called the "bankers blanket bond," a name that is still often used informally to refer to this coverage. Form 24 includes six insuring agreements, as listed below. Agreements D and E are optional. Several additional coverages, such as computer fraud, can be added by endorsement.

A. Fidelity	D. Forgery or alteration
B. On premises	E. Securities
C. In transit	F. Counterfeit currency

Crime General Provisions

The crime general provisions form combines in one document many of the exclusions, conditions, and definitions that are common to forms A through J and O through R. Forms M and N use the separate safe depository general provisions. Forms K and L do not require the attachment of a general provisions form.

The crime general provisions fall into three categories: general exclusions, general conditions, and general definitions. All of the general definitions—of "employee," "money," "securities," and "property other than money and securities"—were discussed earlier in this chapter. The sections that follow describe the general exclusions and selected general conditions.

General Exclusions

The general provisions form contains six exclusions, which apply to all crime coverages included in the policy.

Acts Committed by You or Your Partners

The insurer will not pay for loss resulting from dishonest or criminal acts of the named insured or, if the named insured is a partnership, any partner. The exclusion applies whether the dishonest act is committed by the named insured or a partner acting alone or in collusion with others.

Governmental Action

The insurer will not pay for loss resulting from the seizure or destruction of property by order of governmental authority. The effect of this exclusion is small, since such losses are not likely to result from the covered causes of loss.

Indirect Loss

The policy does not cover any indirect loss resulting from a covered loss. The exclusion lists the following three examples of excluded indirect loss:

- Inability to realize income that would have been realized if the direct property loss had not occurred
- Payment of damages of any type for which the named insured may be held liable except direct compensatory damages arising from a loss covered under the policy
- Expenses incurred by the insured to establish either the existence of a loss or the amount of loss under the policy

Legal Expenses

The insurer will not pay expenses related to any legal action. This exclusion is nullified by those forms that provide liability coverage, such as Form K, which covers the insured's liability for loss of guests' property.

Other Exclusions

The general provisions form also contains the war and nuclear exclusions common to commercial property policies.

General Conditions

The crime general provisions form includes several policy conditions. These conditions are arranged in alphabetical order in the general provisions form but are examined in logical order in this section to facilitate discussion and understanding.

Interests Insured

The following conditions help to clarify issues concerning the interests insured under a crime policy.

Ownership of Property—Interests Covered

The insurance applies only to property owned or held by the named insured or for which the named insured is legally liable. Moreover, the insurance is for the named insured's benefit only.

Joint Insured

The joint insured condition appoints the first named insured as agent for all other insureds with regard to all transactions under the policy. The condition also states that knowledge possessed by any insured or any partner or officer of any insured is considered to be known to all insureds.

Consolidation—Merger

If the insured acquires additional employees or premises by consolidation or merger, the coverage under the policy will be extended automatically to the new employees or premises. The insured must notify the insurer of the acquisition within thirty days and pay the appropriate additional premium.

Where Coverage Applies

Many of the crime coverage forms limit coverage to occurrences taking place inside the premises described in the policy. When coverage is not restricted to the premises, the "territory" provision defines the geographical scope of coverage. This provision limits coverage to acts committed or events occurring within the United States, the U.S. Virgin Islands, Puerto Rico, the Canal Zone, or Canada. Some insurers will broaden the territorial definition to include all U.S. possessions as well as specified foreign countries where the insured needs coverage.

When Coverage Applies

Several conditions, described below, are principally concerned with determining when a loss must occur in order to be covered under a commercial crime policy.

Policy Period and Discovery Period

The insurer will pay only for loss that the named insured sustains through acts committed or events occurring during the policy period. Moreover, the insurer will pay a covered loss only if it is discovered within the **discovery period**: one year after the policy period ends.

The one-year discovery period was developed in recognition of the fact that employee dishonesty losses can go undetected for long periods and sometimes are not discovered until after coverage has terminated. The discovery period therefore creates a potential coverage problem for insureds. However, the provision described below eliminates the problem if the insured has maintained employee dishonesty coverage since the loss occurred and can meet other conditions.

Loss Sustained During Prior Insurance

Under this condition, the insurer agrees to pay a loss that meets all of the following criteria:

1. The loss occurred while prior insurance was in effect.
2. The insured could have recovered the loss under the prior insurance except that the discovery period had expired.
3. The current insurance became effective when the prior insurance was canceled or terminated.
4. The loss would have been covered by the present insurance if the insurance had been in force at the time of loss.

If all four of these requirements are met, the insurer will pay the *lesser* of the amount recoverable under (1) the present insurance or (2) the prior insurance, if it had remained in effect.

To illustrate, assume that Jones Company had employee dishonesty coverage with a $5,000 limit of insurance from IIA Insurance Company. Jones replaced this coverage with $10,000 of employee dishonesty coverage from Malvern Insurance Company. Three years after it purchased coverage from Malvern Insurance Company, Jones discovered that a loss of $7,000 had occurred while the IIA coverage was in effect. Because the IIA policy is no longer in effect and its one-year discovery period has expired, IIA Insurance Company will pay nothing to Jones Company. Because Jones Company has continuously carried similar coverage, Malvern Insurance Company will pay the loss. However, Malvern will pay only the $5,000 limit of insurance that was in effect when the loss occurred.

Loss Covered Under This Insurance and Prior Insurance Issued by Us

In some cases, the same person or persons may commit a series of related dishonest acts over an extended period of time. For purposes of crime insurance, all of these acts are considered to be a single occurrence. If the occurrence takes place over two policy periods, the loss may be covered under both policies. According to the general condition titled "loss covered under this insurance and prior insurance issued by us," if the same insurer covers both policy periods in which the occurrence took place, the insurer is obligated only to pay the higher of the two applicable limits, not the sum of both limits.

Claims Provisions

The provisions described below set forth the procedures and practices to be used following a loss involving covered property.

Duties After Loss, Records

The insured's duties after loss under a crime policy are essentially the same as under other property policies. After discovering a loss or a situation that may result in a loss, the insured must do the following:

1. Notify the insurer as soon as possible.
2. Submit to examination under oath if requested by the insurer.
3. Submit proof of loss within 120 days.
4. Cooperate with the insurer in its investigation of the loss.

The separate "records" condition requires the insured to keep sufficient records to enable the insurer to verify the amount of loss.

Valuation—Settlement

The value of a covered loss is determined differently for each of the three categories of covered property:

- Money is valued at its face value. If foreign money is lost, the insurer has the option of paying for the loss at the face value of the money or at its equivalent U.S. value.

- Securities are valued as of the close of business on the day the loss is discovered. In many cases, duplicate securities can be issued if the insured posts a bond. The insurer will pay the cost of the bond as part of the loss. The insurer has the option of paying the value of lost securities or of replacing them in kind. If securities are replaced, the insured must assign to the insurer all rights, title, and interest in the lost securities.

- If property other than money and securities is lost or damaged, the insurer has the option of paying the actual cash value of the property, repairing the property, or replacing it. If the insured and insurer cannot agree on the actual cash value or the cost to repair or replace, the value or cost will be determined by arbitration. Replacement cost valuation is available by endorsement.

Recoveries

The recoveries condition specifies the method used to divide any subrogation or salvage recoveries between the insurer and the insured. First the insured is reimbursed for any loss greater than the limit of insurance plus the deductible. If any amount of recovery is left, it goes to the insurer until the insurer has recovered all that it paid. Finally, in the unlikely event there is any remaining value to the recovered property, the insured is reimbursed for the deductible amount.

Transfer of Your Rights Against Others

Like most insurance policies, the crime general provisions include a subrogation provision. For any loss the insurance company pays to the insured, the insured must transfer its rights of recovery against others to the insurance company. Moreover, the insured must do nothing *after* loss to impair those rights. (The insured is permitted to waive its rights of action against other parties if the waiver is made *before* loss occurs.)

Other Insurance

The "other insurance" provision states that the insurance will apply as excess coverage over any other insurance available to the insured to cover a loss. In reality, when two policies cover a loss and both purport to be excess over other insurance, the courts usually require both insurers to contribute on a pro rata basis.

Noncumulation of Limit

The limit stated in the declarations is the most that the insurer will pay regardless of the number of years the insurance has been in force or the number of premiums paid. A policy in force ten years with a $5,000 limit will pay a maximum of $5,000, not ten times $5,000. This condition is important to employee dishonesty losses because they often occur over several years.

Rating Commercial Crime Coverage

Each coverage form included in a crime coverage part or in a monoline policy must be rated separately. Rules and loss costs for rating employee dishonesty coverage (Forms A, O, and P) and forgery or alteration coverage (Form B) are published by the Surety Association of America. Rules and loss costs for rating all other crime coverages are published by Insurance Services Office.

The specifics of rating each coverage form are beyond the scope of this text. However, as with commercial property coverage, the rating procedures for crime coverage consider the factors that affect the frequency and severity of expected losses.

For example, rate levels for Form C (theft, disappearance, and destruction of money and securities) depend on the following factors:

1. The type of business being conducted by the insured
2. The fire resistance and crime resistance of the safe or vault used to store covered property
3. The location of the covered premises
4. The number of guards accompanying messengers
5. The types of covered property exposed to loss (cash, payroll checks, and so on)

Summary

The crime insurance coverage forms developed by ISO and the Surety Association of America are available for insuring money, securities, and other property against a variety of perils, including (but not limited to) employee dishonesty, forgery, alteration, robbery, burglary, safe burglary, theft, computer fraud, and extortion. All of the covered crime perils have specific policy definitions that must be fully understood by anyone who wishes to deal effectively with crime insurance. The coverage provided by each of the crime coverage forms can be summarized as follows:

Form A (blanket or schedule) covers money, securities, and property other than money and securities against employee dishonesty.

Forms O and P cover the same property and peril as Form A but are designed specifically for insuring public entities. Form O, like Form A, applies its limit of insurance to *each loss*. Form P applies its limit to *each employee*.

Form B covers loss resulting from forgery or alteration of checks, drafts, and other covered instruments made by or drawn upon the insured.

Form C covers theft, disappearance, or destruction of money and securities (1) inside the premises (or a banking premises) and (2) outside the premises while such property is in the care and custody of a messenger.

Form D covers property other than money and securities against (1) robbery from a custodian or safe burglary (inside the premises) and (2) robbery from a messenger (outside the premises).

Form Q covers money and securities against the perils covered by Form D.

Form E covers property other than money and securities against (1) burglary inside the premises and (2) robbery of a watchperson inside the premises.

Form H covers property other than money and securities against theft (inside the premises) and messenger robbery (outside the premises).

Form F covers money, securities, and other property against computer fraud.

Form G covers money, securities, and other property against extortion.

Form I insures lessees of safe deposit boxes against loss of their property while at the depository premises listed on the schedule. Securities are covered against theft, disappearance, or destruction. Property other than money and securities is covered against burglary or robbery.

Form J covers securities that the insured deposits with others. The perils covered are theft, disappearance, or destruction.

Forms K and L insure innkeepers and similar businesses against their legal liability for loss or destruction of guests' property. Form K covers guests' property while it is inside a safe deposit box. Form L covers the same property while it is anywhere inside the premises or in the insured's possession.

Forms M and N cover safe depository businesses (other than financial institutions) against loss of customers' property inside the depository's premises.

Form R covers loss resulting from the insured's acceptance in good faith of (1) money orders that are not paid upon presentation or (2) counterfeit U.S. or Canadian currency.

Chapter 6

Boiler and Machinery Insurance

Steam boilers and some types of machinery contain tremendous amounts of potential energy. In the rare event that a steam boiler explodes or a piece of machinery undergoes a sudden and accidental breakdown, extensive damage can result.

The building and personal property coverage form covers damage *to* boilers and machinery from a covered cause of loss. However, as discussed in Chapter 3, all three of the commercial property causes-of-loss forms exclude damage to covered property caused by steam boiler explosion, electrical breakdown, or mechanical breakdown. These perils are insurable, but evaluating the pertinent hazards often requires specialized inspection and underwriting skills not generally possessed by commercial property underwriters. Consequently, insurance against these perils is provided under separately underwritten boiler and machinery forms.

Boiler and machinery insurance covers loss resulting from the sudden and accidental breakdown of such objects as boilers, air conditioning and refrigerating systems, pumps, compressors, engines, electrical distribution equipment, and transformers. A **boiler** is a closed container constructed of cast iron or steel in which water is heated to form steam or hot water. Many buildings are heated by boilers, use boilers to generate power for industrial processes, or have air conditioning systems, compressors, electrical switch panels, transformers, or other types of equipment. All of the above items and, in fact, almost anything that can control, transmit, transform, or use mechanical or electrical power can be insured with a boiler and machinery policy.

Boiler and machinery insurance can also cover business income and extra expense losses resulting from the accidental breakdown of covered objects. If, for example, mechanical breakdown of a production machine in a factory shuts down an assembly line for several days until the machine can be repaired or replaced, boiler and machinery time element coverage will cover the resulting loss of business income.

An important part of boiler and machinery insurance is the inspection and loss control services that insurers provide in connection with the insurance policy. Many states, counties, and cities have laws or ordinances that require periodic inspections of boilers and certain types of machinery. In many jurisdictions, inspection by an authorized insurance company representative satisfies the inspection requirement.

Under the ISO commercial package policy program, boiler and machinery insurance can be provided in any of the following:

- The boiler and machinery coverage form
- The small business boiler and machinery coverage form
- The small business boiler and machinery broad coverage form

The latter two forms are used only for the small business boiler and machinery program, which limits eligibility according to the insured's size and business classification and the equipment that qualifies for coverage. This chapter primarily describes the boiler and machinery coverage form (and related time element endorsements), which can be used to cover a wider range of situations than the small business coverage forms. The small business boiler and machinery forms are discussed only briefly.

Boiler and Machinery Coverage Form

The **boiler and machinery coverage form** contains the insurer's promise to pay for direct damage to "covered property" caused by a "covered cause of loss." The policy defines both of the quoted terms, and these definitions are essential to understanding what boiler and machinery insurance covers.

Covered Property

"Covered property" is defined to mean any property that is (1) owned by the named insured or (2) in the named insured's care, custody, or control and for which the named insured is legally liable. Property owned by the named insured can be either real or personal property and is not limited to the "boiler and machinery" items (called "objects") described in the policy. The purpose of boiler and machinery insurance is not only to cover damage to the described objects but also to cover damage to other property that results from accidents involving the objects. As Exhibit 6-1 demonstrates, a boiler explosion can do extensive damage to property other than the boiler itself. The other property might be owned by the insured, or it could be customers' property on the named insured's premises for service or repair.

The scope of coverage for property owned by the insured is very broad; the boiler and machinery coverage form does not exclude the same types of property as are excluded under commercial property forms such as the building and personal property coverage form (BPP). Thus, for example, money and securities, underground pipes, and even automobiles owned by the insured are covered under the boiler and machinery coverage form even though they are excluded under the BPP.

Boiler and machinery insurance does not cover property of others that is *not* in the insured's care, custody, or control. For example, a building owned and used by a neighboring business would not be covered property even if it was damaged by a boiler explosion occurring on the insured's premises.

Covered Cause of Loss

The covered cause of loss for boiler and machinery insurance is defined in terms of two other words with specific policy definitions: an "accident" to an "object" shown in the declarations.

Definition of "Accident"

The definition of "**accident**" can be divided into three parts:

1. A sudden and accidental breakdown of the "object" or a part of the "object"
2. That manifests itself, at the time the breakdown occurs, by physical damage to the "object"
3. That necessitates repair or replacement

An accident has occurred, for example, when a boiler suddenly and accidentally explodes during its operation, resulting in damage that necessitates repair or replacement of the damaged property.

Exhibit 6-1
Building Damage Caused by Boiler Explosion

Courtesy of The Hartford Steam Boiler Inspection and Insurance Company, Hartford, CT

Example of a Boiler and Machinery Loss

A steam boiler explosion in Acme Manufacturing Company's factory damaged Acme's building and personal property, property in Acme's custody that belonged to one of Acme's customers, and the building of a neighboring firm. In addition, the explosion injured several Acme employees as well as a customer who was on Acme's premises. In addition to its own property losses, Acme's customer, its neighbor, and its own employees made liability claims against Acme for their property damage and bodily injury. The claims were covered as shown below.

Covered by Acme's boiler and machinery insurance:

- Destruction of Acme's steam boiler
- Damage to Acme's building
- Damage to Acme's business personal property
- Customer's liability claim for damage to goods in Acme's custody

Not covered by boiler and machinery insurance but covered by Acme's commercial general liability insurance:

- Neighboring firm's liability claim against Acme for damage to its building
- Customer's liability claim for bodily injury

Not covered by boiler and machinery insurance but covered by Acme's workers compensation insurance:

- Acme employees' claim against Acme for their bodily injuries

---

The definition of "accident" includes a list of events not considered to be accidents (and therefore not covered):

- Depletion, deterioration, corrosion, or erosion
- Wear and tear
- Leakage at any valve, fitting, or other connection
- Breakdown of vacuum tubes, gas tubes, or brushes
- Breakdown of electronic data processing equipment
- Breakdown of structures supporting objects or their parts
- The functioning of any safety or protective device

Several of these exceptions reinforce the idea that covered accidents should include only sudden and accidental incidents as opposed to depreciation, which usually occurs over the life of a mechanical device. The wearing out of a mechanical component over time is an example of depreciation.

The exception of breakdown of electronic data processing (EDP) equipment poses a problem, because many production machines are controlled or monitored by computers. Although computers that are used to control insured objects are defined as insured objects (by the object definitions endorsements described below), the exception of EDP equipment breakdown leaves a considerable coverage gap. Consequently, an insured that wants to cover breakdown of computers used to control other insured objects needs to pursue either of two options: (1) pay the boiler and machinery insurer an additional premium to delete the EDP equipment breakdown exception or (2) obtain a separate EDP equipment policy that includes breakdown coverage. EDP equipment policies will be discussed in Chapter 7.

The exception pertaining to the functioning of protective devices is also noteworthy. Although a loss caused by the functioning of safety or protective devices is excluded, losses caused by the *malfunctioning* of such devices are covered. Thus, damage caused by water or steam released by a safety valve when the pressure within a boiler exceeds the release point would not be covered; however, an explosion caused when a safety valve sticks and fails to operate would be covered.

Definition of "Object"

The definition of "**object**" in the boiler and machinery coverage form is simply the equipment described in the declarations. Objects can be described either specifically or in general as a listed group or category. Thus, one policy might describe a specific air compressor owned by a service station, and another policy might state, without any listing of specific objects, that "all pressure and refrigeration objects" are covered.

Any of six **object definitions endorsements** can be attached to the boiler and machinery coverage form:

- Object definitions no. 1—pressure and refrigeration objects
- Object definitions no. 2—mechanical objects
- Object definitions no. 3—electrical objects
- Object definitions no. 4—turbine objects
- Object definitions no. 5—comprehensive coverage (excluding production machines)
- Object definitions no. 6—comprehensive coverage (including production machines)

These endorsements provide a detailed statement of what the equipment described in the declarations includes and does not include. Object definitions nos. 1, 2, 3, and 4 each cover specific groups of objects. Object definitions nos. 5 and 6 (comprehensive coverage), in contrast, take an all-inclusive approach. The only difference between no. 5 and no. 6 is that no. 5 does not cover production machines that process, form, cut, shape, grind, or convey raw materials, materials in process, or finished goods, whereas no. 6 includes such production machines.

Coverage Extensions

The boiler and machinery coverage form contains three extensions of coverage. These apply to expediting expenses, automatic coverage for newly acquired locations, and defense and supplementary payments.

Expediting Expenses

The insurer promises to pay the reasonable extra cost of making temporary repairs, expediting permanent repairs, and expediting permanent replacement of damaged covered property. The purpose of expediting measures is to restore operations promptly, thereby minimizing business income loss resulting from the accident.

An example of **expediting expenses** is the payment of overtime wages to install a replacement for an insured object or the special transportation charges to speed delivery of equipment needed for repairs. Payment is limited to the *lesser* of (1) $25,000 or (2) what is left of the limit of insurance after the insurer pays for the actual loss to covered property. The latter limitation specifies that expediting expenses are to be paid only if loss to covered property—including that owned by others for which the named insured becomes liable—has not exhausted the policy limit. The $25,000 limit can be increased by endorsement, but expediting expenses will still be subject to limitation (2).

Automatic Coverage

The insurer automatically covers accidents to objects at newly acquired locations for up to ninety days after the named insured acquires the property. The object must be in use or connected ready for use at the time of acquisition. It must also be of a type that would be included in an object group description shown in the declarations.

Defense and Supplementary Payments

Property of others in the care, custody, or control of the named insured *for which the named insured is legally liable* is covered if damaged by an accident to an object. An important part of this coverage is the insurer's promise to defend the named insured against any claim or suit alleging liability for damage to such property.

Exclusions

The boiler and machinery coverage form excludes loss caused by ordinance or law, earth movement, nuclear hazard, war and military action, and flood and surface water. These exclusions are similar in most respects to the comparable exclusions under the commercial property causes-of-loss forms discussed in Chapter 3. Additional exclusions eliminate coverage for perils that can be covered under the commercial property coverage part, such as fire and "combustion explosion." Other exclusions eliminate coverage for loss caused by or resulting from the following:

- An accident to any object while being tested. Testing presents an additional hazard. Although some insurers will extend boiler and machinery policies to cover testing, an additional premium is required.
- Delay in or interruption of any business, manufacturing, or processing activity. Business income coverage can be added to a boiler and machinery coverage form by endorsement.

Loss Settlement Provisions

Several provisions in the boiler and machinery coverage form are instrumental in determining how much the named insured can recover for a loss.

Limit of Insurance

The insurer will pay no more than the applicable limit of insurance shown in the declarations for all direct damage to covered property resulting from any "one accident." The form defines "one accident" to include all accidents that result from an initial accident and all accidents at any one location that manifest themselves at the same time and are the result of the same cause.

The boiler and machinery coverage form does not contain an equivalent to the coinsurance clause of commercial property coverage forms. However, ISO manual rules call for the boiler and machinery limit of insurance to be set at 100 percent of the replacement value of all buildings and business personal property at the insured location, including property of others and improvements and betterments to buildings that the insured does not own.

Defense costs and supplementary payments are payable in addition to policy limits. The limits of insurance provision expresses the following limitations. Any payments subject to these limitations reduce the limit of insurance:

1. $25,000 on expediting expenses (as explained above)
2. $25,000 on the cost of cleanup, repair, replacement, or disposal of hazardous substances (other than ammonia)
3. $25,000 on damage resulting from contamination of covered property by ammonia
4. $25,000 on damage by water to covered refrigerating or air conditioning vessels and piping

If these coverage amounts leave the insured with insufficient coverage, the limitations can be increased by endorsement for an additional charge.

Deductible

More than one deductible can be shown in the declarations of a boiler and machinery coverage part. The insured, for example, might want to have a $500 deductible on one group of objects and a $1,000 deductible on all other objects. Accordingly, the boiler and machinery deductible clause states that if there is more than one deductible shown in the policy, only the highest one applies if more than one object is involved in a single accident.

Valuation

The insurer promises to pay what the named insured spends to repair or replace damaged property, not to exceed the smallest of the following:

1. The limit of insurance
2. The cost to repair the property with property of like kind, capacity, size, and quality
3. The cost to replace the property on the same site with other property of like kind, capacity, size, and quality and used for the same purpose
4. The amount that is necessary and actually spent to repair or replace the property

In essence, the boiler and machinery coverage form provides replacement cost coverage. However, if the named insured does not actually repair or replace damaged property within eighteen months after the accident, the insurer will pay only the smaller of the following:

1. What it would have cost to repair the property
2. The actual cash value of the property immediately before the accident occurred

Loss Adjustment Endorsement

When an insured's boiler and machinery insurance and commercial property insurance are provided by separate insurers, the possibility of coverage disputes exists. For example, when a fire breaks out following a boiler and machinery accident, the insurers may disagree on how much of the damage was caused by the "accident" (covered by the boiler and machinery policy) and how much by fire (covered by the commercial property policy).

When such coverage disputes arise, the insured may receive no payment until the insurers settle their differences. The **loss adjustment endorsement** (also known as the joint loss agreement) provides a means for the insured to receive prompt payment. In order for the endorsement to be effective, a similar endorsement must be attached to the commercial property policy. Then, in the event of a disputed loss, the insured will receive payment if (1) both insurers admit to some liability for payment and (2) the insured and the insurers agree on the total amount of loss.

Each insurer will pay the entire amount of the loss that it agrees is covered under its own policy plus one-half of the amount in dispute. The endorsement requires the insurers to settle their differences through arbitration. Thus, the insured receives prompt payment, and the insurers are able to resolve their dispute equitably.

Other Conditions

Although the boiler and machinery coverage form contains numerous conditions in addition to those described above, most are comparable to conditions found under commercial property forms, with some variations. Two notable variations are found in the general conditions pertaining to (1) coverage territory and (2) suspension of insurance.

Coverage Territory

The coverage territory for the boiler and machinery coverage form includes only the United States and Puerto Rico. The coverage territory for the building and personal property coverage form, in contrast, is the United States and Puerto Rico plus Canada and the territories and possessions of the United States. In many cases, insurers broaden the coverage territory to cover boiler and machinery exposures located outside the United States or Puerto Rico.

Suspension

The boiler and machinery coverage form contains a unique condition relating to **suspension of insurance**. This condition states that whenever an object is found to be in a dangerous condition, any representative of the insurer can immediately suspend the insurance against loss from an accident to that object by delivering or mailing written notice to the named insured. Insurance on the object can be reinstated only by endorsement.

Time Element Endorsements

Chapter 4 discussed the need for business income coverage and extra expense coverage as well as the commercial property coverage forms and endorsements used to provide each of these "time element" coverages. A similar need exists for these coverages in connection with boiler and machinery insurance. If covered property is damaged by an accident to an insured object, the insured can suffer a business income loss and incur extra expenses. Business income and extra expense coverage can be added to the boiler and machinery coverage form by various endorsements.

Business income coverage is provided on either a "valued" or an "actual loss sustained" basis. When the valued approach is used, the insured is able to collect a specified amount for each day that business is interrupted because of an accident to an insured object. In addition to the per day limit, the coverage is also subject to a per accident limit and a deductible. The deductible can be expressed as either a specified time period (such as three days) or a dollar amount. The daily amount of insurance is paid regardless of the actual amount of loss. In contrast, the actual loss sustained form (like the business income coverage form) pays only for the insured's actual loss.

The boiler and machinery extra expense endorsement pays for the extra expense of maintaining operations after an accident to an insured object until normal operations can be restored. Boiler and machinery extra expense coverage excludes loss of income. When both coverages are desired, they can be provided through a single endorsement called "combined business interruption and extra expense."

Another boiler and machinery time element endorsement is the **consequential damage endorsement**. It covers spoilage of specified property (such as refrigerated food or flowers) caused by lack of power, light, heat, steam, or refrigeration resulting from an accident to an insured object.

Small Business Forms

The ISO **small business boiler and machinery forms** are designed to provide the property damage, business interruption, and extra expense boiler and machinery coverages needed by insureds with uncomplicated boiler and machinery exposures. These forms are widely used by insureds that meet the applicable eligibility requirements. A simplified rating approach makes the small business forms easier to rate than regular boiler and machinery forms.

Two small business boiler and machinery forms are available:

1. The small business boiler and machinery coverage form (referred to here as the "basic form")
2. The small business boiler and machinery *broad* coverage form (referred to here as the "broad form")

Coverage Features

Most features of the small business forms are comparable to those of the boiler and machinery coverage form. However, the small business forms cover a narrower scope of objects than those that can be insured under the boiler and machinery coverage form. The broad form covers a broader scope of objects than does the basic form. In each case, the scope of objects covered is appropriate for *most* of the smaller organizations that qualify for the program.

The small business forms automatically provide business income and extra expense coverage comparable to the business income and extra expense (actual loss sustained) endorsement that can be added to the boiler and machinery coverage form. However, the business income and extra expense coverage provided by the small business forms is limited to 25 percent of the limit of insurance. Subject to the 25 percent limitation, business income and extra expense claims are paid in addition to the overall limit of insurance. In other words, business income and extra expense claims do not reduce the limit applicable to property damage claims.

Spoilage coverage, comparable to that provided by the boiler and machinery consequential damage endorsement, is available as an option under the broad form but not under the basic form.

Eligibility Criteria

ISO rules require that 80 percent of the replacement value of the insured's building be not more than $5,000,000, which is the maximum amount of insurance available under the small business forms. Thus, any insured whose building has a replacement value of more than $6,250,000 is not eligible for a small business form (.80 x $6,250,000 = $5,000,000).

Eligibility for the basic form is limited to apartment buildings, churches, hotels, motels, office buildings, schools, retail stores, medical buildings, service stations, banks, restaurants, nursing homes, funeral homes, theaters, clubs, and similar small organizations. The broad form can be issued to almost any risk that falls within the replacement value limit. However, neither form can be used for insuring cold storage plants, laundries, processing or manufacturing risks, power, sewage or water plants, or electric substations. In addition, the basic form cannot be used for high-pressure boilers, dry cleaners, greenhouses, or hospitals.

Rating Boiler and Machinery Coverage

Historically, boiler and machinery insurance was rated by calculating individual charges for each insured object. More streamlined methods are now used. As noted earlier in this chapter, different rating methods are used for the small business program and the regular boiler and machinery coverage form.

Small Business Program

Rating the small business boiler and machinery forms is easy. Typically, the insurer's manual shows premiums that depend on the following:

1. The coverage form chosen (basic or broad)
2. The basic type(s) of equipment at the insured's premises
3. The limit of insurance chosen

The premium is not calculated in the usual manner of multiplying a rate times the amount of insurance. The premium is simply "looked up" on the appropriate premium table. This premium is designed for a $500 deductible. If a higher or lower deductible is chosen, the premium is modified accordingly. If optional spoilage coverage is added to the broad form, an additional charge is added to the premium.

Boiler and Machinery Coverage Form

The rating methodology for the boiler and machinery coverage form is more complicated than that for the small business forms. The reason is that the boiler and machinery coverage form is available to insureds of all sizes and business classifications and can be used to cover almost any type of object. Consequently, the rating methodology considers more factors to develop an appropriate premium.

The current rating plan uses one base rate for all insured objects at the insured location. The base rate for a particular location depends on the occupancy classification for that location. The same base rate is used for all occupancies of the same classification. For example, one base rate applies to all breweries, another to all hospitals, and so on.

The base rate for property damage coverage is developed on the assumption that the policy covers all insurable objects. If the policy does not cover all insurable objects, the base rate is reduced accordingly. The base rate also assumes a $500,000 limit and a $500 deductible. For a policy with a higher limit or deductible, the base rate is modified accordingly.

The resulting rate can be further modified in consideration of various factors such as the age, condition, protection, and accessibility of the equipment. This rating feature allows the insurer to adjust the base rate to reflect individual exposures. The final rate is applied to the chosen limit of insurance.

Summary

Boiler and machinery insurance covers damage to or loss of property resulting from an "accident" (sudden and accidental breakdown) to an insured "object" (such as a steam boiler, refrigeration equipment, mechanical equipment, an electrical apparatus, or a turbine). The insurance covers resulting loss or damage to both the object itself and other property owned by the insured or in the insured's care, custody, or control.

Boiler and machinery coverage is necessary because commercial property policies exclude steam boiler explosion, mechanical breakdown, and electrical breakdown. A benefit of boiler and machinery insurance is the inspection service that insurers provide to the insured. Endorsements can be added to the boiler and machinery coverage form to provide coverage for business income, extra expense, and consequential losses.

The ISO small business boiler and machinery program is available to smaller organizations without manufacturing, processing, or other complex boiler and machinery exposures. The rating system used for the small business program is simpler than that used for the boiler and machinery coverage form.

Chapter 7

Inland and Ocean Marine Insurance

Ocean marine insurance covers waterborne exposures—most commonly, damage to vessels and their cargoes, as well as liability arising out of the operation of vessels. Although relatively few organizations own vessels, many organizations are involved in either importing or exporting goods and thus need ocean marine insurance. Almost all organizations are exposed to loss that can be insured through *inland* marine insurance. Inland marine insurance, which evolved from ocean marine insurance, encompasses a far wider range of risks than inland transportation and is thus more prevalent than ocean marine insurance. Both inland and ocean marine insurance are discussed in this chapter because of their logical and historical relationships.

Development of Inland Marine Insurance

What is called "ocean marine insurance" in the United States is known simply as "marine insurance" in the rest of the world. Marine insurance is the oldest and most traditional type of insurance, originating in the Middle Ages. For historical reasons that will be explained below, marine insurance took on a broader definition within the United States and was divided into two branches—inland and ocean.

Inland marine insurance developed in the early 1900s, when American

155

insurers were restricted to writing one of the following general kinds of insurance:

1. Fire (which included insurance against fire and some other causes of property loss)
2. Casualty (liability insurance and miscellaneous lines such as burglary, glass, and steam boilers)
3. Marine (ships and their cargoes)

Although fire insurers could insure buildings and their contents against fire and allied perils, they were not permitted to insure against most crime perils. In addition, they were generally not interested in providing "fire and allied" coverage on property in transit or on valuable property such as jewelry.

In contrast with fire insurers, marine insurers were accustomed to covering ocean cargoes of all types against many different causes of loss, including theft, while the property was either at sea or ashore. Accordingly, marine insurers were willing to provide broad perils or "all-risks" coverage on the types of property that fire insurers avoided. The inventories of jewelry stores, property while in the course of inland transit, tourists' baggage, and even bridges were typical inland properties insured by marine insurers in the early 1900s. Thus, the insurance came to be known as *inland* marine insurance.

By the 1930s, inland marine insurance had grown to include so many types of property that marine insurers and fire insurers sometimes competed intensely for the same properties. To resolve the conflict, the National Association of Insurance Commissioners adopted in 1933 a **Nationwide Marine Definition** that restricted the underwriting powers of marine insurers to specified types of property.

Following legislation in the 1950s that permitted a single insurer to offer fire, casualty, and marine coverages, the definition was no longer needed for restrictive purposes. However, many states continue to use an updated definition to determine whether a particular coverage is an inland or ocean marine coverage under their rating laws. Typically, inland and ocean marine insurance is subject to less rate regulation than other lines. The current Nationwide Marine Definition includes the types of property shown in Exhibit 7-1.

Inland Marine Exposures

Inland marine loss exposures are surveyed below in terms of (1) the items subject to loss, (2) causes of loss, and (3) the economic or financial effect of loss.

Exhibit 7-1
Summary of Nationwide Marine Definition

> A. Imports
>
> B. Exports
>
> C. Domestic shipments
>
> D. Instrumentalities of transportation and communication, such as bridges, tunnels, piers, wharves, docks, pipelines, power and telephone lines, radio and television towers and communication equipment, and outdoor cranes and loading equipment.
>
> E. Various types of property owned or used by individuals, such as jewelry, furs, musical instruments, silverware, coin collections, and stamp collections.
>
> F. Various types of property pertaining to a business, a profession, or an occupation. Examples of such property include mobile equipment, builders risks, property in the custody of bailees, live animals, property at exhibitions, and electronic data processing equipment.

Items Subject to Loss

Inland marine insurance covers the types of property designated in the Nationwide Marine Definition except imports and exports, which are covered under ocean marine insurance. The sections that follow examine distinctive categories of inland marine loss exposures.

Goods in Domestic Transit

Domestic shipments by rail, motor truck, or aircraft, or while in the custody of the U.S. Postal Service, are exposed to loss while in transit. The exposure can be faced by the originator (shipper), the transporter (carrier), or the recipient (consignee), depending on the type of carrier and the terms of sale of the goods being shipped.

Type of Carrier

Carriers of goods are classified as common, contract, or private. **Common carriers** are airlines, railroads, or trucking companies that furnish transportation to any member of the public seeking their services. **Contract carriers** do not serve the general public but furnish transportation for shippers with which they have contracts. **Private carriers** haul their own goods.

Because private carriers mainly transport their own goods, loss of or damage to such goods is a property exposure, not a liability exposure. In contrast, common carriers and contract carriers transport property of others and, depending on the circumstances, can be held legally liable to pay the shipper or consignee for loss of or damage to the cargo. Occasionally, some private carriers haul property of others, in which case the carrier's status changes from private carrier to common carrier or contract carrier, depending on the circumstances. The cargo liabilities of common carriers and contract carriers differ as described below.

Liability of Common Carriers   Common carriers are liable to shippers for the safe delivery of cargo entrusted to them except for losses arising from the following:

- "Acts of God," meaning natural phenomena such as tornadoes or earthquakes that are not reasonably foreseeable
- Acts of public enemies (meaning war risks)
- Acts of public authority
- Neglect or fault on the part of the shipper
- Inherent vice in the cargo itself

When the common carrier is liable for goods damaged in transit, the amount of the liability may be limited by the **bill of lading**, which is the contract between the shipper and the carrier. A *straight* bill of lading fixes no limit on the amount of recovery. A *released value* bill of lading limits recovery to a specified amount. The released amounts of liability are generally low and are usually quoted as dollar limits per pound or parcel. The shipper has the option to pay an additional charge and declare a value for the shipment, thereby increasing the limit of the carrier's liability.

Liability of Contract Carriers   The liability of contract carriers is defined by the contract between the carrier and the shipper. Such contracts often release the carrier from substantial liability except in the case of extreme negligence. However, a contract carrier is generally unable to totally avoid liability to the shipper.

Terms of Merchandise Sale

In ocean marine insurance, "F.O.B." means "free on board" and indicates that the shipper (seller) is responsible for arranging to have the cargo delivered on board the vessel. Once this has been accomplished, both the title to the goods and the responsibility for them change hands from the seller to the buyer. In domestic transactions, "F.O.B." is used more loosely to indicate the point at which ownership and exposure to loss shift from seller to buyer. For example, a contract of sale might stipulate "F.O.B. shipper's loading dock." In that case, the transit exposure would be the buyer's once the goods are on the shipper's loading dock. Many other terms of sale exist, each with specific points at which the exposure shifts from the seller to the buyer.

Property in the Possession of Bailees

A **bailment** exists when goods are left to be held in trust for a specific purpose and returned when that purpose has ended. The **bailor** is the owner of the goods, and the **bailee** is the one in possession of the goods. There are three basic categories of bailments, as follows:

1. Bailment for the benefit of the bailor ("Please keep my dog for the weekend.")
2. Bailment for the benefit of the bailee ("May I borrow your lawn mower?")
3. Bailment for the mutual benefit of bailor and bailee ("Fix my watch. I'll pick it up Friday and pay you for your work.")

Bailments for the mutual benefit of bailor and bailee are also called "commercial bailments." In commercial bailments, the bailor ordinarily pays the bailee to clean, repair, or perform some other service on the bailor's personal property. Examples of commercial bailees are laundries, TV repair shops, furniture upholsterers and refinishers, and industrial equipment repair facilities. As a general rule, a commercial bailee is legally responsible for damage to a customer's property that results from the bailee's negligence. Even if a bailee cannot be held legally liable for damage to a customer's property, the customer is likely to expect the bailee to pay for the loss. Thus, many bailees want to buy insurance that will pay for damage to customers' property regardless of whether the bailee is legally liable.

Movable Equipment and Unusual Property

A wide variety of property is eligible for inland marine insurance. In most cases, such property is subject to frequent movement from place to place or is simply an unusual kind of property. Examples include the following:

- Agricultural equipment, such as tractors and cultivators
- Mobile equipment used by contractors, such as cranes and backhoes
- Physicians' and surgeons' equipment
- Computer equipment
- Farm animals
- Fine arts
- Buildings under construction (builders risks)
- Patterns, molds, and dies
- Partially completed products while at another location for processing
- Property on exhibition

- Sales samples while in the custody of sales representatives
- Valuable papers and records
- Records of accounts receivable
- Theatrical property
- Signs
- Cameras
- Musical instruments

Property of Certain Dealers

One of the first inland marine policies offered was the "jewelers block" policy, so named because it covered a jeweler's unique "block" of exposures, including the jeweler's merchandise in the store or in transit, other property of the jeweler (such as furniture and fixtures), and property of others in the jeweler's care, custody, or control.

In time, inland marine dealer policies were developed for insuring furriers, fine art dealers, coin and stamp dealers, camera dealers, musical instrument dealers, and dealers in mobile or agricultural equipment. The Nationwide Marine Definition permits an inland marine dealers policy to be written for dealers in any type of property that, when in the hands of the final consumer, can be insured under an inland marine form.

Instrumentalities of Communication and Transportation

Property used in transportation such as bridges, tunnels, and pipelines can be insured using inland marine insurance. Inland marine insurance can also cover instrumentalities of communication such as television towers and transmission equipment.

Causes of Loss

Because the kinds of property eligible for inland marine insurance are diverse, the causes of loss to which such property is exposed are also diverse. However, the common thread that runs through most of the inland marine policies is an "all-risks" approach. Often the unique situation or high value of the property exposes it to different causes of loss than property that is generally at a fixed location and insured under commercial property coverage. Even if the property is not exposed to different causes of loss, the degree of exposure to loss may be different.

For example, the merchandise of a jeweler is exposed to fire, but it is more likely that a loss will be from theft. Compact, high-valued property like jewelry or furs is more vulnerable to theft than bulky items of low value like cement or lumber. The probability of loss from the perils of transportation, particularly breakage and theft, is extreme when the property is in transit. Property in the custody of a bailee may be exposed to processing damage. Electronic data processing equipment is subject to electrical injury and mechanical break-down. Mobile equipment and agricultural equipment are exposed to the elements, including earthquake and flood, and can be found at hazardous work sites. Instrumentalities of communication and transportation may be more likely to collapse than other types of stationary property. For inland marine loss exposures, each item subject to loss must be examined separately to determine the causes of loss that may damage or destroy it.

Economic or Financial Effect of Loss

The economic or financial effect of loss to property covered by inland marine policies is no different from the effect of loss to property covered by commercial property forms, with one exception: bailments (discussed below). Lost property must be valued, and the loss may include the loss of use of the property.

The valuation of the property itself can be at replacement cost, actual cash value, or agreed value. When the exposure to loss is of short duration, such as goods in transit, valuation based on selling price or invoice price is most appropriate. Another technique (more common in ocean marine than inland marine) is to add a percentage of the value (such as 10 percent) to the invoice value to cover other costs associated with the loss.

The financial effect of loss of use of the property must also be considered. For instance, damage to a contractor's mobile equipment may necessitate the temporary rental of substitute equipment, and loss of use of a computer can cause extra expenses. Damage to the merchandise of a jeweler or an equipment dealer can also interrupt business.

In bailment situations, the financial effect of the loss will more resemble a liability loss than a property loss. The financial effect of the loss could be set by statute, contract, or the common-law rules of negligence.

There may be a statutory obligation, like regulations that mandate the liability of a common carrier to the shipper. Such laws could limit liability to a specific dollar amount per pound or per parcel for certain kinds of property, and this would be the extent of the loss to the common carrier. However, the loss to the shipper or the consignee could be much greater.

A contract between the parties in a bailment situation could stipulate the amount owed. A common carrier that accepts goods for transportation under a released bill of lading can tell in advance the amount owed the shipper if there is damage. Furriers, as another example, usually have their customers declare a value on furs before they are taken in for repair or storage. The measure of the loss of that garment to the furrier is the value set by the customer and agreed to by the furrier.

In other cases, the financial effect on the bailee may be determined by common law through the courts. This would be the case if a laundry was found negligent and thus became obligated to pay damages to customers for their goods destroyed in a fire.

Inland Marine Insurance

There are many kinds of inland marine policies covering many kinds of loss exposures. Insurance regulatory authorities have recognized this diversity by dividing inland marine policies into two categories: filed and nonfiled.

Filed policies are those for which the policy forms and rates must be filed with the state insurance department. Filed policies are characterized by (1) a large number of potential insureds and (2) reasonably homogeneous loss exposures. Examples are policies that cover musical instruments and photographic equipment. In many states, the filed policies are the same as those filed by Insurance Services Office (ISO) and the American Association of Insurance Services (AAIS) on behalf of their member insurers. Thus, the filed policies for state regulatory purposes also tend to be standardized forms.

Nonfiled policies are those for which neither policy forms nor rates are filed with the state insurance department. Nonfiled policies are characterized by a relatively small number of potential insureds, diverse loss exposures, or both. The contractors equipment floater is a good example. The property covered might range from simple hand tools and small power equipment to very large cranes and earthmovers. The property might be used in a desert, in a rain forest, or on the arctic tundra. It might be used to build roads, buildings, pipelines, or other structures. Policies must be drafted, rates calculated, and underwriting keyed to all of these variables. The fact that these policies do not need to be filed with state regulators allows insurers the flexibility needed to determine appropriate policy provisions and rates for individual risks.

Nonfiled Inland Marine Coverages

The largest classes of inland marine insurance (as measured by premiums written) are nonfiled. Typically, each insurer develops its own form. The form may range from a preprinted form and endorsements that the insurer uses for most insureds to a one-of-a-kind manuscript policy drafted for an unusual risk. Some important nonfiled policies are described below, though there are many other nonfiled inland marine policies.

Contractors Equipment

Contractors equipment is the largest class of commercial inland marine insurance. The equipment used by contractors when constructing buildings, highways, dams, tunnels, and bridges ranges from small hand tools to large machines worth hundreds of thousands or even millions of dollars. Such equipment may include cranes, earthmovers, tractors, stone crushers, bulldozers, mobile asphalt plants, portable offices, and scaffolding. All such equipment can be insured under a **contractors equipment floater.** (The term "floater" is often used to denote an inland marine policy that covers floating property, or property that is moved between different locations.)

The property eligible for a contractors equipment floater is not limited to that used by contractors. For example, contractors equipment floaters are used to insure mobile equipment used in mining and lumbering operations as well as snow removal and road repair equipment owned by municipalities.

A contractors equipment floater for a small or medium-sized contractor with perhaps two or three dozen pieces of equipment normally contains a schedule listing each piece of equipment with its own limit of insurance. A policy may also provide blanket coverage on hand tools and miscellaneous equipment.

It is difficult, if not impossible, to keep an up-to-date insurance schedule of all items when several hundred pieces of equipment are used by an insured. A large contractor may therefore obtain blanket coverage applying to all equipment, whether owned, rented, or borrowed by the contractor.

Coverage may be on an "all-risks" basis or for named perils. When coverage is on a named perils basis, the following perils are commonly included: fire, lightning, explosion, windstorm, hail, vandalism, theft, earthquake, flood, collision, overturn, and collapse of bridges and culverts.

Contractors equipment floaters frequently include rental reimbursement coverage, which pays the cost of renting substitute equipment when covered property has been put out of service by a covered cause of loss. Rental reimbursement coverage is comparable to the extra expense coverage provided by the business income coverage form.

Builders Risk

Although there is an ISO builders risk form that can be issued as a component of a commercial property coverage part, buildings or other structures (such as a bridge) in the course of construction can also be insured under a nonfiled inland marine form. The nonfiled approach is often preferred by both insureds and insurers because it allows more flexibility in coverage and rating.

Inland marine builders risk policies typically cover the structure being built, temporary structures at the building site, and building materials that have not yet become part of the building. Building materials are covered while on the insured location, in transit, or in storage at another location. Business income coverage may be provided as part of the policy.

Inland marine builders risk policies usually cover on an "all-risks" basis, and many insurers will provide coverage for losses that are excluded under an ISO builders risk policy, such as the following:

- Flood
- Earthquake
- Collapse occurring during construction
- Theft of building materials that have not been installed

Many insurers that write inland marine builders risk policies offer an endorsement providing "soft costs" coverage. **Soft costs coverage** insures various incidental expenses that may result from a physical loss by a covered peril to a building project, such as the following:

1. Additional interest on funds borrowed to finance reconstruction or repairs
2. Additional real estate taxes
3. Additional advertising expenses
4. Additional costs and commissions from having to renegotiate leases

Closely related to the builders risk policy is the installation floater. An **installation floater** usually insures a contractor's interest in building supplies or in fixtures that the contractor has been hired to install. It does not cover the entire building, as in the case of a builders risk policy.

Transit

Transit insurance, also called transportation insurance, covers owners of property against damage to their property while in the course of transit by carriers. This coverage is desirable for shippers because their property may be damaged in circumstances under which the carrier has no legal obligation to pay the shipper's loss. Transit policies may also cover property being transported on the insured's own vehicles.

Two basic types of transit insurance are available. The **trip transit policy**, purchased by occasional shippers, covers the particular shipment of goods specified in the policy. The **annual transit policy**, designed for frequent shippers, covers all shipments made or received by the insured throughout a one-year policy period. The provisions typically found in annual transit policies are summarized below.

Any annual transit policy excludes certain types of property. Contraband, for example, is not insurable as a matter of public policy, and most policies make this clear by excluding it. Other types of property are commercially insurable, but they are especially attractive to thieves and therefore expensive to insure. Examples are precious metals, furs, jewelry, and money and securities. Most annual transit policies exclude these items. If coverage for such items is wanted and the insured is willing to pay an additional premium, the exclusions can be deleted or modified to provide coverage. (Coverage might also be obtained under another policy, such as a jewelers or furriers block policy or a crime policy covering money and securities.)

Most annual transit policies cover on an "all-risks" basis. The approach is similar to that of the causes of loss—special form. However, an annual transit policy typically does not contain as many exclusions as the special form and thus covers a broader scope of perils. For example, flood and earthquake are usually covered.

Many annual transit policies cover only within the continental United States, Alaska, and Canada, including airborne shipments between those places. The "continental United States" does not include Hawaii, Puerto Rico, or any overseas possessions. Such wording precludes the insurer from having to cover air or water shipments to or from overseas locations. Overseas shipments by plane or ship are usually insured under ocean marine cargo policies.

Property covered under an annual transit policy is usually valued at the amount of invoice if the property is being transported between buyer and seller. When no invoice applies (such as when a company is shipping its own property between its own locations), the property may be valued at actual cash value.

Motor Truck Cargo

As discussed earlier, a motor carrier, whether operating as a common carrier or a contract carrier, can be held liable for damage to the property it is transporting in certain circumstances. A motor carrier can cover this exposure by purchasing **motor truck cargo insurance**.

This form of insurance applies only to cargo damage for which the carrier is legally liable. It is not a direct property insurance for the benefit of the cargo owner. For example, a cargo loss may have resulted from an "act of God" (such as a hurricane) without any negligence on the part of the carrier. The carrier would not be liable under such circumstances, and the insurance would not cover the loss.

In addition to limiting coverage to losses for which the insured is legally liable, some policies also limit coverage to losses caused by specified perils. Other forms cover any loss for which the insured is liable as long as the loss is not subject to any of the exclusions expressed in the form. The exclusions are comparable to those generally found in "all-risks" property forms.

The description of covered property is usually broad enough to encompass most property accepted by the insured for transportation. However, certain types of valuable property likely to be targeted by thieves are commonly excluded, such as precious metals, jewelry, and fine arts. Some policies exclude liquor and cigarettes, two other commodities that attract hijackers. A carrier that transports such commodities can usually have the exclusions deleted in return for an additional premium.

The property is covered only while in or on a land vehicle operated by the insured (including connecting carriers) or while located at the insured's terminal. Terminal coverage, however, is usually limited to a certain number of hours, such as seventy-two. The insurer will usually extend the duration of terminal coverage for an additional premium.

Difference in Conditions

Difference in conditions (DIC) insurance can serve a variety of needs. Its basic purpose is to fill in gaps left by the insured's commercial property insurance. Originally, a DIC policy was a means of providing "all-risks" coverage to insureds whose basic policy provided only named perils coverage. DIC policies are still used for that purpose, but with the widespread availability of "all-risks" commercial property policies, the purposes for buying DIC policies now include the following:

1. To provide coverage for flood and earthquake exposures not covered by basic policies

2. To provide excess limits over flood and earthquake coverages included in basic policies

3. To cover loss exposures not covered in basic policies, such as property in transit or loss of business income resulting from theft or transit losses

4. To cover property at overseas locations

DIC policies are a nonfiled class of inland marine insurance in most states. Thus, insurers have great flexibility in arranging the insurance to address the specific needs or exposures of their insureds.

Electronic Data Processing Equipment

"Electronic data processing equipment" basically means "computer equipment." Although such equipment is covered as business personal property in the building and personal property coverage form and other commercial property forms, an inland marine **electronic data processing (EDP) equipment floater** can provide added benefits. Many EDP equipment floaters cover special perils such as mechanical or electrical breakdown. They also typically insure covered property while in transit. Moreover, since EDP equipment is a nonfiled class of inland marine in most states, an EDP equipment floater can be tailored to meet the individual needs of insureds.

An EDP floater typically covers equipment, data, and media owned by the insured, as well as similar property of others in the insured's care, custody, or control. The policy definition of "equipment" usually includes (but is not limited to) mainframe computers, minicomputers, microcomputers, terminals, monitors, printers, disk drives, and modems. The term "data" includes both computer programs (which direct the processing of data) and data files (which store processed data, such as a customer mailing list). "Media," such as disks and tapes, are the materials used to store data.

Coverage for extra expenses incurred as the result of covered loss is usually included in an EDP policy. Business income coverage can often be added when the insured requests it.

Coverage is usually on an "all-risks" basis but with fewer of the exclusions found in the causes of loss—special form. In addition, breakdown coverage can usually be added to an EDP policy. Subject to a separate deductible, breakdown coverage insures loss to equipment resulting from such perils as mechanical failure, electrical disturbance, and changes in temperature resulting from breakdown of air conditioning equipment.

Equipment and data are usually subject to separate valuation methods. Equipment may be valued at its actual cash value, replacement cost, or upgraded value. Upgraded value is the cost to replace the property with the latest, comparable, state-of-the-art equipment available. For data and media, property can be valued at the actual cost of reproduction or for an agreed dollar amount.

Many EDP floaters exclude loss of or damage to covered property while in transit. Because it is fairly common to transport computers to repair shops, many insureds may wish to have the floater amended to cover the property while in transit and while at other locations.

Bailees

Bailee policies are written for dry cleaners, repair shops, public warehouses, and many other types of businesses with large amounts of customers' goods in their possession. There are two major types of bailee policies. A **bailee liability policy** covers damage to customers' goods only if the insured is legally liable for the damage. A **bailees customers policy** covers damage to customers' goods without regard to the bailee's liability. Because a bailees customers policy allows the bailee to pay customers' losses even when there is no legal obligation to do so, it is also called "goodwill" insurance.

Instrumentalities of Transportation and Communication

Property essential to transportation or communication can be insured under an inland marine policy. The major types of properties in this class are bridges, tunnels, pipelines, and radio and television broadcasting equipment.

Filed Inland Marine Coverages

ISO and AAIS file several inland marine coverage forms. These forms can be combined with inland marine declarations, a commercial inland marine conditions form, and any applicable endorsements to make up a commercial inland marine coverage part. The coverage part can be included in a commercial package policy or issued as a monoline policy.

The ISO commercial inland marine coverage forms are briefly described below. Comparable AAIS forms are also available. The ISO forms cover risks of direct physical loss to covered property except those causes of loss that are specifically excluded (that is, they are "all-risks" forms). Valuation is typically on an actual cash value basis. However, ISO manual rules permit the valuation clause to be modified to provide for any other basis of valuation to which the insurer and the insured might agree.

Commercial Articles

The **commercial articles coverage form** covers photographic equipment and musical instruments used commercially by photographers, motion picture producers, professional musicians, and others. It is not intended for dealers of these types of property. Coverage can be provided on a scheduled or blanket basis.

Equipment Dealers

The **equipment dealers coverage form** is intended primarily to cover the stock in trade of dealers in agricultural and construction equipment. Customers' equipment in the care, custody, or control of the named insured is also covered. Coverage under a reporting form is available.

Camera and Musical Instrument Dealers

The **camera and musical instrument dealers coverage form** covers the stock in trade of dealers in cameras and musical instruments. Similar property of others in the insured's care, custody, or control is also covered. Coverage can be provided by endorsement for other types of equipment while it is on the insured's premises.

Physicians and Surgeons Equipment

The **physicians and surgeons equipment coverage form** is used to insure the professional equipment, materials, supplies, and books of physicians, surgeons, and dentists and, at the insured's option, similar property of others used by the insured in his or her profession. Coverage is also provided for the insured's office equipment, including furniture and fixtures, and for improvements and betterments if the insured does not own the building. Coverage can be added by endorsement for (1) office equipment while off premises for no more than thirty consecutive days, (2) extra expenses following a covered loss, (3) money and stamps on premises, (4) personal effects of the insured or others while on premises, and (5) valuable records.

Signs

The **signs coverage form** is used to insure neon, fluorescent, automatic, or mechanical signs. The covered signs must be scheduled with a limit of insurance shown for each item. The signs form is used by many businesses because commercial property forms exclude or severely limit coverage for signs.

Theatrical Property

The **theatrical property coverage form** covers stage scenery, costumes, theatrical properties, and other similar personal property used in theatrical productions. It covers similar property of others in the insured's care as well as property owned by the insured. The insured must have used or must intend to use the property in a production stated in the declarations.

Film

The **film coverage form** insures exposed motion picture film and magnetic tapes or videotapes, including related soundtracks or sound records. Each production must be scheduled with an amount of insurance in the declarations. The amount of insurance reflects the cost of reshooting the film if it is lost or damaged. Coverage can also be provided on a reporting form basis.

Floor Plan

A floor plan is a financing technique in which a manufacturer or finance company holds title to merchandise but permits a dealer to display and sell the merchandise. It is used extensively for agricultural equipment, construction equipment, major home appliances, and similar merchandise. The **floor plan coverage form** may be used to insure (1) the interest of the dealer in floor-planned property, (2) the interest of the manufacturer or finance company, or (3) both interests. Coverage is written on a reporting form basis.

Jewelers Block

The **jewelers block coverage form** was designed to meet the needs of small retail jewelers. This filed coverage form covers damage to the insured's stock of jewelry, precious and semiprecious stones, watches, precious metals, and similar merchandise, along with "other stock used in [the named insured's] business." Similar property of others in the insured's care, custody, or control is also covered.

Nonfiled jewelers block policies are used to insure (1) retailers with average inventories exceeding $250,000, (2) jewelry wholesalers, and (3) jewelry manufacturers.

Mail

The **mail coverage form** is written for banks, trust companies, insurance companies, investment brokers, and similar firms that frequently ship securities by mail. It covers securities and other negotiable instruments while in transit by first-class mail, certified mail, express mail, or registered mail.

Accounts Receivable

Many businesses would be unable to collect their accounts receivable if the records of those accounts were destroyed. This exposure can be significant and easily overlooked during the process of identifying loss exposures.

The **accounts receivable coverage form** covers the insured's records of accounts receivable. In the event of loss, the insurer pays the amount of accounts receivable the insured is unable to collect because of the destruction of records. The form also covers the cost to reconstruct accounts receivable records, interest on loans made necessary by an inability to collect accounts receivable, and increased collection costs resulting from loss of records. Coverage may be written on either a reporting or nonreporting form.

Valuable Papers and Records

The **valuable papers and records coverage form** is used to insure against loss to valuable papers and records. Such valuable papers might include prescription records in a drug store, plans and blueprints belonging to an architectural or engineering firm, and similar records. The policy covers the cost of necessary research to reconstruct the records. Irreplaceable records, such as valuable manuscripts, are scheduled with an agreed value shown for each item.

Rating Inland Marine Coverage

Rating methods for the filed commercial inland marine forms discussed in this chapter are based on rate factors, loadings, and credits contained in the ISO *Commercial Lines Manual (CLM)*. In most cases, base rates for these filed lines are derived from the contents rates that apply to standard commercial property coverage and are increased or decreased for use in inland marine premium determination.

The *CLM* does not contain rating methods for the nonfiled classes of inland marine insurance. However, many nonfiled inland marine policies are so widely written that both their coverage provisions and rates have become standardized to an extent. Motor truck cargo insurance, for example, is a common form of inland marine coverage, and the rates for it are based on many years of loss experience. Insurance companies active in insuring truck shipments have developed their own manuals and rate schedules for this coverage.

In other cases, the property being insured under a nonfiled policy may be so unusual or the coverage terms so specialized that there is not enough previous loss information to give the insurance company a statistically accurate idea of what the coverage should cost. What is a fair price for transporting a priceless painting from one museum to another for a special exhibit? How much should be charged for "all-risks" coverage on a one-of-a-kind piece of machinery that could be damaged as it is custom-fitted and installed in a new factory? How do you rate coverage on a drawbridge?

When faced with questions like these, inland marine underwriters must rely on their best judgment to set rates. **Judgment rating** (as opposed to manual rating, the method used to determine the premium for filed lines of insurance) requires a thorough knowledge of the business for which coverage is being written. An underwriter might have to draw on expertise in any of several specialized fields—fine arts, heavy equipment, construction, communications—to determine an adequate rate for the unique risks that are eligible for inland marine coverage.

Ocean Marine Exposures

Overseas trade by oceangoing vessels creates several loss exposures. These loss exposures exist not only for the owners of the cargo being shipped, such as manufacturers, importers, and exporters, but also for the owners of the vessels in which the cargo is being transported. (The owner of a vessel that transports property of others may operate as either a common carrier or a contract carrier.)

For the owners of the cargo there is the possibility of loss to the cargo while it is in the course of transit, either aboard the ship or on land between the ship and the cargo's point of origin or destination. For the owners of the ships there is the chance of loss of or damage to their vessels—or "hulls"—by largely the same perils that can damage or destroy the cargo they carry. These perils include the action of wind and waves, striking of rocks or other vessels, shifting of cargo, fire, war, and breakage of machinery.

A carrier that is prevented by an accident from delivering the cargo aboard its ship may face an additional exposure, called loss of **freight** (the compensation the carrier receives for transporting cargo). If the cargo cannot be delivered as promised, the carrier may lose the freight that the cargo owner (also called the "shipper") would otherwise have paid. More frequently, however, the shipper guarantees that freight charges will be paid whether the cargo is delivered or not, provided the failure to deliver the cargo results from causes beyond the carrier's control. When freight is guaranteed, it is the shipper, and not the carrier, who is primarily exposed to loss of freight.

Finally, a carrier faces the exposure to legal liability for damage to cargo, damage to other property, and bodily injury to crew members, passengers, and other persons. If, for example, an oil tanker operator's negligence resulted in a collision with another vessel, the operator could become liable to the cargo owner for loss of oil being carried; to the owner of the struck ship for damage to its hull and cargo and loss of freight; to persons on either vessel injured in the accident; and for the costs of cleaning up a resulting oil spill.

Ocean Marine Insurance

Ocean marine insurance is used to insure the cargo, hull, freight, and liability exposures described above. To a large degree, the same coverages are used to insure commercial vessels on rivers, lakes, and other inland waterways and even yachts and pleasure craft. Miscellaneous forms of ocean marine insurance are used to cover boat dealers, marina operators, shipbuilders, ship repairers, stevedores, wharf operators, and other maritime businesses.

Ocean marine insurance is written using a variety of forms. Because there can be considerable variation from one ocean marine policy to another, this discussion describes the general characteristics of the three most common types of ocean marine policies: (1) cargo, (2) hull, and (3) protection and indemnity.

Cargo Insurance

There are two basic types of cargo policies. A **voyage policy** covers cargo for a single trip described in the policy. In contrast, an **open cargo policy** is essentially a reporting form policy that covers all goods shipped or received by the insured during the term of the policy. The insured periodically pays premiums to the insurer based on reports from the insured of covered shipments. The open cargo policy is well suited to the needs of an insured who frequently ships or receives goods overseas. Open cargo policies are often extended to cover air shipments as well as ocean shipments.

The open cargo policy also permits the insured to prepare "special policies" or certificates of insurance as may be required in ocean commerce. A special policy is a complete insurance policy that is sometimes required to accompany a shipment of cargo and is assignable to anyone having an insurable interest in the property during the course of transit. In some transactions, a shorter form of the special policy, called a certificate, is used. In either case, the insured with an open cargo policy is ordinarily permitted to prepare and issue the document without having to obtain the insurer's consent.

Valuation of Property

If a policy covers only one particular voyage, the property can be insured for a specific agreed value. It would be impractical, however, for an open cargo policy to list an individual valuation for every shipment made under that policy, especially if the insured makes many shipments each year. Consequently, the usual practice is to value a shipment of cargo by a formula typically including the amount of invoice, all freight charges, and a stated percentage to cover additional expenses. The stated percentage varies depending on the circumstances, but 10 percent is often used.

Open cargo policies are ordinarily subject to a maximum limit of insurance for cargo shipped on any one vessel. There may also be a separate limit for "on deck" shipments, since they present a greater hazard than cargo stowed under deck. Open cargo loss payments are usually subject to a dollar deductible.

Warehouse to Warehouse Clause

Many importers and exporters are not located in a seaport. Consequently, their overseas shipments may be exposed to loss while in transit by truck or railcar to the port facility, while aboard the cargo ship, and while being transported again by land to the final destination. To accommodate shippers' needs for continuous coverage during the entire course of transit, including inland transportation, ocean cargo policies usually contain a **warehouse to warehouse clause**. This clause provides that the insured cargo is covered during the ordinary course of transit from the time the cargo leaves the point of shipment until it is delivered to its final destination. If the cargo is discharged at the final port and not delivered to an inland destination, coverage ceases after a stipulated number of days.

The warehouse to warehouse clause is often supplemented by the so-called **marine extension clauses**, which expand the coverage to include (1) unavoidable deviations from the ordinary course of transit or (2) delays caused by natural disasters, orders of civil authorities, or strikes of port workers. For example, a ship may become damaged and have to dock for repairs at an unintended port. If the cargo owner arranges for transshipment to the final destination, the policy will cover the remainder of the trip. The insured must pay the additional premium required by the insurer.

Covered Causes of Loss

Traditionally, ocean cargo policies insured against specified causes of loss. Today, most ocean cargo policies use the "all-risks" approach. When cargo insurance is written on an "all-risks" basis, the insurer covers any unexpected or fortuitous loss not specifically excluded. Typically, an "all-risks" open cargo policy excludes loss caused by delay, inherent vice, war, strikes, riots, or civil commotion. Coverage for loss caused by strikes, riots, or civil commotion is reinstated in virtually every open cargo policy by means of the **strikes, riots, and civil commotion (SR&CC) endorsement**. Loss caused by war can usually be insured under a separate **cargo war risk policy** issued at the same time as the ocean cargo policy.

Sue and Labor Expenses

Virtually every cargo policy contains a **sue and labor clause**. In the event of loss to the covered property, the sue and labor clause requires the insured to take reasonable measures to protect the property from further damage. In return, the insurer agrees to pay expenses the insured incurs in carrying out this duty.

General Average and Salvage Charges

Cargo policies specifically cover the insured's liability for general average and salvage charges. In marine terminology, "average" means partial loss, and **general average** is partial loss that is to be shared by all parties to the venture. **Particular average**, in contrast, is partial loss that is borne by only one party (such as a cargo owner).

General average situations arise when some of the ship's cargo is jettisoned (thrown overboard) or otherwise sacrificed in order to save the entire venture. Under maritime law, all parties to the venture, including the shipowner and all cargo owners, are required to share the losses of the owners whose property was sacrificed. Similarly, if the shipowner incurs certain expenses (such as the cost of being towed to a port of refuge) in order to ensure the safety of a voyage following a collision or other casualty, all owners of cargo aboard the vessel may be required to share the expenses.

Salvage refers to situations in which owners of cargo aboard a ship that falls in distress become liable to pay awards to those who put themselves at risk to rescue the ship.

Hull Insurance

A "hull" is the body of a vessel. **Hull insurance** covers damage to or loss of an insured vessel's structure. Also covered are machinery, boilers, and fuel supplies owned by the insured. Equipment installed for use on board the ship that the insured does not own is usually covered as well, if the insured has assumed responsibility for its safety. Hull insurance also covers provisions and stores for the operation of the ship. Hull policies ordinarily exclude any cargo on board the vessel, as well as personal effects of passengers and crew.

Covered Causes of Loss

Hull insurance policies usually cover on a specified perils basis rather than an "all-risks" basis. The following causes of loss are typically covered:

- "Perils of the seas." **Perils of the seas** are accidental causes of loss that are peculiar to the sea and other bodies of water. Examples include abnormally high winds and rough seas, strandings, groundings, and collision with other vessels or objects.
- Fire, lightning, earthquake. The inclusion of earthquake provides coverage for the possibility that a vessel might be damaged by earthquake while docked.
- Barratry. Barratry is serious misconduct by the vessel's master or crew that is contrary to the owner's interest, such as a fraudulent or criminal act that causes damage to the vessel.

- All other like perils. "All other like perils" refers to perils *similar* to the perils specifically listed in the policy. The phrase does not provide "all-risks" coverage.

In addition to the basic perils listed above, many hull policies include an additional perils clause covering losses caused by several other perils, such as electrical breakdown, bursting of boilers, breakage of shafts, latent defects, and negligence of the crew.

Hull policies exclude loss caused by war, piracy, strikes, riots, and virtually any situation in which the vessel is taken by another party. Coverage for many of the excluded perils can be added to the policy by endorsement.

Types of Policies

Hull insurance can be written as either a voyage policy or a time policy. A **voyage policy** covers a specified voyage "at and from" the port named, with coverage typically ending after the ship has moored safely at its destination for twenty-four hours. Voyage policies are primarily used for ships taking hazardous voyages or operating irregularly and without established routes.

A **time policy** covers the insured vessel(s) for a specified period of time, typically a year. It may cover voyages anywhere in the world or restrict coverage to certain areas. Time policies are often written for fleets of ships, in which case the policy may be arranged to cover all ships owned or acquired by the insured, including nonowned ships that the insured charters. Most time policies stipulate that if the policy expires while an insured vessel is at sea, in distress, or at a port of refuge or a port of call, the insurance will continue in effect until the vessel reaches its port of destination; however, the insured must notify the insurer and pay any additional premium required.

Other types of hull policies include port risk policies and builders risk policies. Port risk policies are used to insure vessels that are confined to port and not subject to navigation hazards. Builders risk policies are written to insure vessels during the course of construction.

Valuation of Property

A vessel is normally insured for a value agreed on by the insurer and the insured. If the vessel sustains a total loss caused by a covered cause of loss, the insurer pays the "agreed value" stated in the policy. In the event of a partial loss, the insurer pays the cost of repairs.

Underwriters consider several factors in determining the agreed value of a vessel. These factors include the vessel's replacement cost, its age and condition, the current market value if the vessel could be sold, the freight the vessel could earn during its remaining useful life, and its scrap value at the end of its useful life. A relatively new ship may be valued at close to its replacement cost, while an older vessel for which there is little demand may be valued at its present market value, which may be only a small fraction of its replacement cost.

Types of Loss Covered

Ordinarily, a hull policy applies to both partial and total losses, including general average, salvage, and sue and labor charges, subject to a flat deductible. However, some hull policies are written to cover total loss only. A total-loss-only policy might be used for an older ship chartered for a single voyage or for a ship that is engaged in a hazardous undertaking.

Collision Liability Clause

Most hull policies contain a **collision liability clause** (also known as a "running down clause"), which covers the insured's liability for collision damage to other ships and their cargoes, including resulting loss of freight charges and loss of use of the other owner's ship. Collision liability coverage is a separate amount of insurance ordinarily equal to the amount of insurance on the hull. The costs of defending a suit alleging covered damages are also covered, and such costs do not reduce the amount of insurance available for paying damages.

The collision liability clause does not cover liability for bodily injury, nor does it cover property damage resulting from some cause other than collision. Usually, it also does not apply to liability for collision damage to any property besides other ships and their cargoes. For these reasons and because an insured may want higher collision liability limits than the amount of insurance on the hull, shipowners usually purchase an additional form of liability insurance, called protection and indemnity.

Protection and Indemnity

Protection and indemnity (P&I) insurance covers shipowners against various liability claims resulting from operating the insured vessel. P&I insurance is usually provided in a separate policy. Some of the important sources of liability claims that may be covered by P&I insurance are as follows:

1. Damage to bridges, piers, wharves, and other structures along waterways
2. Injury to passengers, crew, and other persons on the ship
3. Injury to persons on other ships
4. Damage to cargo of others aboard the insured vessel

P&I policies cover several miscellaneous exposures as well, such as expenses incurred to remove the wreck of an insured vessel, the costs of entering an unscheduled port to obtain medical assistance for a passenger or crew member, and fines resulting from the violation of laws. Some P&I policies do not cover the insured's liability for discharging pollutants. Separate pollution liability insurance for shipowners is available from underwriting syndicates or industry pools.

Although conventional insurers write P&I insurance, a significant portion of P&I insurance is issued by P&I "clubs." A P&I club is a mutual insurer, owned by the shipowner policyholders, that writes P&I insurance exclusively for its owners.

Rating Ocean Marine Insurance

There is no advisory organization that computes ocean marine loss costs. Moreover, ocean marine insurance is generally not subject to rate filing laws in the various states. Thus, each insurer writing ocean marine insurance develops its own ocean marine rates, guided by the judgment of its underwriters and the forces of competition in the marine insurance market.

A marine underwriter's judgment may be influenced by many factors. For example, a cargo underwriter usually considers past loss experience, the product being shipped, the type of packing, the trade route over which the product is to be shipped, the volume of shipments, port conditions, the ocean and inland carriers, and, significantly, the management and reputation of the shipper. Hull and P&I underwriters consider past loss experience; the size, type, and age of the insured vessel; the area of navigation; the trade in which the vessel is employed; the nation in which the vessel is registered (the loss experience of ships registered under one flag may differ dramatically from ships under another flag); and the management and reputation of the shipowner.

Summary

Inland marine insurance evolved from ocean marine insurance in the early 1900s to meet consumers' needs in an inflexible regulatory environment. Inland marine insurance covers a broad range of exposures and is needed by most insureds. Ocean marine insurance is needed by owners of vessels and by importers and exporters.

Some common inland marine exposures are goods in domestic transit, property in the possession of bailees, movable equipment and unusual property, property of certain dealers, and instrumentalities of communication and transportation. These items of property may be subject to unusual perils. Financial effects of inland marine losses include a decrease in value, extra expenses, loss of business income, and bailee liability.

Some inland marine policies are "filed," and others are "nonfiled." Filed policies must be filed with state regulators. Nonfiled policies do not have to be filed and thus allow more flexibility for insuring unusual exposures. ISO and AAIS file various forms on behalf of their members. However, the largest classes of inland marine insurance are nonfiled and include contractors equipment, builders risk and installation, transit, motor truck cargo, difference in conditions, and electronic data processing equipment.

Rates for filed inland marine policies are derived from the insurer's commercial property rates, which are increased or decreased according to certain factors, loadings, and credits. Nonfiled policies, in contrast, must be judgment rated when there are insufficient statistics to support a manual rating approach.

The principal ocean marine loss exposures can be summarized as follows:

- Loss to cargo being carried on vessels
- Loss to vessels
- Legal liability for various accidents arising out of the operation of vessels

These exposures can be insured by three basic types of marine insurance: (1) cargo insurance, (2) hull insurance, and (3) protection and indemnity (P&I) insurance.

The open cargo policy covers all goods shipped or received by the insured during the term of the policy. Property is usually valued at invoice cost plus freight plus a stated percentage of the invoice value (such as 10 percent). Shipments are covered on a "warehouse to warehouse" basis, including transit by water and land. The policy is often extended to cover air shipments as well. Coverage is usually on an "all-risks" basis. Although excluded by the open cargo form, strikes, riots, and civil commotion are usually covered by endorsement. War is also excluded but can be covered in a companion war risk cargo policy. Open cargo policies also cover sue and labor expenses and the insured's liability for general average and salvage charges.

Hull insurance covers the vessel, its machinery, fuel, and supplies. Although a hull policy can be written to cover a specified voyage, the more common approach is a time policy covering the insured's vessels for a one-year term. Each vessel is usually insured for an amount agreed on by the insured and the insurer. In the event of a total loss, the agreed value is paid. For partial losses, the insurer pays the cost of repairs. Hull policies typically cover "perils of the seas" and several other named perils. Coverage for loss caused by war, piracy, or seizure of the vessel can be added by endorsement. The hull policy also provides collision liability coverage, which covers the insured's liability for damage to other vessels and their cargoes resulting from collision with the insured vessel.

Protection and indemnity (P&I) insurance covers shipowners against various liability claims resulting from the operation of the insured vessel. Some of the liability exposures commonly covered by P&I include the following:

- Injury to crew members, passengers, or other persons on the vessel
- Injury to persons on other vessels
- Damage to cargo of others being carried on the vessel
- Damage to piers, docks, and other property

Each insurer writing ocean marine insurance develops its own rates, guided by the judgment of its underwriters and the forces of competition in the marine insurance market.

Chapter 8

Commercial General Liability Insurance

The preceding chapters of this text have focused on property loss exposures and the corresponding types of commercial insurance. This chapter describes *liability* loss exposures and begins the examination of **commercial general liability insurance**, the foundation of liability insurance protection for most organizations. The examination of commercial general liability insurance continues in Chapter 9. Policies covering other types of liability exposures, such as automobile liability and workers compensation obligations, will be discussed in later chapters.

Liability Loss Exposures

All businesses and other organizations face liability loss exposures. A **liability loss exposure** is the possibility of experiencing a liability loss. A liability loss includes all costs to a person or an organization as the result of a specific legal claim or suit against that person or organization.

For example, Speedy Convenience Store could be sued for injuries resulting from a dangerous condition (such as a slippery floor) on its premises. The possibility that such a suit could occur is a liability loss *exposure*. If Debbie, one of Speedy's customers, slips and falls on Speedy's floor and sues Speedy to recover for her medical expenses and lost wages resulting from the accident, the store will experience a liability loss. At the very least, the store's liability loss will include the costs of investigating and defending against the suit. If Debbie wins her suit, the store's liability loss will include the cost of paying damages to compensate Debbie for her medical expenses, lost wages, and perhaps even pain and suffering. Investigation and defense costs and damages are covered under general liability policies. Other consequences of liability claims, which are generally *not* covered, include the following:

- Costs incurred by the sued organization to reduce the chance of additional, related losses in the future. For example, a business that has been sued because of injuries occurring on its property may adopt several new loss control measures.

- Hidden costs, including the time consumed in defending against a claim and the adverse publicity that comes from being sued.

To be able to identify, analyze, and properly handle an organization's liability loss exposures, one must understand (1) the concept of legal liability and (2) the common sources of liability loss exposures. Both topics are explored below.

Legal Liability

Legal liability describes a legally enforceable obligation of a person or an organization to pay a sum of money (called **damages)** to another person or organization. When a person or an organization becomes legally liable to pay damages, the person or organization suffers a liability loss. Anyone who wishes to evaluate an organization's liability loss exposures must understand the various ways in which the organization could become legally liable.

As illustrated in the example above, an organization can experience a liability loss even if it is not held legally liable. All that the other party (called the "claimant") must do is *allege* that the organization is legally liable to pay damages. The accused organization (or its liability insurer) must then incur expenses to investigate and defend against the claimant's allegation of legal liability. Even if the claim is eventually found to be invalid, the organization (or its insurer) will have incurred a liability loss. If the claimant succeeds in proving legal liability, the loss will be increased by the amount that must be paid as damages.

A liability insurance policy typically obligates the insurance company to defend the insured against allegations that, if true, would be covered under the policy. In addition, the policy obligates the insurance company to pay damages for which the insured is legally liable. Most liability claims never go to court. If the insurer believes that its policyholder is legally liable, the insurer ordinarily attempts to settle the claim (by offering to pay a certain amount of damages to the claimant) and avoid the additional expense of going to court.

Thus, being able to determine whether the insured is legally liable is a fundamental skill for insurance claims personnel.

Civil Law and Criminal Law

Legal liability can be imposed by civil law, criminal law, or both. **Civil law** provides a means to settle disputes between parties, whereas **criminal law** imposes penalties for wrongs against society. Liability insurance responds to liability imposed by civil law. Insurance is not available for criminal liability. Such insurance would be against public policy and is prohibited by law.

The same conduct can constitute both a civil wrong and a crime. For example, if a driver causes the death of a pedestrian, government authorities may charge the driver with vehicular homicide, a criminal act. The driver may also be subject to a civil action by the estate of the deceased pedestrian for medical bills, funeral expenses, loss of support, and other damages that the law allows. Insurance coverage would not respond to the criminal charges. It could, however, provide payment for the civil claims.

Civil liability can be based on torts, contracts, or statutes.

Legal Liability Based on Torts

A **tort** is a civil wrong against another person other than a breach of contract. Most of the liability claims covered by liability insurance are based on the law relating to torts (tort law). Tort law protects the rights of individuals. These legally protected rights originally included the rights to security of person, property, and reputation. Over the years, legal changes have established other rights of individuals, such as the right to privacy. Where there is a right, there is also a duty on the part of others to respect that right and to refrain from any act or omission that would impair or damage that right. Any wrongful invasion of legally protected rights entitles the injured party to bring an action against the wrongdoer for damages.

The numerous types of torts recognized by law can be classified into three broad types: (1) negligence, (2) intentional torts, and (3) strict liability torts.

Negligence

The tort of **negligence** is based on four elements: (1) a duty owed to another person, (2) a breach of that duty, (3) the occurrence of injury or damage, and (4) a close causal connection between the negligent act and the resulting harm. Negligence occurs when a person exposes others to an unreasonable risk of harm because of failure to exercise the required degree of care. For example, negligence exists when a motorist drives at an unsafe and excessive speed and, as a result, causes an accident that injures another motorist.

Intentional Torts

If a person foresees (or should be able to foresee) that his or her act will harm another person, the act is classified as an **intentional tort.** The act does not necessarily have to be performed with malicious or hostile intent. An example of an intentional tort is libel, the publication of a false statement that damages a person's reputation.

Strict Liability Torts

In various situations, tort liability can be imposed when the defendant acted neither negligently nor with intent to cause harm. This type of legal liability is commonly referred to as **strict liability** (or absolute liability). Common examples of strict liability include liability for abnormally dangerous instrumentalities (such as wild animals), ultrahazardous activities (such as blasting), and dangerously defective products.

The term "strict liability" is also used to describe liability imposed by certain statutes, such as workers compensation laws. Strict liability imposed by statute, as opposed to strict liability based on tort, is described in a separate section below.

Legal Liability Based on Contracts

In addition to torts, contracts are another basis for imposing legal liability. A **contract** is a legally enforceable agreement between two or more parties in which each party makes some promise to the other. If one party fails to honor the promise, the other may go to court to enforce the contract. Liability based on contracts can arise out of either a breach of contract or an agreement to assume the liability of another party.

Breach of Contract

A common type of **breach of contract** involves the promise (called a warranty) made by a seller regarding its product. If the product fails to live up to the promise, the warranty has been breached, and the buyer can make claim against the seller. The warranty may be either expressly stated or implied by law. For example, the law implies a warranty that every product is fit for the particular purpose for which it is sold. If the product is unfit for its intended purpose and the buyer is injured as a result, the seller may be held legally liable for damages.

Liability for injury or damage resulting from a seller's breach of warranty is commonly insurable. Other consequences of breach of contract are not insurable. For example, if a builder fails to complete a new store by the completion date promised, the store owner's claim for loss of revenue is normally not insurable under the builder's general liability insurance.

Assumption of Liability

Many contracts contain a provision that obligates one of the parties to assume the legal liability of another party. Such a provision is often called a **hold harmless agreement** because it requires the affected party to "hold harmless and indemnify" the other party against liability arising from the activity or product that is the subject of contract.

For example, a lease on a building may obligate the tenant to hold the landlord harmless against any liability claims made against the landlord by any person injured on the leased premises. The tenant, in this case, is agreeing by contract to pay claims for which the tenant would not otherwise have been legally liable. This type of liability—often called **contractual liability** or assumed liability—is commonly covered under liability insurance policies.

Legal Liability Based on Statutes

In addition to torts and contracts, statutes are a third major basis for imposing legal liability. A **statute** is a written law passed by a legislative body, at either the federal or state level. Written laws at the local level are usually referred to as ordinances. Statutes and ordinances can modify the duties that persons owe to others. Thus, the duties imposed by statute or ordinance may be used as evidence of a person's duty of care in a tort action. Apart from playing that role in tort actions, a statute can also impose legal liability on certain persons or organizations regardless of whether they acted negligently, committed any tort, or assumed liability under a contract.

In other words, a statute can give certain persons or organizations an absolute legal obligation to compensate other persons if certain events occur. This type of obligation is a form of strict liability, like that discussed earlier, except that it is based entirely on requirements imposed by statute rather than on tort law. An important example of liability imposed by statute is the workers compensation system, which requires employers to pay prescribed benefits for occupational injuries or illness of their employees. The employer must pay these benefits even if an employee's injury or illness did not result from the employer's negligence. (The workers compensation system will be discussed in Chapter 12.)

Sources of Liability Exposures

A wide range of exposures, arising from various sources, can spawn liability losses. One major source of liability exposures is the operation of automobiles. Another major source of liability exposures is employees, since most employers are obligated by workers compensation laws to pay for occupational injuries of their employees. Those two sources of liability exposures will be examined in later chapters. The present chapter focuses on liability exposures covered under commercial general liability (CGL) insurance. CGL insurance provides coverage primarily for liability losses arising from premises, operations, products, and completed operations, although it also covers other exposures.

Premises Liability Exposure

The **premises liability exposure** exists when there is ownership, occupancy, or use of property (the premises). The standard of care imposed on an owner-occupant, a landlord, or a tenant is that the property be maintained as a reasonable and prudent person would maintain it. For example, a reasonable and prudent person would be expected to keep floors dry and free of objects that might cause injury to another person.

Operations Liability Exposure

The **operations liability exposure** relates to activity in addition to the occupancy of property. The operations could be those of any kind of business, but this exposure is generally associated with manufacturers, processors, or contractors. For example, a contractor paving a road has an operations liability exposure. If a member of the public is injured as a result of negligent construction activity while the project is underway, any resulting liability claim against the contractor will be said to have arisen out of the operations liability exposure.

Products Liability Exposure

The **products liability exposure** of an organization is the possibility that a member of the general public might be injured by a product manufactured, sold, or distributed by the organization. If, for example, a child is injured by a dangerously defective toy, the injury can be said to have arisen out of the toy manufacturer's products liability exposure. Products liability can be imposed on a manufacturer, seller, or distributor of products under several different legal theories, including negligence, breach of contract, and strict liability in tort.

Completed Operations Liability Exposure

Although the **completed operations liability exposure** is traditionally linked with the products liability exposure, the two exposures are distinguishable in liability insurance. The products liability exposure is associated with any items or goods sold by an organization, which might be the manufacturer, the wholesaler, or the retailer of the goods. The completed operations liability exposure typically relates to an organization's liability for work it has performed and finished, including any materials provided by the organization doing the work.

For example, a furnace sold by its manufacturer to a heating contractor is within the manufacturer's *products* liability exposure. After the contractor who bought the furnace has installed it in a customer's home, the furnace and all labor and parts included in the installation job are within the contractor's *completed operations* liability exposure.

The word "completed" is important. If an injury had occurred because of the contractor's negligence during the course of the work (before the work was *completed*), the claim would be said to have arisen out of the contractor's operations liability exposure, not its *completed* operations liability exposure.

Other CGL Exposures

Other liability exposures covered by the CGL policy include liability assumed under certain contracts and liability for some intentional torts (such as libel and slander). These additional exposures, as well as those described above, will become more apparent as the corresponding provisions of commercial general liability insurance are described in the remainder of this chapter.

Overview of Commercial General Liability Insurance

Most organizations have, at the least, premises or operations liability exposures and therefore commonly purchase commercial general liability (CGL) insurance to cover those exposures. CGL insurance can therefore be viewed as the foundation for most organizations' liability insurance programs. Additional types of liability insurance, such as automobile liability insurance, are frequently added to this foundation in order to insure exposures that the CGL policy excludes.

The most commonly used standard form for providing CGL insurance is the commercial general liability coverage form of Insurance Services Office (ISO). This coverage form can be combined with CGL declarations and any applicable endorsements to form a CGL coverage part. Like the other ISO coverage parts, this one can be either included in a commercial package policy or issued as a monoline policy.

The CGL coverage form comes in two versions: the occurrence form and the claims-made form. "Occurrence" and "claims-made" refer to the events that trigger coverage under the forms (a point that will be explained in more detail later in this chapter). The two forms differ only in their provisions respecting these coverage triggers. Because the occurrence form is much more widely used than the claims-made form, it is described first. The claims-made form will be discussed in the next chapter.

Both versions of the CGL coverage form provide three separate coverages:

- Coverage A: bodily injury and property damage liability
- Coverage B: personal and advertising injury liability
- Coverage C: medical payments

This chapter describes the insuring agreements and applicable exclusions for each of these coverages as found in the 1996 revised edition of the CGL coverage form.

Coverage A: Bodily Injury and Property Damage Liability

Coverage A insures against claims arising out of the premises, operations, products, completed operations, and contractual liability exposures described earlier. The main provisions for Coverage A consist of a broad insuring agreement that is limited by several exclusions. If a claim against an insured meets all of the criteria of the insuring agreement and does not come within the scope of any of the exclusions, it is covered, subject to policy limits and conditions.

Coverage A Insuring Agreement

The Coverage A insuring agreement consists of two distinct promises made by the insurer: (1) a promise *to pay damages* on behalf of the insured and (2) a promise *to defend* the insured against claims or suits seeking damages covered under the policy.

Insurer's Duty To Pay Damages

The insuring agreement imposes several conditions on the insurer's duty to pay damages. All of the following conditions must be fulfilled:

1. The insured must be legally obligated (legally liable) to pay damages.
2. The damages must result from "bodily injury" or "property damage" as defined in the policy (see below).

3. The policy must apply to the bodily injury or property damage.

4. The bodily injury or property damage must be caused by an "occurrence" (see definition below).

5. The occurrence must take place in the "coverage territory."

6. The bodily injury or property damage must occur during the policy period. (The claims-made form contains a different provision in this regard.)

1. Legally Obligated To Pay Damages

Whether the insured is legally obligated to pay damages is a question that can be settled either in court or by the insurer's claim investigation. Often, the insurer's investigation reveals that the insured is legally liable. If the insurer also believes that the policy covers the claim, it will usually attempt to negotiate with the third-party claimant and try to arrange an out-of-court settlement.

The basic types of damages that a court might award consist of the following:

- Special damages, for such out-of-pocket costs as medical expenses and loss of earnings

- General damages, for such intangibles as pain and suffering

- Punitive damages, awarded to punish or make an example of the wrong-doer

Although the insurer promises to pay all damages for which the insured is liable, a few states do not recognize the concept of punitive damages, and some other states do not permit insurers to pay punitive damages on behalf of an insured. Even in states that do allow insurers to pay punitive damages, insurers are not likely to pay them in an out-of-court settlement.

2. "Bodily Injury" and "Property Damage"

The CGL coverage form broadly defines **bodily injury** as "bodily injury, sickness or disease sustained by a person, including death resulting from any of these at any time." The insuring agreement contains a statement that damages because of "bodily injury" include damages for care, loss of services, or death. Damages for pain and suffering are part of "bodily injury."

The policy definition of **property damage** includes both of the following:

- *Physical injury to tangible property, including resulting loss of use of that property.* An example of physical injury is the destruction of a customer's building by fire caused by the insured contractor's negligence. "Resulting loss of use" would include the loss of income sustained by the customer until the building could be rebuilt.

- *Loss of use of tangible property that is not physically injured.* An example is loss of business income suffered by a stock brokerage firm because utility services were interrupted for several hours as a result of utility company negligence.

3. Injury or Damage to Which the Insurance Applies

The insurer is not obligated to pay damages if any of the Coverage A exclusions applies to the claim or if the claim is not covered for any other reason. The Coverage A exclusions are described in a later section of this chapter.

4. Caused by an "Occurrence"

To be insured, the bodily injury or property damage must be caused by an "occurrence." The policy definition of **occurrence** is "an accident, including continuous or repeated exposure to substantially the same general harmful conditions."

The term "accident" is not defined in the policy. However, the intent is to provide coverage for any adverse condition that continues over a long period and eventually results in bodily injury or property damage, as well as for an event that happens suddenly and results in immediate bodily injury or property damage. In either case, the bodily injury or property damage would be caused by an "occurrence."

Unintended results of intentional acts generally qualify as accidents. For example, in using a propane torch to thaw out a customer's frozen water pipe (an intentional act), a plumber might accidentally set the building on fire. The fire, because it was an unintended result, would qualify as an accident. In contrast, if a plumber intentionally set a customer's house on fire, perhaps to get back at a customer who refused to pay for the plumber's services, the fire (an example of arson) would not be considered an accident or, by extension, an "occurrence."

5. "Coverage Territory"

Coverage A applies only to occurrences that take place in the "coverage territory" defined in the policy. The coverage territory that applies to most claims is the United States (including its territories and possessions), Puerto Rico, and Canada. International waters and international airspace are included in the coverage territory unless the injury or damage occurs in the course of travel or transportation to or from any place not included in the basic coverage territory described above.

The coverage territory also includes the entire world with respect to the following:

- Goods or products made or sold by the named insured in the basic coverage territory described above
- Activities of a person whose home is in the basic coverage territory but who is away for a short time while pursuing the named insured's business

In either case, the insured's liability for damages must be determined either in a suit filed in the basic coverage territory (the United States, its territories or possessions, Puerto Rico, or Canada) or in a settlement to which the insurer agrees.

6. Injury or Damage Occurring During the Policy Period

The occurrence version of the CGL coverage form requires that, in order for a claim to be covered, the bodily injury or property damage must occur during the policy period. This requirement is the so-called **occurrence coverage trigger.** In other words, the policy that applies to a particular claim is the one that is in effect when the bodily injury or property damage occurs. This is so even if the claim is not made until many years after the policy period ends.

Significantly, the claims-made version of the CGL coverage form contains a different coverage trigger. Basically, the *claim* for bodily injury or property damage must be first made during the policy period. However, several additional conditions apply. The claims-made form will be described in more detail in Chapter 9.

Insurer's Duty To Defend

The Coverage A insuring agreement also expresses the insurer's right and duty to defend the insured against any suit seeking damages for bodily injury or property damage to which the insurance applies. The policy defines the word "suit" to include informal civil proceedings and arbitration proceedings, as well as formal lawsuits.

Courts frequently describe the insurer's duty to defend as being broader than its duty to pay damages. The insurer must defend its insured whenever a claimant alleges a wrongful act or omission of the insured that could conceivably fall within the coverage of the policy. The duty to defend exists even if the allegations are later proved to be groundless, false, or fraudulent. In many cases, a plaintiff will allege various acts or omissions, some of which may be clearly outside the scope of coverage. However, as long as at least *one* of the alleged acts or omissions is conceivably covered, the insurer is usually obligated to defend the insured against the entire complaint.

Coverage A Exclusions

Fourteen exclusions, labeled *a* through *n* in the CGL coverage form, apply to Coverage A. Many of these exclusions contain exceptions that restore coverage for certain types of claims.

Many of the exclusions eliminate coverage for exposures (such as automobile liability, workers compensation, and pollution liability) that are customarily insured under other policies or that can be insured, for an additional premium, under endorsements to the CGL coverage form. A smaller number of exclusions deal with exposures (such as intentional injury or product recall) that are uninsurable or, at best, difficult to insure.

Expected or Intended Injury

Exclusion *a* eliminates coverage for bodily injury or property damage expected or intended by the insured. Thus, there would be no coverage if the insured intentionally injured the claimant. However, the exclusion does not apply to bodily injury resulting from the use of reasonable force to protect persons or property. For example, a store owner might use *reasonable* force to restrain a customer from defacing merchandise. This act of protecting property would be covered even though the store owner intentionally used force. However, even acts undertaken to protect persons or property are not covered if *excessive* force is used.

Contractual Liability

Exclusion *b* eliminates coverage for liability assumed by the insured under a contract. This exclusion applies only if the liability would not have existed in the absence of the contract. That is, if liability for a claim could have been imposed by tort law, the exclusion will not apply even though the insured might also have assumed liability for the claim under a hold harmless agreement.

More significantly, the exclusion also does not apply to liability assumed under an "insured contract" if the bodily injury or property damage occurs after the contract or agreement is executed. Therefore, the CGL form *covers* liability assumed under any contract that meets the policy definition of "insured contract"—as long as the bodily injury or property damage occurs after the contract is executed.

Definition of "Insured Contract"

The policy definition of **insured contract** includes the following:

1. A lease of premises, but not that portion of a lease of premises that indemnifies another party for fire damage to premises rented to or temporarily occupied by the insured

2. A railroad sidetrack agreement

3. Any easement or license agreement, except in connection with construction or demolition within fifty feet of a railroad

4. An obligation to indemnify a municipality if required by ordinance, except in connection with work performed for the municipality

5. An elevator maintenance agreement

6. Any other contract or agreement pertaining to the insured's business under which the insured assumes the *tort* liability of another

Item 6 above covers contracts not specifically listed in items 1 through 5. Thus, for example, if the insured assumed the tort liability of another party under a hold harmless agreement in a construction contract, such an agreement would be an "insured contract."

However, the following types of contracts are specifically excluded from the definition of "insured contract" and therefore are not covered:

1. Contracts to indemnify a railroad for bodily injury or property damage arising from construction or demolition operations within fifty feet of a railroad property and affecting any railroad bridge or trestle, tracks, roadbeds, tunnel, underpass, or crossing

2. Contracts to indemnify architects, engineers, or surveyors for their errors or omissions in performing their professional duties

3. Contracts under which architects, engineers, or surveyors assume liability for injury or damage arising from their errors and omissions in performing their professional duties

Defense Costs Assumed Under Contract

In many cases, a hold harmless agreement will obligate the insured to pay the other party's defense costs in addition to its damages. Earlier versions of the CGL policy did not specifically address defense costs assumed under contract. Although some insurers paid such costs under their CGL policies, other insurers held that CGL contractual liability coverage only applied to damages and not to defense costs.

In 1996 ISO introduced in many states a new edition of the CGL coverage form that obligates the insurer to pay reasonable attorney fees and necessary litigation expenses assumed by the insured under an insured contract. However, such expenses paid by the insurer are treated as "damages" and thus are subject to the policy limits. In contrast, the insurer is obligated to pay regular defense costs (those incurred in defending the insured against direct claims) *in addition* to policy limits.

Liquor Liability

Exclusion *c* applies only to insureds who are in the business of manufacturing, distributing, selling, serving, or furnishing alcoholic beverages. It eliminates coverage if liability arises from causing or contributing to the intoxication of any person, from furnishing alcoholic beverages to a person under the legal drinking age, or otherwise violating the laws governing the sale and distribution of such beverages. The liquor liability exclusion does not apply to the casual or occasional distribution of alcoholic beverages, such as at an annual company picnic or holiday office party, as long as the insured is not in the alcoholic beverage business.

Workers Compensation and Employers Liability

Exclusions *d* and *e* deal with injuries to any employee of the insured. Exclusion *d* eliminates coverage for obligations of the insured under any workers compensation, disability benefits, unemployment compensation, or similar law.

Exclusion *e* eliminates coverage for bodily injury to any employee of the insured if the injury arises out of and in the course of employment. The exclusion applies regardless of whether the insured is liable in a capacity other than as an employer. It also applies to obligations to share damages with someone else or to repay someone who has paid damages. However, the exclusion does not apply to liability assumed by the insured under an insured contract.

The CGL coverage form defines "employee" to include a "leased worker." Thus, exclusion *e* applies to both normal employees and leased workers as defined. A "leased worker" is a worker leased to the insured by a labor-leasing firm to perform duties related to the insured's business. Many businesses use leased workers in an attempt to reduce record keeping and paperwork, provide better employee benefits at lower cost, and achieve other savings. A temporary worker—that is, a worker furnished to the insured to substitute for a permanent employee on leave or to meet seasonal or short-term workload conditions—is not included in the definition of "leased worker."

Pollution

Exclusion *f* eliminates coverage for pollution liability claims related to the insured's premises and operations. The exclusion is worded very broadly in order to encompass the many ways pollutants might enter the environment. It deals with bodily injury and property damage resulting from pollution and with the cost or expense involved with the cleanup of pollutants.

The exclusion is virtually absolute with regard to the insured's premises, sites, or locations (past and present) as well as premises, sites, or locations used by the insured for the handling, storage, disposal, processing, or treatment of waste. The exclusion expresses two exceptions, which provide coverage for the following:

- Bodily injury or property damage caused by heat, smoke, or fumes from a hostile fire. A hostile fire is a fire that becomes uncontrollable or breaks out from where it was intended to be.

- Bodily injury or property damage resulting from the escape of fuels, lubricants, or other operating fluids needed to perform the normal functions of mobile equipment. The fuels, lubricants, or operating fluids must escape from a vehicle part designed to hold them, and the escape must be accidental.

By inference from the wording of the exclusion, the exclusion does not apply to bodily injury or property damage resulting from pollution caused by the insured's products or completed operations away from the insured's premises. For example, a family might be taken ill by chemical vapors emanating from carpeting sold by the insured. The family's claim for bodily injury would not be excluded.

By inference, the exclusion also does not apply to work being performed away from the insured's premises by the insured or contractor or subcontractor working on the insured's behalf as long as the following are true:

1. The pollutants are not brought onto the site by the insured, the contractor, or the subcontractor.

2. The operations do not in any way involve working with pollutants.

To illustrate, the insured, an excavation contractor, might accidentally run a bulldozer into another contractor's oil storage tank at a work site. As long as the insured did not bring the oil onto the site, any liability that the insured might have for resulting bodily injury or property damage would be covered under the insured's CGL policy. Cleanup costs, however, are excluded in all cases.

Aircraft, Autos, and Watercraft

Exclusion *g* eliminates coverage for bodily injury and property damage arising from the ownership, maintenance, or use of any aircraft, "auto," or watercraft. As defined by the form, an **auto** is a land motor vehicle, trailer, or semitrailer designed for travel on public roads, including any attached machinery or equipment. However, any land motor vehicle that is included within the definition of "mobile equipment" (discussed below) is not an "auto."

The exclusion also applies to the **loading or unloading** of aircraft, autos, and watercraft. As defined in the coverage form, loading or unloading occurs when property is handled during the following periods:

• After it is moved from the place where it is accepted for movement into or onto an aircraft, auto, or watercraft

• While it is on such a conveyance

• While it is being moved from the conveyance to the place where it is finally delivered

Loading or unloading includes the movement of property by a hand truck but not the movement of property by any other mechanical device that is not attached to the conveyance.

To illustrate the definition of loading or unloading, assume that an appliance store sold a deep freezer to a customer and agreed to deliver the freezer to the customer's home and place it in the basement. The store employees delivering the freezer accidentally gouged wood trim and wallboard while carrying the freezer down the basement stairs. According to the definition, the damage occurred during loading or unloading (that is, while the freezer was being moved from the store's truck "to the place where it is finally delivered"). Thus, the customer's claim for property damage will not be covered under the store's CGL policy. It will, however, be covered under the store's auto liability insurance as long as the delivery truck is a covered auto.

Some coverage for claims involving aircraft, autos, and watercraft is provided through the following exceptions to exclusion g:

1. Claims arising from watercraft while ashore on the insured's premises are covered.

2. Claims arising out of nonowned watercraft are covered if the craft is less than twenty-six feet long and is not being used to carry persons or property for a fee.

3. Liability assumed under an insured contract for the ownership, maintenance, or use of aircraft or watercraft (but not autos) is covered.

4. The operation of certain types of equipment (such as a cherry picker) attached to autos is covered.

5. Claims arising from parking an auto on or next to the insured's premises are covered if the auto is not owned by, rented to, or loaned to any insured.

The last exception listed above primarily benefits organizations that provide valet parking service. If, for example, a restaurant employee, while parking a patron's car in the restaurant's parking lot, negligently struck another car and injured its driver, the restaurant's CGL policy would cover the damage to the other car and the injury to its driver. Damage to the customer's auto would not be covered by the CGL, however, because of exclusion *j*, discussed below. Liability for damage to customers' autos in the insured's care, custody, or control can be covered through garagekeepers insurance, discussed in Chapter 10.

Mobile Equipment

The only CGL exclusion that specifically applies to mobile equipment is exclusion *h*, which applies only in narrow circumstances. Thus, the CGL form generally covers liability arising out of the ownership, maintenance, or use of mobile equipment.

The mobile equipment exclusion eliminates coverage for the following:

1. The transportation of "mobile equipment" by an auto that is owned, operated, rented, or borrowed by an insured
2. The use of mobile equipment in a prearranged racing, speed, or demolition contest or in a stunting activity

The policy definition of **mobile equipment** includes a variety of motorized land vehicles and any machinery or equipment attached to them. The types of vehicles included in the definition of "mobile equipment" are presented in Exhibit 8-1. The exhibit also lists the types of equipment that are considered "autos." Although most claims involving autos are excluded from CGL coverage, claims arising from the operation of "mobile equipment" as defined are covered as long as they are not excluded by exclusion *h*.

Note that a truck can be classified as mobile equipment if it is used solely on or next to the insured's premises. Thus, an accident involving a truck used only to move beams around the storage yard of an iron and steel wholesaler would be covered under the wholesaler's CGL policy.

War

It is unlikely that an insured would be held directly liable for bodily injury or property damage resulting from war. However, an insured might become obligated under an "insured contract" for some war-related claims. Consequently, exclusion *i* of the CGL form excludes liability resulting from war if the liability is assumed under a contract or other type of agreement.

Damage to Property

Exclusion *j* eliminates coverage for damage to any of the following:

1. Property owned, rented, or occupied by the named insured
2. Premises the named insured has sold, given away, or abandoned if the damage arises out of any part of such premises

Exhibit 8-1
Distinction Between "Mobile Equipment" and "Autos" in the
CGL Coverage Form

"Mobile Equipment"

The following types of land vehicles, including attached equipment:

  a. Bulldozers, farm machinery, forklifts and other vehicles designed for use principally off public roads

  b. Vehicles maintained for use solely on or next to premises owned or rented by the named insured

  c. Vehicles that travel on crawler treads

  d. Vehicles (self-propelled or not) maintained primarily to provide mobility to permanently mounted power cranes, shovels, loaders, diggers, drills, or road construction or resurfacing equipment such as graders, scrapers, or rollers

  e. Vehicles that are not self-propelled and are maintained primarily to provide mobility to permanently attached equipment of the following types: air compressors, pumps, and generators (including spraying, welding, building cleaning, geophysical exploration, lighting, or well servicing equipment) and cherry pickers and similar devices used to raise or lower workers

  f. Vehicles not described above that are maintained primarily for purposes other than transportation of persons or cargo

"Autos"

Land motor vehicles, trailers, or semitrailers designed for travel on public roads, including any attached machinery or equipment

Self-propelled vehicles with the following types of permanently attached equipment:

Snow removal

Road maintenance (not construction or resurfacing)

Street cleaning

Cherry pickers and similar devices mounted on automobile or truck chassis and used to raise or lower workers[1]

Air compressors, pumps, and generators, including spraying, welding, building cleaning, geophysical exploration, lighting, and well servicing

---

1. The operation of these types of attached equipment is covered under the CGL. However, the operation of the vehicles to which the equipment is attached is *not* covered by the CGL.

3. Property loaned to the named insured

4. Personal property in the care, custody, or control of an insured

5. That particular part of any real property on which work is being done by the named insured or any contractor or subcontractor working for the named insured if the damage arises from the work

6. That particular part of any property that must be restored, repaired, or replaced because the named insured's work was incorrectly performed on it

It is usually possible to purchase other policies to cover many of the excluded items. The insured's property, excluded by item 1, can be insured by the building and personal property coverage form or by another property insurance form. Other property in the insured's custody, excluded by items 1, 3, and 4, can be covered in a property insurance form or in various inland marine forms.

Item 2 does not apply to premises that are the named insured's work if they were never occupied, rented, or held for rental by the insured. This exception provides coverage for a builder who constructs a building for sale and later becomes liable for damage to the building after it has been sold. Furthermore, since the exclusion applies only to property damage, bodily injury arising out of premises the named insured has sold, given away, or abandoned would be covered.

Items 5 and 6 sometimes cause confusion. Item 5 excludes only "that particular part" of *real property* on which the named insured is working. The exclusion does not, therefore, apply to *personal property* under any circumstances, and it applies only to "that particular part" of real property on which the insured is working. To illustrate, say that the insured is an electrician who is installing electrical components in a building under construction. If, while working on an electrical control panel, the electrician negligently causes a fire that burns down the entire building, item 5 will only exclude damage to "that particular part" on which the insured was working. "That particular part" would presumably be limited to the control panel. Damage to the rest of the building would be covered.

Item 6 applies to "that particular part" of either real property or personal property that must be repaired or replaced because the insured's work on it was done incorrectly. In other words, the insurer will not pay the cost of redoing the insured's faulty work. The insurer will, however, pay for damage to property other than "that particular part" that must be redone.

To illustrate the application of item 6, assume that a remodeling contractor installed a faulty roof on a home addition that he was constructing. Before the addition was completed, rainwater entered the addition and damaged the inside of the addition, and the owner made claim against the contractor for resulting damages. Item 6 under the contractor's CGL policy would exclude the cost of repairing the roof, but it would not exclude the cost of repairing the other parts of the building that were damaged because of the faulty roof.

Insured's Products and Work

The remaining CGL exclusions (*k* through *n*) relate to the insured's products and work. In general, they exclude claims for damage to the insured's products or to work performed by or on behalf of the insured if the damage arises from defects in the insured's products or work. The primary purpose of this group of exclusions is to prevent the insurer from having to pay for failures of the insured's products or work—other than bodily injury or damage to property besides the insured's own product or work. The CGL form contains detailed definitions of "your product" and "your work," which will not be restated here.

Damage to Your Product

Exclusion *k* eliminates coverage for any damage to the insured's product if the damage results from a defect in any part of the product. For example, if cabinets that the insured manufactured collapse because of a defect in the cabinets, the damage to the cabinets would not be covered. However, the insured's CGL policy would cover claims for breakage of the contents of the cabinets.

Damage to Your Work

Exclusion *l* is similar to exclusion *k*, but it applies to claims for injury or damage resulting from a defect in the insured's work rather than the insured's products. The exclusion applies only to completed work—not to work that is still being performed when the property damage occurs. (Damage to property being worked on is addressed by exclusion *j*.)

Exclusion *l* does not apply to claims if either the damaged work or the work from which the damage arose was performed for the insured by a subcontractor. For example, assume that defective plumbing caused extensive damage to a house built by Miller Construction Company but not owned by Miller at the time of the damage. If Miller did all of the work, including the plumbing, there would be no coverage for any claim based on damage from the plumbing. If a subcontractor did the plumbing, then claims against Miller for damage caused by the work of the plumbing subcontractor would be covered.

Damage to Impaired Property or Property Not Physically Injured

Exclusion *m* eliminates coverage for claims for property damage to "impaired property" or property that has not been physically injured if the damage arises from (1) a defect in the insured's product or work or (2) failure of the insured or anyone acting on behalf of the insured to complete a contract or agreement in accordance with its terms.

The form defines "impaired property" as tangible property other than the insured's product or work that cannot be used or is less useful because (1) it includes the insured's defective product or defective work or (2) the insured has failed to fulfill a contract or agreement.

To illustrate the application of the exclusion to impaired property, assume that BC Company manufactures small electric motors that are incorporated in drills produced by other companies. If the BC motors are defective and must be replaced so that the drills will function properly, the drills would be "impaired property." Accordingly, BC's CGL policy would not cover claims against BC for the loss in value of the drills or for the cost of replacing the motors.

The exclusion also applies to property damage to "property that has not been physically injured." Remember that the definition of "property damage" includes loss of use of property that has not been physically injured. However, the exclusion under consideration eliminates coverage for such loss-of-use claims when the cause is a defect in the insured's product or work or the insured's failure to perform a contract.

To illustrate this aspect of the exclusion, suppose that Acme Heating Company installed a furnace in a new office building. However, the furnace was defective and did not provide sufficient heat for the building. Consequently, occupancy of the building was delayed for several weeks while a new furnace was ordered and installed. The building owner sustained a loss of income because the building could not be occupied. The owner might have a valid legal claim against Acme, but it would not be covered under Acme's CGL policy because of exclusion *m*: the loss of use of the building (which was not physically injured) resulted from a defect in Acme's product.

However, the exclusion contains an important exception. The exclusion does not apply if loss of use of property other than the insured's product or work arises out of *sudden and accidental damage* to the insured's product or work after it has been put to its intended use.

Returning to the example of Acme Heating Company, suppose that the building opening was delayed because the furnace had been suddenly and accidentally damaged by an explosion inside its firebox. In this case, the impaired property exclusion would not apply, and Acme's CGL policy would cover the building owner's claim for the resulting loss of use of the building.

(Damage to the furnace itself would still be excluded, because of the "damage to your product" exclusion.)

Recall of Products, Work, or Impaired Property

Exclusion *n* eliminates coverage for any loss, cost, or expense resulting from loss of use, withdrawal, recall, inspection, repair, replacement, adjustment, removal, or disposal of (1) the insured's product, (2) the insured's work, or (3) impaired property.

Manufacturers must often recall products that are found to pose a risk of serious injury to users or others. Even though such a recall may avoid claims that would be covered by the policy, the CGL policy does not (because of exclusion *n*) cover the cost of the recall. Such recalls can be extremely expensive. Johnson & Johnson spent over $100 million removing Tylenol from store shelves after the deaths of seven persons who ingested cyanide-contaminated capsules.[1]

Fire Damage Coverage

An exception to exclusions *c* through *n* at the end of the Coverage A exclusions grants coverage for fire damage to premises rented to or temporarily occupied by the named insured. This coverage, widely known as **fire legal liability coverage,** insures claims that would otherwise be excluded by exclusion *j*, which applies to property that the named insured rents or occupies.

To illustrate the application of fire legal liability coverage, assume that the insured occupies, under lease, part of a multi-tenant building. Assume also that the insured's negligence causes a fire in its own part of the building. In this case, the insured's liability to the building owner for fire damage to that part of the building would be covered by the fire legal liability coverage in the insured's CGL policy; that is, the exclusion of damage to property rented or occupied by the insured would not apply. The insured's liability for damage to any *other* parts of the building would also be covered, regardless of the fire legal liability coverage, since the other parts of the building are not rented or occupied by the insured.

Coverage B: Personal and Advertising Injury Liability

Coverage B of the CGL form insures against claims based on torts such as libel, slander, and wrongful eviction. The provisions relating to Coverage B, like those relating to Coverage A, consist of an insuring agreement and several exclusions.

Coverage B Insuring Agreement

The Coverage B insuring agreement parallels the Coverage A insuring agreement in several ways. The insurer agrees to pay those sums that the insured becomes legally obligated to pay as damages. In addition, the insurer agrees to defend the insured against any suit seeking such damages. However, instead of responding to claims for bodily injury and property damage, Coverage B responds to claims for "personal injury" and "advertising injury" to which the insurance applies.

The CGL policy defines **personal injury** and **advertising injury** to include several specific torts. These policy definitions are reproduced in Exhibit 8-2.

Exhibit 8-2
CGL Policy Definitions of "Personal Injury" and "Advertising Injury"

"Personal Injury"

"Personal injury" means injury, other than "bodily injury," arising out of one or more of the following offenses:

a. False arrest, detention or imprisonment;

b. Malicious prosecution;

c. The wrongful eviction from, wrongful entry into, or invasion of the right of private occupancy of a room, dwelling or premises that a person occupies by or on behalf of its owner, landlord or lessor;

d. Oral or written publication of material that slanders or libels a person or organization or disparages a person's or organization's goods, products or services; or

e. Oral or written publication of material that violates a person's right of privacy.

"Advertising Injury"

"Advertising injury" means injury arising out of one or more of the following offenses:

a. Oral or written publication of material that slanders or libels a person or organization or disparages a person's or organization's goods, products or services;

b. Oral or written publication of material that violates a person's right of privacy;

c. Misappropriation of advertising ideas or style of doing business; or

d. Infringement of copyright, title or slogan.

Both definitions include injury arising out of one or more of the offenses listed in the definition. Although the CGL form does not define *injury*, the word has a broad meaning and can include (but is not limited to) physical harm or impairment, mental anguish or injury, fright, shock, humiliation, and loss of reputation. Courts can award damages for any of the above types of harm that result from torts.

However, the "personal injury" definition excludes bodily injury. If the insured causes bodily injury as the result of committing a personal injury or advertising injury offense, any damages the insured becomes liable to pay because of the bodily injury are payable under Coverage A, as long as they are not otherwise excluded by the policy. Although the legal profession uses the term "personal injury" to mean bodily injury, this difference in usage should not cause confusion. In the insurance business, "personal injury" is a defined term that specifically excludes bodily injury.

To be covered, any personal injury offense or advertising injury offense must be committed in the CGL coverage territory, as described earlier.

Under the occurrence CGL coverage form, the coverage trigger for Coverage B is a personal injury offense or advertising injury offense committed during the policy period. That is, the policy in effect when the insured committed the offense is the policy that covers any damages resulting from that offense (even if claim is not made until after the policy has expired).

Coverage B Exclusions

Coverage B is subject to ten exclusions. Five of them apply to both personal injury and advertising injury. The remaining exclusions apply only to advertising injury.

The five exclusions that apply to both personal and advertising injury eliminate coverage for the following:

1. Injury arising out of oral or written publication of material if done by or at the direction of the insured with knowledge of its falsity

2. Injury arising out of oral or written publication of material whose first publication occurred before the beginning of the policy period

3. Injury arising out of the willful violation of a penal statute or ordinance committed by or with the consent of the insured

4. Injury for which the insured is liable solely because of a contract or agreement

5. Injury resulting from the release of pollutants

The exclusions that apply only to advertising injury eliminate coverage arising out of the following:

1. Breach of contract, other than misappropriation of advertising ideas under an implied contract

2. The failure of goods, products, or services to conform with the advertised quality of performance

3. The wrong description of the price of the goods, products, or services

4. An offense committed by an insured whose business is advertising, broadcasting, or telecasting

5. Requests or demands to clean up or in any other way respond to pollutants

The first three advertising injury exclusions deal with "business risks" for which insurance is not generally available. The fourth exclusion eliminates advertising liability coverage for advertising agencies and similar businesses, which are ordinarily insured under separate advertisers liability policies. The pollution cleanup exclusion, like the pollutant exclusion that applies to personal injury and advertising injury, is intended to clarify that Coverage B does not apply to pollution liability or cleanup orders.

Supplementary Payments

The CGL coverage form contains a section titled "supplementary payments," which completes the insuring agreements for Coverages A and B. Both of those insuring agreements obligate the insurer to defend any claim or suit seeking damages if such damages would be covered under the policy. The supplementary payments section describes the specific items that the insurer will pay (in addition to damages).

The supplementary payments are payable in addition to the limits of insurance that apply to CGL coverage. However, the insurer's obligation to pay these supplementary payments ends as soon as the applicable limit of insurance has been used up in paying damages for judgments or settlements. The supplementary payments consist of the following:

• All expenses incurred by the insurer, such as fees for attorneys, witness fees, cost of police reports, and similar items.

• Up to $250 for the cost of bail bonds required because of accidents or traffic law violations involving any covered vehicle (typically mobile equipment).

• The cost of bonds to release any property of the insured's held by a plaintiff to ensure payment of any judgment that may be rendered against the insured. The insurer is not required to provide either of the bonds described above; its only obligation is to pay the premium.

- Reasonable expenses incurred by the insured at the insurer's request, including loss of earnings (up to $250 a day) if the insured must miss work to testify, attend court, or otherwise assist in the defense.

- Court costs or other costs (other than actual damages) assessed against the insured in a suit.

- Interest on judgments awarded against the insured. In some cases, courts will award either prejudgment interest or post-judgment interest, or both, to a plaintiff. Prejudgment interest is interest that accrues on the amount of a judgment before entry of the judgment. Post-judgment interest is interest that accrues after the judgment is entered but before the judgment is paid to the plaintiff. Under the CGL coverage form, the insurer agrees to pay either type of interest. However, if the insurer offers to pay the applicable limit of insurance to a third-party claimant, the insurer will not pay any prejudgment interest for the period of time after the offer is made.

The supplementary payments of the 1996 edition of the CGL coverage form contain an additional provision, relating to the costs of defending a party (called an "indemnitee") that the insured has agreed to hold harmless or indemnify under an "insured contract."

As discussed earlier in this chapter, the contractual liability exclusion states that any defense costs paid to an indemnitee under an insured contract are payable *within policy limits*. In contrast, the supplementary payments provision states that the insurer will pay an indemnitee's defense costs *in addition to policy limits* if an indemnitee and an insured are both named as parties in the same suit.

This supplementary payment applies only if the insured has assumed the obligation to defend the indemnitee under an insured contract and no conflict appears to exist between the interests of the insured and the interests of the indemnitee. Moreover, the indemnitee must cooperate with the insurer in the defense and perform essentially the same duties as any other insured would have to perform. The insurer's duty to defend ends when the insurer has paid the applicable limit of insurance.

Coverage C: Medical Payments

Medical payments coverage is not liability insurance, because it pays regardless of whether the insured is legally liable. However, the coverage provides a modest amount of insurance for settling minor injury cases without having to make a determination of liability. In that sense, the coverage provides a means of making prompt settlements, satisfying potential liability claimants, and avoiding possibly larger liability claims.

Coverage C Insuring Agreement

The insurer agrees to pay medical expenses (including funeral expenses) for bodily injury caused by an accident occurring on or next to premises that the insured owns or rents. Bodily injury caused by an accident that occurs away from the insured's premises or next to them is covered if the accident results from the named insured's operations.

The accident must occur in the CGL coverage territory and during the policy period. The medical expenses must be incurred and reported to the insurer within one year after the date of the accident. An injured person who wishes to receive medical payments coverage must agree to be examined by a physician designated by the insurance company.

Coverage C Exclusions

CGL medical payments coverage does not apply to bodily injury to the following persons:

1. Any insured
2. Anyone hired to do work for an insured or for a tenant of an insured
3. A person injured on that part of the named insured's premises which the person normally occupies
4. A person entitled to workers compensation benefits for the injury
5. A person injured while taking part in athletics

Medical payments coverage also does not apply to the following:

1. Bodily injury included within the products-completed operations hazard
2. Bodily injury excluded under Coverage A
3. Bodily injury caused by war

Summary

A liability loss exposure is the possibility of experiencing a liability loss. A liability loss includes all costs to an organization as the result of a specific legal claim or suit against that organization.

The person making claim or suit against the organization (the claimant) ordinarily attempts to prove that the organization is legally liable to pay damages. Anyone who wishes to evaluate an organization's liability loss exposures must understand the various ways in which the organization could become legally liable. Broadly speaking, civil liability (in contrast with criminal liability) can be based on torts, contracts, or statutes.

- Torts, which are civil wrongs, consist of negligence and various intentional torts.
- A contract is a legally enforceable agreement between two or more parties. Legal liability can result from breach of contract or from a "hold harmless" agreement.
- A statute is a written law. Statutes can either modify the duties that persons owe to others, or, as in the case of workers compensation statutes, they can create obligations to pay benefits to other persons regardless of fault.

Liability exposures covered under commercial general liability (CGL) insurance are commonly categorized as premises, operations, products, and completed operations. Other liability exposures covered by CGL insurance include liability assumed under contract and liability for some torts such as libel and slander.

The CGL coverage form provides three basic coverages:

1. Coverage A—bodily injury and property damage liability
2. Coverage B—personal and advertising injury liability
3. Coverage C—medical payments

The Coverage A insuring agreement expresses the insurer's promise to (1) pay damages for which the insured is legally liable and (2) defend the insured against claims or suits alleging bodily injury or property damage covered under the policy. The bodily injury or property damage must be caused by an occurrence, and the occurrence must take place in the coverage territory. Moreover, under the occurrence version of the CGL form, the bodily injury or property damage must occur during the policy period.

Coverage A is subject to several exclusions that further define the coverage. Subject to some exceptions, the exclusions eliminate coverage for the following:

- Injury or damage expected or intended by the insured
- Liability assumed under contract (other than an "insured contract")
- Liquor liability if the insured is in the business of selling or serving alcoholic beverages
- Injury to employees of the insured
- Liability arising from the release of pollutants
- Liability for aircraft, autos, and watercraft
- Mobile equipment while being transported by an auto or used in racing

- Damage to property owned, rented, or borrowed by the insured or to personal property in the insured's care, custody, or control
- Damage to that particular part of real property on which the insured is working
- Damage to the named insured's products or work
- Damage to "impaired property" or property not physically injured
- The cost of recalling the named insured's products or work

Coverage B of the CGL form covers claims for "personal injury" or "advertising injury" as defined in the form. This coverage insures against liability for various torts, such as libel, slander, and wrongful eviction.

Coverage C of the CGL form pays for medical expenses of persons injured on the insured's premises or as a result of the insured's operations. Coverage does not apply to bodily injury to any insured, to anyone who is entitled to workers compensation benefits for the same injury, or to bodily injury excluded under Coverage A.

Chapter Note

1. Brian O'Reilly, "J & J is on a Roll," *Fortune Magazine*, December 26, 1994, p. 192.

Chapter 9

Commercial General Liability Insurance, Continued

The preceding chapter described Coverage A (bodily injury and property damage liability), Coverage B (personal and advertising injury liability), and Coverage C (medical payments) of the commercial general liability (CGL) coverage form. This chapter continues the discussion of the CGL coverage form and covers the following topics:

- Who is an insured
- Limits of insurance
- CGL conditions
- Claims-made provisions
- CGL endorsements
- Rating CGL coverage

This chapter also describes several miscellaneous liability coverage forms developed by Insurance Services Office. These forms are used to cover special situations or loss exposures.

Who Is an Insured?

Depending on the circumstances, many different persons or organizations may be insured under the CGL coverage form. These persons and organizations are discussed under the following three categories:

1. Named insured
2. Employees of the named insured
3. Other persons and organizations

Named Insured

The named insured may be an individual, a partnership, a joint venture, a corporation, or a limited liability company.

If the named insured is an individual, both the named insured and his or her spouse are insured. However, coverage applies only to claims arising from the conduct of a business owned solely by the named insured. The named insured and spouse are not covered for their nonbusiness activities.

If the named insured is a partnership or joint venture, the named partnership or joint venture and all partners or members and their spouses also are insured, but only for liability claims arising out of the conduct of the business of the partnership or joint venture.

If the named insured is a limited liability company (an entity that in some ways resembles a partnership and in other ways resembles a corporation), the named company is insured, as are the following:

1. The "members" of the company (the persons who receive the company's income), but only with respect to the conduct of the named insured's business
2. The managers of the company, but only with respect to their duties as managers of the named insured

If the named insured is an organization other than a partnership, joint venture, or limited liability company (for example, a corporation, a school district, a municipality, or an association), then all executive officers, directors, and stockholders are insured, but only with respect to their liability as officers, directors, or stockholders.

Employees of the Named Insured

Employees of the named insured are covered for liability claims arising from their duties as employees. However, an employee is not an insured for the following:

- Bodily injury or personal injury to the named insured, to the named insured's partners or members (if the named insured is a partnership or joint venture), or to a co-employee while in the course of his or her duties as such

- Bodily injury or personal injury arising out of the employee's providing or failing to provide professional health-care services (for example, a doctor employed by the named insured who provides improper medical treatment to a co-employee or a guest visiting the named insured's place of business)

- Property damage to property owned, occupied, or used by any of the following: the named insured, the named insured's employees, or the named insured's partners or members

Other Persons and Organizations

In addition to the named insured and the named insured's employees, several other persons and organizations are insured under certain circumstances. These other persons and organizations include the following:

1. Real estate managers
2. Legal representatives
3. Mobile equipment operators
4. Newly acquired organizations

Real Estate Managers

Any person (other than an employee) or organization acting as real estate manager for the named insured is an insured. Coverage applies only while the person or organization is serving as real estate manager for the named insured.

Legal Representatives

If the named insured dies, any person or organization having proper temporary custody of the named insured's property is insured under the CGL until a legal representative is appointed. The coverage for a temporary custodian applies only to liability arising out of the maintenance or use of the property. The appointed legal representative is also an insured, but only with respect to his or her duties as legal representative.

Mobile Equipment Operators

The insureds described above would be covered while operating mobile equipment in most circumstances. In addition, the CGL coverage form insures certain additional persons or organizations for liability claims arising from operating mobile equipment registered in the name of the named insured under any motor vehicle registration law. Those additional insureds are the following:

1. Any person while driving the named insured's mobile equipment along a public highway with the permission of the named insured
2. Any other person or organization responsible for the conduct of the driver

However, coverage applies only if liability arises from operating the equipment and only if no other insurance is available to the person or organization. Coverage does not apply to bodily injury to a co-employee of the driver. It also does not apply to damage to property owned by, rented to, in the charge of, or occupied by the named insured or the employer of the driver.

Newly Acquired Organizations

Any subsidiary or affiliated organization of the named insured that is in existence at or before the inception of the CGL policy must be shown in the declarations as a named insured in order to be covered. If the named insured acquires or forms a new organization during the policy period, the new organization qualifies as a named insured and is covered for ninety days or to the end of the policy period, whichever comes first. This provision does not extend to partnerships, joint ventures, or limited liability companies that are not named in the policy.

Moreover, Coverage A does not apply to bodily injury or property damage occurring before the organization was acquired or formed, and Coverage B does not apply to personal injury or advertising injury arising out of any offense committed before the organization was acquired or formed.

Limits of Insurance

CGL coverage is subject to the following limits of insurance:

1. General aggregate limit
2. Products-completed operations aggregate limit
3. Personal and advertising injury limit
4. Each occurrence limit
5. Fire damage limit
6. Medical expense limit

The dollar amount of each limit is shown on the CGL declarations page. How these limits apply is explained below and illustrated in Exhibit 9-1.

Exhibit 9-1
Illustration of the CGL Limits of Insurance

Adapted with permission from International Risk Management Institute, Inc.,
Commercial Liability Insurance, vol. 1, p. IV.E.18. Copyright © 1994.

Aggregate Limits

An **aggregate limit** is the most the insurer will pay under a policy for the sum of covered claims during the policy period (usually one year beginning on the effective date of the coverage part or an anniversary of the effective date). When an aggregate limit is exhausted by payment of applicable claims, the insurer is no longer obligated to pay damages or defend claims subject to that aggregate limit. Aggregate limits are restored (for purposes of future occurrences only) when the policy is renewed for a new policy period.

The CGL coverage form contains two aggregate limits:

1. The **general aggregate limit** is the most the insurer will pay for the sum of the following:

    *   Damages under Coverage A except for damages included in the "products-completed operations hazard"
    *   Damages under Coverage B
    *   Medical expenses under Coverage C

2. The **products-completed operations aggregate limit** is the most the insurer will pay under Coverage A for damages included in the "products-completed operations hazard."

The **products-completed operations hazard**, as defined in the CGL coverage form, includes all bodily injury and property damage occurring away from premises owned or rented by the named insured and arising out of the named insured's product or work. The term does not include the following:

1. Products that are still in the named insured's physical possession
2. Work that has not been completed or abandoned

Injury or damage resulting from item 1 or 2 above is part of the premises and operations liability exposure and would be subject to the general aggregate limit. To illustrate, suppose that a customer is shopping inside the insured's store. If the customer is injured by a defective product held for sale by the insured, the customer's claim would be subject to the *general aggregate* limit because the accident occurred on the insured's premises. If the injury had occurred after the customer bought the product and took it away from the insured's premises, the resulting claim would be subject to the products-completed operations aggregate limit.

Personal and Advertising Injury Limit

The **personal and advertising injury limit** is the most the insurer will pay for the sum of all personal injury and advertising injury to one person or organization. All sums paid under this limit reduce the general aggregate limit.

Each Occurrence Limit

The **each occurrence limit** is the most the insurer will pay for the sum of the following arising out of a single occurrence:

1. Damages for bodily injury and property damage under Coverage A
2. Medical expenses under Coverage C

The each occurrence limit is the most the insurer will pay for a single occurrence, regardless of the number of persons insured, the number of claims or suits brought, or the number of persons or organizations making claim. All sums paid under this limit reduce the general aggregate limit or the products completed operations limit, depending on the nature of the claim.

Fire Damage Limit and Medical Expense Limit

The **fire damage limit** is the most the insurer will pay under Coverage A for the named insured's liability for fire damage to premises rented to or temporarily occupied by the named insured.

The **medical expense limit** is the most the insurer will pay for Coverage C medical expenses resulting from bodily injury to one person. No other limit applies to medical payments coverage other than the each occurrence limit.

All sums paid under either the fire damage limit or the medical expense limit are subject to the each occurrence limit and also reduce the general aggregate limit.

Application of CGL Limits

An example will clarify the application of the CGL limits. Assume that beginning January 1, the Always Best Corporation (ABC) was insured for a one-year period under an occurrence CGL coverage form with the following limits:

General aggregate	$2,000,000
Products-completed operations aggregate	2,000,000
Personal and advertising injury	1,000,000
Each occurrence	1,000,000
Fire damage	50,000
Medical expense	5,000

Occurrence 1: On February 1, a fire in a building rented to ABC caused the following losses for which ABC was held liable (except for the medical payments, which were paid without regard to liability):

Fire damage to the rented building	$150,000
Medical payments to ten injured customers ($1,000 each)	10,000
Bodily injury to others	300,000

The medical payments claims and bodily injury claims would be paid in full, for $310,000. Only $50,000 of the fire legal liability claim would be payable because of the fire damage limit. The total of $360,000 is within the each occurrence limit. The remaining general aggregate limit is $1,640,000 ($2,000,000 – $360,0000).

Occurrence 2: On July 10, an elevator fell in the building rented to ABC, injuring fifteen customers. ABC was held liable for $1,500,000 in damages for the customers' injuries.

The $1,500,000 in damages resulting from the elevator collapse exceeds the each occurrence limit of $1,000,000. Thus, the insurer will pay only $1,000,000 for that occurrence. The general aggregate limit is now reduced to $640,000 ($1,640,000 – $1,000,000).

Occurrence 3: On November 27, ABC committed an advertising injury offense when it improperly used a picture of an actor in its advertising material. The damages awarded to the actor were $800,000.

The $800,000 damages for the advertising injury offense are within the personal and advertising injury limit. However, the general aggregate has been reduced to $640,000. Consequently, the insurer is only liable for $640,000. ABC would bear the balance of the loss itself.

Occurrence 4: On December 8, one of ABC's customers was injured by a defective product sold by ABC. The customer won a judgment of $900,000 in damages against ABC.

The insurer would pay $900,000. The bodily injury was within the products-completed operations hazard and thus subject to the products-completed operations aggregate limit. The products-completed operations aggregate limit was not reduced by prior claims during the policy period, and the $900,000 damages were less than the $1,000,000 each occurrence limit.

If this claim had been one that was subject to the general aggregate limit (for example, a claim by a customer who tripped and fell on a slippery floor), the insurer would have had no duty to defend the insured or pay damages. The general aggregate limit was used up by occurrence 3, above.

CGL Conditions

The CGL coverage form contains several conditions that supplement the common conditions discussed in Chapter 2. The CGL conditions, listed below, are described in the corresponding sections that follow:

1. Bankruptcy
2. Duties in the event of occurrence, offense, claim, or suit
3. Legal action against us
4. Other insurance
5. Premium audit
6. Representations
7. Separation of insureds
8. Transfer of right of recovery against others to us
9. When we do not renew

Bankruptcy

Bankruptcy or insolvency of the insured does not relieve the insurer of any of its policy obligations. The insurer remains obligated to defend the insured and pay judgments or settlements as though the insured had remained solvent.

Duties in the Event of Occurrence, Offense, Claim, or Suit

If the insured does not perform the duties required by this condition, the insurance company may be relieved of its duty to defend and pay claims. Thus, it is crucial that the insured understand these duties and fulfill them.

Whenever the insured becomes aware of an occurrence or an offense that may result in a claim, notice must be given to the insurer as soon as practicable. The notice may be either oral or written, and it should state the following:

1. How, when, and where the occurrence happened
2. The names and addresses of any injured persons and any witnesses
3. The nature and location of any damage or injury resulting from the occurrence or offense

When a claim or suit is actually brought against any insured, the named insured must do the following:

1. Immediately record the details of the claim or suit and the date received
2. Notify the insurer in writing as soon as practicable

The named insured (or any other insured involved in a claim or suit) is required to do the following:

1. Immediately forward to the insurer copies of any legal papers received in connection with the suit
2. Authorize the insurer to obtain any legal records or other documents
3. Cooperate with the insurer in the investigation or settlement of the claim or in the insurer's defense against the suit
4. Assist the insurer in any action against any third party that may be liable to the insured because of the injuries or damage for which claim is made

Finally, the condition states that no insured may make voluntary payment, assume any obligation, or incur any expense without the insurer's consent. Any voluntary payments made by an insured or expenses incurred by an insured without the insurer's consent must be paid by the insured. The only exception is that the insured may incur expenses for first aid at the time of the occurrence.

Legal Action Against Us

The legal action condition provides that no person or organization can bring the insurer into any suit seeking damages from an insured. Insurers feel that a suit that includes an insurance company as a defendant may encourage a jury to award higher damages or to award damages in cases where damages would not be awarded otherwise. (Some states permit third-party claimants to sue insurers directly, regardless of this provision.)

The condition also states that no person or organization can bring suit to enforce the CGL coverage part unless that party has fully complied with all policy conditions. For example, the insured could not sue the insurer (to get the insurer to pay a third-party claim) unless the insured had first forwarded all legal papers to the insurer, cooperated in the defense, and so on.

Other Insurance

The other insurance condition explains how the amount the insurer is obligated to pay on a claim is determined if the insured has other insurance that also covers the claim. For the purposes of the other insurance condition, all applicable coverages are classified as either excess insurance or primary insurance.

When CGL Is Excess

CGL coverage is excess insurance if the other insurance is any of the following:

1. Fire, extended coverage, builders risk, installation risk, or similar coverage on the named insured's work

2. Fire insurance on premises rented to the named insured or that the named insured temporarily occupies with the owner's permission

3. Aircraft, auto, or watercraft coverage

If CGL coverage is excess, the insurer has no obligation to provide defense for any claim or suit that another insurer has a duty to defend against. However, if no other insurer provides defense, the excess (CGL) insurer will do so. In such a case, the excess insurer takes over the insured's right to recover defense costs from the other insurer.

If a claim is covered by two or more excess insurers, they share the amount of loss in excess of all primary insurance. The procedure is discussed under "Methods of Sharing" below.

When CGL Is Primary

All applicable insurance not defined as excess is considered primary and begins to pay at the first dollar of loss or when the deductible or self-insured amount, if any, is exceeded. Primary insurers are obligated to provide defense for covered claims until their limits of insurance have been exhausted by the payment of settlements or judgments. If two or more primary insurers cover the claim, they share the loss up to their combined limits of insurance.

Methods of Sharing

If two or more policies apply at the same level, either primary or excess, the policy provides for two methods of sharing: (1) contribution by equal shares and (2) contribution by limits. If all applicable policies permit contribution by equal shares, that method is used. Otherwise, contribution by limits is used.

Contribution by Equal Shares

Under **contribution by equal shares**, each insurer contributes an equal amount to the payment of the claim until the claim is fully paid or until each insurer exhausts its limit of insurance, whichever occurs first. Assume, for example, that Luckless Manufacturing Company (LMC) has two liability claims arising from separate occurrences and that these claims are covered under two of LMC's primary liability policies. The applicable each occurrence limits of insurance for the two policies are as follows:

Insurer	Limit
A	$500,000
B	$1,000,000

For a claim of $300,000, each insurer would contribute $150,000. That amount would cover the claim in full and is within the limits of both policies.

A claim of $1,200,000 would be distributed in two stages. First, each insurer would contribute $500,000, equal to A's limit. Since Insurer B has not exhausted its limit, it would contribute an additional $200,000 to cover the rest of the claim.

Contribution by Limits

Under **contribution by limits**, each insurer pays that proportion of the claim that its limit bears to the total of all applicable insurance. However, no insurer will pay more than its applicable limit of insurance.

Using the policies of LMC as described above, Insurer A's limit ($500,000) is one-third of the total applicable limits ($1,500,000) of both policies. Consequently, Insurer A would pay one-third of each claim, but not more than its limit of $500,000. Insurer B's limit ($1,000,000) is two-thirds of the total applicable limits. Thus, Insurer B would pay two-thirds of any claim, but not more than its limit. Using contribution by limits, the two claims against LMC would be distributed as follows:

Insurer	$300,000 Claim	$1,200,000 Claim
A	$100,000	$400,000
B	$200,000	$800,000

Notice that Insurer A paid less when the claims were shared using contribution by limits. As a general rule, contribution by equal shares is more advantageous to the insurer with the higher limits, and contribution by limits is more advantageous to the insurer with the lower limits.

Premium Audit

CGL policies are often issued with estimated premiums. The final premium is determined after the policy has expired, based on the insured's payroll, sales, attendance, or some other rating base that could not be determined precisely at the policy inception. The **premium audit** condition requires the named insured to keep adequate records to permit correct calculation of the premium and to make such records available to the insurer on request. The named insured must promptly pay for any additional premiums resulting from the audit. If the audit shows the earned premium to be less than the original estimate, the insurer is obligated to return the excess to the named insured, subject to any policy minimum premium.

Representations

The representations condition states that the named insured, by accepting the policy, agrees to the following:

1. The statements in the declarations are accurate and complete.
2. The statements in the declarations are based on representations made by the named insured to the insurer.
3. The insurer has issued the policy in reliance on the named insured's representations.

This condition places a heavy burden on the named insured to read the policy declarations and to be sure that the representations made in the negotiation of the policy are accurate.

Separation of Insureds

The separation condition states that the insurance provided by the policy applies separately to each person insured. This condition can benefit an insured under certain circumstances. For example, one insured might intentionally injure a third party. The policy should not provide any coverage for the insured who caused the injury (unless inflicted with reasonable force to protect a person or property from harm). However, because of the separation condition, the policy would still provide coverage for any other insured (such as an employer or partner) who might be liable for the injury. Also, if one insured sues another insured, coverage is still provided for the insured who has been sued, subject to the other conditions and exclusions of the policy.

The condition is subject to two restrictions. First, the limits of insurance apply to all persons insured and are not increased because two or more persons are insured. Second, any rights or duties specifically assigned to the first named insured are not applicable to any other insured.

Transfer of Right of Recovery Against Others to Us

If the insured has any right to recover from any third party all or any part of a claim paid by the insurer, that right must be transferred to the insurer. In legal terminology, the insurer is subrogated to the rights of the insured to recover the amount paid. The insured must do nothing after a loss to impair this right and, upon the insurer's request, must assist the insurer in any reasonable manner to enforce the right of recovery. This policy condition was known as the *subrogation* provision in earlier policies. The insurer's right to subrogate arises because the insurer defends and pays damages on behalf of the insured.

When We Do Not Renew

If the insurer opts not to renew the policy, it must give written notice of nonrenewal to the first named insured at least thirty days before the expiration date of the policy. If the notice is mailed, proof of mailing is adequate proof of notice.

Many states have adopted specific regulations that supersede this policy provision. In such cases, a mandatory endorsement is attached to the policy detailing the required provisions. Even if the endorsement is not attached to the policy, the regulations would supersede the policy renewal provision.

Liability Insurance for Farms and Ranches

Although the CGL coverage form is used to insure most organizations, farms and ranches are usually insured under specially designed property-liability package policies. Under the ISO farm program, the farm liability coverage form is comparable to the CGL coverage form, with some differences to make the form more suitable for insuring a farm family's business and personal loss exposures.

The farm liability form limits coverage of business pursuits to farming and ranching, including the operation of roadside stands for selling the insured's produce. Products liability is covered but is subject to the same aggregate limit as all other claims.

The farm liability form excludes farming operations that the insured performs for others for a fee if the named insured's receipts from such activities exceed a stipulated amount during the twelve months immediately before the date of the occurrence for which coverage is sought. Full coverage for such operations (known as "custom farming") can be added by endorsement.

The farm liability form contains the broad pollution exclusion found in the CGL coverage form. By endorsement, this exclusion can be modified to allow limited coverage for discharge of smoke or farm chemicals, liquids, or gases used in normal farming operations. Crop-dusting operations, however, are not covered.

Employers liability coverage can be added to the farm liability form by endorsement. In many states, farm workers are not covered by workers compensation statutes and can therefore sue their employers for job-related injury or illness due to negligence on the part of the employer. Employers liability insurance pays (1) the cost of defending against such suits and (2) damages that the insured farmer becomes legally obligated to pay.

Farm liability coverage also provides the equivalent of homeowners liability coverage to cover the personal liability exposures of an insured farm family.

Claims-Made CGL Coverage Form

The occurrence version of the CGL coverage form has been the basis for discussion in this chapter and in Chapter 8. However, insurers prefer to insure some organizations on the claims-made version of the CGL coverage form.

The occurrence CGL form covers bodily injury or property damage that occurs during its policy period, *regardless of when claim is made*. A claim made today for injury that occurred twenty years ago could be covered under an occurrence policy that was in effect twenty years ago. If the injury was considered to have been "occurring" during the intervening years as well, coverage might even be triggered under any occurrence-basis policies in effect during those years. In recent years, many such "long-tail" claims have been made for latent injury caused by exposure to asbestos and other substances.

For example, in 1993, two leading insurance companies agreed to pay up to $3 billion for claims on policies they had issued almost forty years earlier for Fibreboard Corporation, a manufacturer of asbestos products. Fibreboard faced claims from over 145,000 people who maintained they were injured by its products as far back as 1950.

A problem posed for insurers by these long-tail claims is that their ultimate cost cannot be accurately predicted when the insurer develops the premium for the policy. The insurer may not realize that the insured's product can cause latent injury, and the unanticipated claims, made many years in the future, may be subject to liberalized law or inflated monetary values. As a result, the policy premiums charged by the insurer may be inadequate to pay covered claims. This poses significant challenges to insurance capacity and even insurer solvency.

The claims-made CGL coverage form was developed to address this problem. The discussion that follows describes the principal features of the claims-made form. These features include the following:

- Claims-made trigger
- Retroactive date
- Extended reporting periods

Claims-Made Trigger

In the claims-made coverage form, Coverage A and Coverage B are both subject to a **claims-made coverage trigger.** The basic requirement of the trigger is that the claim for bodily injury, property damage, personal injury, or advertising injury must be first made against any insured during either the policy period or an extended reporting period provided by the policy. (Extended reporting periods are described in more detail below.)

The claims-made form states that a claim will be deemed to have been made at the earlier of the following times: (1) when notice of the claim is received and recorded by any insured or by the insurer or (2) when the insurer settles the claim. The form also states that notice of an *occurrence* (such as "Today a customer slipped and fell on our floor. . . .") is not notice of a *claim or offense* (such as "Today we received suit papers from a customer who slipped and fell on our floor last month. . . .").

Retroactive Date

An additional requirement of the claims-made form is that the injury or damage for which claim is made must have occurred on or after the policy's retroactive date, if any, but not after the end of the policy period. Similarly for Coverage B claims, the personal or advertising injury offense must have been committed on or after the retroactive date but not after the end of the policy period. Thus, the **retroactive date** is the date on or after which injury or damage must occur in order to be covered.

A claims-made policy may contain no retroactive date, a retroactive date that is the same as the policy inception date, or a retroactive date that is before the policy inception date.

- If it has no retroactive date, the policy will cover claims first made during its policy period, regardless of when the injury occurred.

- If the policy has a retroactive date (shown in the CGL declarations), the policy will not cover claims for injury that occurred before the retroactive date, even if claim is first made during the policy period.

Extended Reporting Periods

Claims-made policies have a feature called an **extended reporting period**, often referred to as a "tail." An extended reporting period is a time period following the termination date of a claims-made policy. The insurer agrees to pay any claim first made during the extended reporting period if the claim is for an injury that occurred after the retroactive date and before the policy expiration date. In other words, an extended reporting period only extends the period within which claim can be made. It does not extend the period within which the injury must have occurred.

The claims-made CGL coverage form automatically includes a basic extended reporting period for no additional premium. The basic tail runs for five years from the policy expiration date. Claims first made within that five-year tail are covered, but only if both of the following conditions are met:

1. The injury occurred (or the offense was committed) on or after the retroactive date, if any, and before the policy expiration date

2. The insured reported the occurrence to the insurer within sixty days after the policy expired

The claims-made CGL form also permits the insured to obtain, for an additional premium, a supplemental extended reporting period. The supplemental tail lasts forever and does not require that the occurrence be reported within sixty days after policy expiration. In addition, the supplemental tail restores the policy's aggregate limits to their original levels.

Illustration of Retroactive Date

LMC purchased a one-year claims-made CGL policy with an inception date of January 1, 1994. The retroactive date was also January 1, 1994. On January 1, 1995, the policy was renewed for an additional year. The retroactive date for the renewal policy remained January 1, 1994. Before January 1, 1994, LMC was covered by occurrence form policies.

On July 1, 1995, claim was first made against LMC for injury B, which occurred on December 1, 1994. Given these facts, as depicted on the time line below, the claim was covered under the 1995 policy, since it was the policy in effect when the claim was made and the injury occurred after the policy's retroactive date.

On November 1, 1995, another person first made claim against LMC for injury A, which occurred on July 1, 1993. This claim would not be covered by the 1995 policy, since the injury occurred before the retroactive date. The claim would be covered under the occurrence policy that was in effect in 1993.

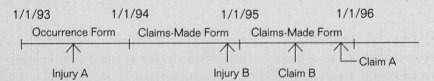

If the retroactive date of the renewal policy had been advanced to January 1, 1995, claim B would not have been covered under the 1995 policy. Even though claim would have been made during the policy period, the injury would have occurred before the retroactive date.

Non-ISO Claims-Made Forms

The ISO claims-made CGL form has not achieved widespread acceptance. Most organizations are still insured under occurrence policies for their general liability exposures. However, claims-made forms are widely used to provide professional liability and other specialty coverages (which will be described in Chapter 13). These forms are independently developed by the insurers that use them, and their claims-made features usually differ from those of the ISO form. For example, independent forms seldom include an automatic extended reporting period. Any extended reporting period must be purchased separately and is usually limited to one to three years rather than the unlimited reporting period offered by the ISO supplemental tail.

CGL Endorsements

A wide variety of endorsements are available for modifying the CGL coverage form to meet particular needs. These endorsements can be categorized as follows:

1. State endorsements
2. Exclusion endorsements
3. Classification endorsements
4. Miscellaneous endorsements

State Endorsements

Some states have laws or regulations requiring special policy provisions. They may, for example, require earlier notice of cancellation or nonrenewal than that provided by the standard policy. Other states restrict the insurer's right to cancel coverage midterm or require the insurer to state the reason for cancellation. State endorsements are usually mandatory and must be attached to all policies providing coverage in the states to which they apply.

Exclusion Endorsements

ISO provides many exclusion endorsements, all of which restrict coverage in some way. Examples of such endorsements are listed below:

1. The *advertising injury exclusion endorsement* modifies Coverage B of the CGL form by eliminating coverage for claims arising from advertising by the insured.
2. The *employment-related practices exclusion endorsement* eliminates coverage for bodily injury arising from employment practices of the insured, such as refusal to employ, termination of employment, coercion, demotion, harassment, discrimination, and similar practices.
3. The *total pollution exclusion endorsement* eliminates coverage for any injury, damage, or cleanup costs resulting from the actual, alleged, or threatened discharge of pollutants.
4. The *designated product exclusion endorsement* excludes liability arising out of specified products of the insured.

Some of the classification endorsements discussed below also fit the category of exclusion endorsements.

Classification Endorsements

Many endorsements are available for adapting the CGL policy to the needs of certain classes of business organizations. These endorsements may either restrict or expand coverage under the form. Two examples of endorsements that restrict coverage are as follows:

- The *exclusion—germination failure (seed producers or distributors) endorsement* is attached to policies issued to seed producers or distributors to exclude liability for failure of seeds to germinate.

- The *exclusion—professional services (blood banks) endorsement* excludes professional liability claims against blood banks.

In contrast, the *optical and hearing aid establishment endorsement* extends the policy to cover the professional liability exposure of such businesses. The *druggists* endorsement does the same for pharmacies.

Miscellaneous Endorsements

Some of the miscellaneous endorsements that can be used to add coverages, deductibles, or insureds to a CGL policy are briefly discussed below. Other miscellaneous endorsements amend certain coverages or the limits of insurance, and others modify the claims-made CGL form to provide supplemental extended reporting periods or to exclude specified locations, products, or work.

The *liquor liability exclusion—exception for scheduled activities endorsement* can be used to cover bodily injury or property damage arising out of the selling, serving, or furnishing of alcoholic beverages at activities specified in the endorsement.

The *deductible liability insurance endorsement* enables the insured to apply deductibles to the bodily injury and property damage liability coverages, either separately or combined. The deductibles may be on either a per-claim or a per-occurrence basis.

Over twenty endorsements are available to include specific types of persons or organizations as insureds under a CGL policy. For example, the *additional insured—vendors endorsement* includes as an insured any person or organization (the vendor) specified in the endorsement. The vendor is covered for bodily injury or property damage liability arising from distributing or selling any of the named insured's products listed in the endorsement.

Other endorsements can be used to include such additional insureds as club members, condominium unit owners, townhouse associations, volunteers, lessors of leased equipment, state or political subdivisions, users of golf carts, charitable institutions, and elected or appointed executive officers of public or municipal corporations.

Certificates of Insurance

Many organizations demand that firms doing business with them provide evidence of insurance. Furthermore, rating rules for both workers compensation and general liability insurance require that the insured either obtain proof of insurance from contractors or subcontractors employed by the insured or pay a higher premium. The customary method of providing such evidence is a **certificate of insurance.** A certificate of insurance is a brief outline of the coverage in force when the certificate is issued. An example of a certificate is shown in Exhibit 9-2.

Two problems arising from certificates of insurance for general liability insurance are (1) the requirements for notice of cancellation and (2) the inclusion of additional insureds.

Most certificate holders want to receive written notice of cancellation from the insurer if the insurer cancels the insurance described in the certificate. The cancellation provision included in the certificate states that the insurer will attempt to mail written notice but that failure to mail such notice will not impose any liability on the insurer. Only an endorsement to the policy can obligate the insurer to give notice.

In addition to requiring certificates of insurance, some organizations want to be added as additional insureds to the policies covering the firms with whom they do business. Merely adding wording to that effect to the certificate without endorsing the policy has been held to be ineffective. Again, an endorsement to the policy is required.

Certificates are frequently prepared by insurance producers. Extreme care is necessary when preparing a certificate to be sure that the coverage described in the certificate accurately reflects the policy coverage. Furthermore, certificates should only be prepared by producers who have been authorized to do so by the insurer. Making an error or exceeding authority when preparing a certificate can expose the producer to professional liability.

Rating CGL Coverage

The formula used to determine the premium for a CGL policy is as follows:

$$\text{Rate} \times \text{Rate exposure} = \text{Premium}$$

The rate depends on the nature of the insured organization and its susceptibility to liability losses. The rate exposure reflects the size of the business operations

Exhibit 9-2

Certificate of Liability Insurance

ACORD™ **CERTIFICATE OF LIABILITY INSURANCE**	10/1/96

PRODUCER	THIS CERTIFICATE IS ISSUED AS A MATTER OF INFORMATION ONLY AND CONFERS NO RIGHTS UPON THE CERTIFICATE HOLDER. THIS CERTIFICATE DOES NOT AMEND, EXTEND OR ALTER THE COVERAGE AFFORDED BY THE POLICIES BELOW.
A.M. Able Agency 250 Main St. Workingtown, PA 19000 (215) 697-0000	**COMPANIES AFFORDING COVERAGE**
	COMPANY A — Insurance Company A
INSURED	COMPANY B — Insurance Company B
BLS Construction 3000 Industrial Highway Workingtown, PA 19000	COMPANY C — Insurance Company C
	COMPANY D

COVERAGES

THIS IS TO CERTIFY THAT THE POLICIES OF INSURANCE LISTED BELOW HAVE BEEN ISSUED TO THE INSURED NAMED ABOVE FOR THE POLICY PERIOD INDICATED, NOTWITHSTANDING ANY REQUIREMENT, TERM OR CONDITION OF ANY CONTRACT OR OTHER DOCUMENT WITH RESPECT TO WHICH THIS CERTIFICATE MAY BE ISSUED OR MAY PERTAIN. THE INSURANCE AFFORDED BY THE POLICIES DESCRIBED HEREIN IS SUBJECT TO ALL THE TERMS, EXCLUSIONS AND CONDITIONS OF SUCH POLICIES. LIMITS SHOWN MAY HAVE BEEN REDUCED BY PAID CLAIMS.

CO LTR	TYPE OF INSURANCE	POLICY NUMBER	POLICY EFFECTIVE DATE (MM/DD/YY)	POLICY EXPIRATION DATE (MM/DD/YY)	LIMITS	
A	**GENERAL LIABILITY** [X] COMMERCIAL GENERAL LIABILITY [ ] CLAIMS MADE [X] OCCUR [ ] OWNER'S & CONTRACTOR'S PROT	SP 0002	7/1/96	7/1/97	GENERAL AGGREGATE	$2,000,000
					PRODUCTS - COMP/OP AGG	$2,000,000
					PERSONAL & ADV INJURY	$1,000,000
					EACH OCCURRENCE	$1,000,000
					FIRE DAMAGE (Any one fire)	$50,000
					MED EXP (Any one person)	$5,000
A	**AUTOMOBILE LIABILITY** [X] ANY AUTO [ ] ALL OWNED AUTOS [ ] SCHEDULED AUTOS [ ] HIRED AUTOS [ ] NON-OWNED AUTOS	SP 0002	7/1/96	7/1/97	COMBINED SINGLE LIMIT	$1,000,000
					BODILY INJURY (Per person)	$ -NA-
					BODILY INJURY (Per accident)	$ -NA-
					PROPERTY DAMAGE	$ -NA-
	GARAGE LIABILITY [ ] ANY AUTO				AUTO ONLY - EA ACCIDENT	$
					OTHER THAN AUTO ONLY:	
					EACH ACCIDENT	$
					AGGREGATE	$
B	**EXCESS LIABILITY** [X] UMBRELLA FORM [ ] OTHER THAN UMBRELLA FORM	3XS-1522-25	7/1/96	7/1/97	EACH OCCURRENCE	$5,000,000
					AGGREGATE	$10,000,000
						$
C	**WORKERS COMPENSATION AND EMPLOYERS' LIABILITY** THE PROPRIETOR/ PARTNERS/EXECUTIVE OFFICERS ARE: [X] INCL [ ] EXCL	29984-31	7/1/96	7/1/97	[X] WC STATUTORY LIMITS [ ] OTHER	
					EL EACH ACCIDENT	$100,000
					EL DISEASE - POLICY LIMIT	$500,000
					EL DISEASE - EA EMPLOYEE	$100,000
	OTHER					

DESCRIPTION OF OPERATIONS/LOCATIONS/VEHICLES/ SPECIAL ITEMS
Building Contractor / Work site at Certificateholder's Premises

CERTIFICATE HOLDER	CANCELLATION
CCC Real Estate 25 2nd St. Workingtown, PA 19000	SHOULD ANY OF THE ABOVE DESCRIBED POLICIES BE CANCELLED BEFORE THE EXPIRATION DATE THEREOF, THE ISSUING COMPANY WILL ENDEAVOR TO MAIL 10 DAYS WRITTEN NOTICE TO THE CERTIFICATE HOLDER NAMED TO THE LEFT, BUT FAILURE TO MAIL SUCH NOTICE SHALL IMPOSE NO OBLIGATION OR LIABILITY OF ANY KIND UPON THE COMPANY, ITS AGENTS OR REPRESENTATIVES.
	AUTHORIZED REPRESENTATIVE A. M. Able

ACORD 25-S (1/95)   © ACORD CORPORATION 1988 to be insured, not the type of losses to which the business is susceptible. For example, because of its production volume, the manufacturer of 1,000,000 toys a year is more likely to be sued for products liability than a manufacturer that produces 50,000 similar toys a year. Such differences are reflected in the rate exposure. The unit in which the rate exposure is measured is called the **premium base**.

An insurer that writes CGL insurance develops a rate for each business classification that it is willing to insure. The classifications used to reference these rates are listed in the classification table of the ISO *Commercial Lines Manual*. The classification table lists more than 1,000 types of operations, each assigned an identification number called the **class code**. The class code used for a particular organization represents the description in the classification table that best fits the operations of the organization. For some businesses, more than one class code applies because the business operations involve two or more separately described classifications.

Two CGL rates apply for most classifications:

1.   A premises-operations rate

2.   A products-completed operations rate

For organizations having little or no risk of incurring products-completed operations liability losses (such as photo finishing labs or florists), only a premises-operations rate is used. The small cost of providing products liability coverage for such insureds is included in their premises-operations rate.

Premium Base

The premium base used in rating CGL coverage for any given business is also indicated in the classification table. In general, organizations of the same kind have the same premium bases:

- Mercantile businesses (retail stores, for example) are rated using a premium base of gross sales.

- Contracting businesses are rated on the basis of payroll.

- Building and premises risks (apartments and hotels) may be rated on the basis of area, gross sales, or the number of units in the building.

- Special events (concerts, sporting events, exhibitions, and so on) might be rated on the number of admissions to the event.

Once the premium base to be used in the rating of a particular policy is known, information about the organization must be gathered carefully and completely in order to measure rate exposure accurately. Specific rules govern what is and is not to be included in any of the rate exposures used to rate CGL insurance.

As explained earlier in connection with the premium audit condition, the actual premium for a CGL policy is often calculated at the end of the policy period after the rate exposure can be determined accurately. That premium is then reconciled with the estimated premium the insured paid at the beginning of the policy period.

Other Rating Considerations

Depending on the coverage choices that an insured has made, other factors are considered in determining a CGL premium. Increased limits factors are used to generate higher premiums for policies written with coverage amounts higher than the basic limits. If the insured has chosen not to buy certain coverages included automatically in the CGL form—personal and advertising injury, medical payments, or fire damage liability, for instance—premium credits are given for such reductions in coverage. Coverage can be written subject to a deductible, which reduces the premium.

When coverage is written on a claims-made basis, the usual rates are modified by claims-made factors. These factors reduce the usual rates slightly to account for the fact that claims-made policies do not (unless an additional premium is paid) cover some accidents that occur during the policy period but result in claims made after the policy has expired. An occurrence policy covers such accidents regardless of when claim is made.

Miscellaneous Liability Coverage Forms

In addition to the CGL coverage form, several miscellaneous liability coverage forms are filed by ISO. Some of these forms cover significant exposures (liquor liability and pollution liability) that are excluded under the CGL form. Another form is specially designed to allow a contractor to purchase general liability insurance in the name of a project owner.

Liquor Liability Coverage Form

Bars, restaurants, liquor stores, and other businesses that serve or sell alcoholic beverages are exposed to what is commonly called "liquor liability." Liquor liability may be established through principles of common law or imposed by state statutes known as dram shop acts. ("Dram shop" is the archaic term for a bar or tavern.) A dram shop act gives persons a right of action against the provider of alcoholic beverages when they are injured or their property is damaged by the actions of an intoxicated person.

Dram shop laws ordinarily do not allow the intoxicated person to recover damages—only those who have been injured by the intoxicated person. However, under common law in some jurisdictions, even an injured intoxicated person can recover damages from a provider who continued to serve the person after he or she became intoxicated.

The CGL coverage form excludes liquor liability if the insured is "in the business of manufacturing, distributing, selling, serving or furnishing alcoholic beverages." To cover their liquor liability exposures, such businesses can purchase liquor liability insurance under a separate ISO coverage form that is issued in a monoline policy or as part of a commercial package policy. (Liquor liability insurance is also written by insurers who use independently developed forms.)

ISO maintains two versions of the **liquor liability coverage form**—one with an occurrence trigger, the other with a claims-made trigger. Both coverage forms agree to pay those sums that the insured becomes legally obligated to pay as damages because of bodily injury or property damage resulting from the selling, serving, or furnishing of any alcoholic beverage.

Exclusions

The liquor liability coverage form contains only three of the exclusions that appear in the CGL coverage form. These exclusions apply to expected or intended injury, obligations under workers compensation and similar laws, and bodily injury to employees of the insured.

In addition, the liquor liability form excludes injury resulting from the consumption of any alcoholic beverage sold, served, or furnished while any required license is suspended or after the license has expired or been revoked.

The liquor liability form also excludes injury arising out of the insured's products. The purpose of this exclusion is to eliminate coverage for products liability claims that would be covered under a regular CGL policy. Examples of incidents that would be excluded by this exclusion are as follows:

- A customer drank a glass of contaminated wine served by the insured and became ill.

- A customer was cut by a defective "pop top" on a can of beer sold by the insured.

- A customer swallowed broken glass that was in a bottle of beer served by the insured.

This exclusion contains exceptions which make it clear that the exclusion does not eliminate coverage for liability resulting from the following:

- Causing or contributing to the intoxication of any person
- Furnishing alcoholic beverages to a person under the legal drinking age or under the influence of alcohol
- Any statute, ordinance, or regulation relating to the sale or distribution of alcoholic beverages

The liquor liability form does not exclude liability arising out of the use of an auto, aircraft, watercraft, or mobile equipment. Consequently, the insurance covers liquor liability of the insured even if the intoxicated person was operating an auto, an aircraft, a watercraft, or a piece of mobile equipment at the time of the injury. Liquor liability often results from accidents caused by drunk driving.

Limits

The liquor liability form is subject to two limits of insurance: an aggregate limit and an "each common cause" limit. The "each common cause" limit is the most the insurer will pay for all injury sustained by one or more persons as the result of the selling or serving of any alcoholic beverage to any one person. If, for example, a drunk driver injures five persons in five separate incidents after leaving Joe's Bar, the most that Joe's liquor liability insurance will pay for the claims of all five persons is the "each common cause" limit.

Pollution Liability Coverage Form

Any organization that sells, processes, transports, stores, disposes, or in any other way handles toxic or hazardous substances is exposed to liability for bodily injury or property damage resulting from the release of those substances into the environment. Liability may be based on tort principles or on any of various state and federal statutes. In addition to paying for injury to others caused by pollution incidents, the responsible party may also be ordered by governmental authorities to pay for cleanup of a toxic spill or a contaminated site. Cleanup costs can easily exceed damage to property and health.

As discussed in Chapter 8, the CGL coverage form excludes most pollution liability claims. An organization with minimal exposure may be able to obtain limited pollution liability coverage through endorsements to its CGL policy. Organizations with severe exposure—such as hazardous waste treatment plants or landfill operators—must usually buy separate insurance if they wish to insure their pollution liability exposures. Many organizations obtain pollution liability insurance in order to satisfy financial responsibility requirements imposed by statutes and governmental regulations.

Because of the potential severity, only a few insurers write pollution liability insurance (also known as environmental impairment liability insurance). Often, the forms used to provide this insurance are independently developed. Nevertheless, ISO has developed two versions of a **pollution liability coverage form,** titled as follows:

1.   Pollution liability coverage form (designated sites)
2.   Pollution liability limited coverage form (designated sites)

Both forms cover liability for bodily injury and property damage to which the insurance applies. The broader of these forms also covers government-mandated cleanup costs incurred by the insured because of environmental damage occurring away from the insured's premises and waste facilities. The pollution liability limited coverage form does not cover cleanup costs.

Exclusions

The coverage forms are subject to many of the exclusions found in the CGL coverage forms, such as expected or intended injury, contractual liability (but with no exception for "insured contracts"), workers compensation and employers liability, damage to property, and liability arising out of aircraft, autos, or watercraft. Additional exclusions apply to liability resulting from the following:

1.   Pollution incidents that began before the policy's retroactive date
2.   Products and completed operations
3.   Offshore facilities
4.   Closed waste sites
5.   Rolling stock (rail cars)
6.   Wells
7.   Failure to comply with environmental laws

Claims-Made Provisions

Both of the ISO pollution liability forms apply on a claims-made basis. The insured can obtain only a one-year extended reporting period, and the insured must pay an additional premium. Independently developed pollution liability policies also typically have similarly restrictive tail provisions.

Underground Storage Tank Policy

Pollution caused by leakage from underground storage tanks (USTs) is an exposure faced by many businesses ranging from small gas stations to large industrial complexes. The Environmental Protection Agency, pursuant to the

Resource Conservation and Recovery Act, requires that owners and operators of USTs used to store petroleum products demonstrate their financial ability to clean up UST leaks and pay for any damages that others may suffer because of such leaks.

Certain types of storage tanks are exempt from the regulations, such as tanks on farms, tanks used to store heating oil for use on the same premises, and tanks with a capacity of 110 gallons or less. However, even owners and operators of tanks that are exempt from the requirement to show financial responsibility still face a liability exposure in the event of a leak.

One way to demonstrate financial responsibility is by purchasing liability insurance. Some states have established facilities (called "state funds") for providing this insurance. In other states, UST liability insurance is offered by commercial insurance companies. ISO has developed an **underground storage tank policy** that insurers can use to provide this insurance.

The ISO form covers (1) bodily injury and property damage resulting from accidental releases of pollutants from tanks described in the policy and (2) cleanup costs that the insured becomes legally obligated to pay. Coverage is on a claims-made basis with an automatic six-month extended reporting period. A two-year supplemental extended reporting period can be obtained for an additional premium.

Owners and Contractors Protective Liability Coverage Form

As a general rule, a property owner is not held liable for the negligent acts or omissions of independent contractors doing work for the owner. However, some exceptions exist. Courts have held that property owners cannot escape liability for the breach of certain nondelegable duties.

In one case, for example, a property owner was held liable for injuries suffered by a child who fell in a hole that an independent contractor had dug and left uncovered on the owner's land. The court ruled that a property owner has the duty to monitor the work of a contractor and make reasonable efforts to correct dangerous conditions that could injure the public.

Although a property owner's CGL insurance will cover this exposure, some property owners feel that the contractor should bear the cost of insuring the exposure. Accordingly, property owners sometimes require their contractors to provide a special form of premises and operations liability insurance for the benefit of the owner. The insurance, known as **owners and contractors protective (OCP) liability coverage**, is purchased by the contractor, with the property owner shown as the named insured. OCP coverage can also be purchased by a subcontractor to protect a general contractor.

The OCP form developed by ISO covers the named insured's liability for bodily injury or property damage that arises out of either of the following:

1. The operations of the contractor at the specified location
2. Acts or omissions of the named insured in connection with the general supervision of such operations

The OCP form does not cover the named insured for liability arising out of any other activities, such as the named insured's usual business operations. Otherwise, the terms of coverage are comparable in most respects to those of the occurrence version of the CGL coverage form. However, the OCP form does not cover the products-completed operations hazard. OCP coverage automatically terminates as soon as the contractor's work is completed or put to its intended use.

Summary

In addition to the named insured, various other persons and organizations may also be insured under the CGL coverage form. These other insureds include (but are not limited to) spouses of individual named insureds, partners and their spouses (if the named insured is a partnership), employees of the named insured, the named insured's real estate manager or legal representative, operators of the named insured's mobile equipment, and organizations newly acquired by the named insured.

The CGL coverage form carries the following limits of insurance:

- General aggregate limit—the most the insurer will pay during the policy period for medical expenses under Coverage C, damages under Coverage B, and damages under Coverage A other than damages included in the "products-completed operations hazard"

- Products-completed operations limit—the most the insurer will pay for Coverage A damages included in the "products-completed operations hazard"

- Personal and advertising injury limit—the most the insurer will pay for damages under Coverage B

- Each occurrence limit—the most the insurer will pay for medical expenses under Coverage C and damages under Coverages A and B arising out of any one occurrence

- Fire damage limit—the most the insurer will pay for the named insured's liability for fire damage to premises rented to or temporarily occupied by the named insured
- Medical expenses limit—the most the insurer will pay for Coverage C medical expenses resulting from bodily injury to one person

The conditions included in the CGL coverage form relate to bankruptcy of the insured, the insured's duties in the event of loss, legal action against the insurer, other insurance, premium audits, representations, separation of insureds, subrogation, and the insurer's duties when it does not renew the policy.

Insurers use a claims-made version of the CGL coverage form for insuring some organizations that have long-tail liability exposures. The claims-made CGL coverage form covers claims first made during the policy period for injury or damage that occurred after the retroactive date, if any, shown in the policy. The claims-made coverage form contains a basic extended reporting period provision. This provision provides limited coverage for claims first made after the end of the policy period because of injury or damage that occurred before the policy period ended. For an additional premium, the insured can obtain a supplemental extended reporting period, which lengthens the basic extended reporting period.

Endorsements to the CGL policy serve several purposes, such as meeting requirements of individual states, adding or excluding coverages, making special provisions for certain classes of business, or including other persons or organizations as additional insureds.

The premium for a CGL policy is determined by multiplying applicable rates by the insured's rate exposure. The premises-operations and products-completed operations rates for a given organization depend on its class code. The rate exposure is a measure of the size of the organization stated in units of the applicable premium base: gross sales, payroll, and area are common examples.

In addition to the CGL coverage form, several miscellaneous liability coverage forms are filed by ISO to meet special needs. These coverage forms include the following:

- Liquor liability coverage form
- Pollution liability coverage form
- Underground storage tank policy
- Owners and contractors protective liability coverage form

Chapter 10

Commercial Automobile Insurance

The ownership, maintenance, or use of automobiles creates both property and liability loss exposures. These automobile loss exposures are generally excluded in commercial property and general liability coverage forms, but they can be covered under commercial auto insurance.

This chapter examines three widely used commercial auto coverage forms. One of these forms, the **business auto coverage form**, meets the needs of the majority of organizations. The other two forms are designed to meet the needs of two specific types of insureds:

- The **garage coverage form** is used to insure "auto businesses," such as auto dealers, service stations, and auto repair shops.

- The **motor carrier coverage form** is used to insure businesses that use automobiles to transport property of others or, in some cases, their own property.

Automobile Loss Exposures

Automobile loss exposures include both property exposures and liability exposures.

Property Exposures

Any organization that has a financial interest in one or more automobiles is exposed to loss if those vehicles are damaged or destroyed. The main consequences of damage to or destruction of an auto are as follows:

1. Decrease in or loss of the auto's value
2. Loss of use of the auto until it can be repaired or replaced

Auto physical damage insurance can be used to cover damage to or destruction of an auto. Ordinarily, the insurer pays the cost of repairing the vehicle or its actual cash value, whichever is less.

To a limited extent, loss of use of an auto is insurable under a rental reimbursement endorsement to auto physical damage insurance. If a covered auto is disabled by a covered cause of loss, the insurer will reimburse the insured, up to a stated limit, for the cost to rent a substitute vehicle. In that way, the insured can continue operations and avoid loss of income.

Automobiles are subject to many of the same causes of loss that can damage property at a fixed location, such as fire, hail, windstorm, and vandalism. Because autos are mobile, they are highly susceptible to some additional perils, such as collision, overturn, and theft. The mobility of autos also makes them less susceptible than fixed property to certain other perils. For example, a car can often be quickly driven away from rising floodwaters, an approaching forest fire, or other perils that could destroy stationary property.

Liability Exposures

Most organizations own or use autos and are thus exposed to auto liability. Liability can arise from the business use of hired or borrowed autos or even from the operation of employees' autos on behalf of the business. One organization can also assume the auto liability of another organization by contract. These different aspects of the auto liability exposure are described in more detail below.

Owned Autos

Perhaps the most likely way a business can incur auto liability is when an employee of the business, while operating an auto owned by the business, negligently injures other persons or damages their property. As long as the employee operates the vehicle within the scope of his or her employment, the liability for resulting injuries and damage ordinarily falls on the employer as well as the employee. This rule of placing liability on the employer, known as the doctrine of *respondeat superior* ("let the employer answer"), is based on the fact that the employee was acting on behalf of the employer at the time of loss. The employer's liability in this situation is also referred to as **vicarious liability**.

Under the common law, the owner of an auto is not liable for negligent operation of the vehicle by someone who is not acting on behalf of the owner. To illustrate, suppose that John's Garage allows a customer to borrow one of John's business vehicles as a loaner while the customer's car is being serviced. If the customer injures another person by negligently operating John's vehicle, John should not have any liability for resulting damages.

The common-law rule does not apply in some states, however. Those states have enacted laws that make the owner of an auto liable for injuries arising out of the use of the auto by borrowers.

Commercial auto insurance covers liability of the insured arising out of the "ownership, maintenance, or use" of a covered auto. Thus, the insured's liability in any of the situations described above would be covered by commercial auto insurance, assuming the owned auto is a covered auto.

Autos Not Owned

There are several situations in which an organization can become liable for injury or damage to others resulting from the use of autos it does not own. In addition, a business that services, repairs, or otherwise attends to customers' autos can become liable for damage to cars left in its custody.

Hired and Borrowed Autos

An organization may hire autos from others for terms ranging from a few hours to a number of years. A rental period of six months or longer is usually referred to as a "lease," and shorter rental periods are typically called "rentals." In either case, the organization hiring the auto can be held legally liable for injury resulting from operating the vehicle. Similarly, the person or organization that borrows an auto from another can be held liable for injury arising from operating the borrowed vehicle.

An organization that hires or borrows autos can also become liable for damage to the hired or borrowed auto itself. This liability may be based either on negligence of the user or on a contractual duty to return the auto in the same condition as when hired, normal wear and tear excepted. These *liability* exposures are typically insured by purchasing auto *physical damage* insurance on hired autos.

Liability Assumed Under Contract

An auto rental agreement or lease may contain a hold harmless agreement whereby the renter, or lessee, agrees to indemnify the owner for the owner's liability to others arising out of use of the hired auto. As already discussed, the lessee is normally liable for damage resulting from use of the vehicle, even in the absence of the contract. However, the hold harmless agreement could have the further effect of obligating the lessee to reimburse the owner for amounts the owner is required to pay for injury to others arising out of the owner's faulty maintenance of the auto. Subject to certain restrictions, commercial auto insurance covers auto liability assumed by the insured under contracts, including auto rental agreements and leases.

Employers Nonownership Liability

Some employees use their own cars in performing their job duties. A sales representative, for example, may use his or her own car to drive to customers' offices. Because the auto is being used to further the employer's business, the employer is exposed to liability for such use. The exposure has traditionally been referred to as **employers nonownership liability**. Insurance for this exposure can be arranged under each of the commercial auto forms described in this chapter.

Bailee Loss Exposures

Some businesses, such as repair shops, service stations, and parking lots, must by the nature of their business take temporary possession of customers' autos. Accordingly, these "auto businesses" face the bailee loss exposures described in Chapter 7 in connection with inland marine insurance. A bailee is legally liable for damage to customers' property only if the damage occurs as a result of the bailee's negligence. However, in order to maintain good customer relations, many bailees choose to make "goodwill" payments for customers' losses even when the bailees are not legally obligated to do so. The garage coverage form, discussed later in this chapter, contains optional garagekeepers insurance provisions for covering customers' autos.

Operations Difficult To Separate From the Auto Exposure

Particularly in the case of garages, it may be difficult to determine whether the negligence that causes injury is associated with an auto or with the premises. For example, suppose an auto falls from a service hoist, injuring a nearby customer. Is this a premises exposure or an auto exposure? To the injured customer it makes no difference. It is also of little importance to the repair shop owner, who is liable in either case.

The point is that the auto can be only one aspect of the exposure, particularly with regard to legal liability to third parties, and it is sometimes difficult to determine which activity at a garage caused a particular loss. The provisions for garage liability insurance overcome this difficulty by combining both auto liability coverage and commercial general liability coverage under a single insuring agreement.

Other Auto Exposures

In addition to auto physical damage and auto liability insurance, other types of auto insurance can be purchased to cover loss exposures besides those described above.

Auto No-Fault

In an attempt to reduce litigation arising from auto accidents, several states have enacted no-fault auto accident laws. These laws require motorists to purchase (or require insurers to make available) insurance that provides minimum first-party benefits to injured persons without regard to fault or negligence. Some of these laws also limit the injured person's right to sue unless the injuries meet a certain threshold. In some states, the threshold is expressed in terms of a dollar quantity of damages resulting from the injury. (For example, motorists cannot sue for accidents resulting in less than $2,000 in damages.) In other states, the threshold is expressed as a definition of "serious injury" or the like. Unless a motorist sustains "serious injury" as defined, he or she cannot sue.

Where no-fault auto laws are in effect, motorists must buy auto no-fault coverage (also known as personal injury protection). This coverage can be added to the business auto coverage form by endorsement.

Uninsured Motorists

Uninsured motorists laws are in effect in most states. They establish that a vehicle owner can obtain insurance, under his or her auto policy, to pay for injuries caused by another motorist who is uninsured (or underinsured) and, as a result, unable to pay. Some states allow the coverage to be rejected if the policyholder signs a release stating that the coverage is not wanted. Uninsured (and underinsured) motorists insurance can be added to the business auto policy by endorsement.

Auto Medical Payments

Auto medical payments coverage provides insurance to pay for medical expenses incurred by occupants of a covered auto, regardless of whether the driver of the covered auto was at fault in the accident. Medical payments coverage, by paying a small bodily injury claim without any determination of liability, can perhaps avoid a costlier liability claim by a passenger against the driver. Auto medical payments coverage is not mandatory in any state. (When medical coverage is required by a no-fault law, the coverage is provided through a special no-fault endorsement.)

Business Auto Coverage Form

The **business auto coverage form** is used for insuring all types of organizations other than "auto businesses" and motor carriers. The business auto coverage form, along with business auto declarations and any applicable endorsements, can be included in a commercial package policy or issued as a monoline policy.

The business auto declarations form is longer and more detailed than the declarations for most other coverage forms. Thus, in addition to the usual information contained in any declarations form, the business auto declarations form includes various schedules for recording applicable coverages, covered autos, limits, deductibles, premiums, and rating and classification information.

The business auto coverage form consists of the following five sections:

Section I—Covered Autos

Section II—Liability Coverage

Section III—Physical Damage Coverage

Section IV—Business Auto Conditions

Section V—Definitions

Sections I through IV are discussed in the same order below. The various definitions, however, are related as the defined terms are encountered in Sections I through IV.

Section I—Covered Autos

The business auto coverage form allows great flexibility in designating covered autos for the various coverages available under the policy. A coverage chosen by the named insured need not apply to all covered autos. For example, the insured might want to provide liability coverage for all vehicles and medical payments coverage for private passenger vehicles only.

The mechanism used to indicate the vehicles to which each coverage applies is a series of nine numerical **coverage symbols**, defined in Section I of the coverage form. The appropriate symbol or symbols are entered beside each coverage in the schedule of coverages and covered autos in the declarations. An illustration of how the schedule might be completed is shown in Exhibit 10-1. Each of the coverage symbols is described below.

Symbol 1—Any Auto

If symbol 1 is entered for a coverage, that coverage is provided for any auto, including autos owned by the named insured, autos the named insured hires or borrows from others, and other nonowned autos used in the insured's business. Ordinarily, this symbol is used for liability coverage only.

An auto, as defined in the business auto form, is a land motor vehicle, trailer, or semitrailer designed for travel on public roads but is not "mobile equipment." The business auto definition of "mobile equipment" is the same as that of the commercial general liability (CGL) coverage form.

Symbol 2—Owned Autos Only

If symbol 2 is entered for a coverage, that coverage applies to all autos owned by the named insured. For liability insurance only, coverage is also provided for a nonowned trailer while it is attached to a power unit owned by the named insured. ("Power unit" is not defined in the coverage form, but the term refers to a truck tractor used to pull a semitrailer. "Trailer," defined in the coverage form, includes, but is not limited to, a semitrailer.) Symbol 2 does not cover hired or borrowed autos or other autos the named insured does not own. Symbol 2 is also used for physical damage and medical payments coverages.

Symbol 3—Owned Private Passenger Autos Only

When a 3 is entered beside a coverage, that coverage is provided only for private passenger autos owned by the named insured. This symbol does not include trucks or buses owned by the named insured or any kind of auto not owned by the named insured.

Symbol 4—Owned Autos Other Than Private Passenger Autos

If a 4 is entered for a coverage, that coverage is provided for all autos owned by the named insured except private passenger autos.

Symbol 5—Owned Autos Subject to No-Fault

Symbol 5 is normally entered only on the personal injury protection (PIP) or

Exhibit 10-1

Schedule of Coverages and Covered Autos

ITEM TWO

SCHEDULE OF COVERAGES AND COVERED AUTOS

This policy provides only those coverages where a change is shown in the premium column below. Each of these coverages will apply only to those "autos" shown as covered "autos". "Autos" are shown as covered "autos" for a particular coverage by the entry of one or more of the symbols from the COVERED AUTO Section of the Business Auto Coverage Form next to the name of the coverage.

COVERAGES	COVERED AUTOS (Entry of one or more of the symbols from the COVERED AUTOS Section of the Business Auto Coverage Form shows which autos are covered autos)	LIMIT THE MOST WE WILL PAY FOR ANY ONE ACCIDENT OR LOSS	PREMIUM
LIABILITY	1	$	
PERSONAL INJURY PROTECTION (or equivalent No-fault coverage)	5	SEPARATELY STATED IN EACH PIP ENDORSEMENT MINUS $ Ded.	
ADDED PERSONAL INJURY PROTECTION (or equivalent added No-fault coverage)	5	SEPARATELY STATED IN EACH ADDED PIP ENDORSEMENT	
PROPERTY PROTECTION INSURANCE (Michigan only)		SEPARATELY STATED IN THE P.P.I. ENDORSEMENT MINUS $ Ded. FOR EACH ACCIDENT	
AUTO MEDICAL PAYMENTS		$	
UNINSURED MOTORISTS	6	$	
UNDERINSURED MOTORISTS (When not included in Uninsured Motorists Coverage)	6	$	
PHYSICAL DAMAGE COMPREHENSIVE COVERAGE	7, 8	ACTUAL CASH VALUE OR COST OF REPAIR, WHICHEVER IS LESS MINUS $ Ded. FOR EACH COVERED AUTO. BUT NO DEDUCTIBLE APPLIES TO LOSS CAUSED BY FIRE OR LIGHTNING. See ITEM FOUR for hired or borrowed "autos".	
PHYSICAL DAMAGE SPECIFIED CAUSES OF LOSS COVERAGE		ACTUAL CASH VALUE OR COST OF REPAIR, WHICHEVER IS LESS MINUS $25 Ded. FOR EACH COVERED AUTO FOR LOSS CAUSED BY MISCHIEF OR VANDALISM. See ITEM FOUR for hired or borrowed "autos".	
PHYSICAL DAMAGE COLLISION COVERAGE	7, 8	ACTUAL CASH VALUE OR COST OF REPAIR, WHICHEVER IS LESS MINUS $ Ded. FOR EACH COVERED AUTO. See ITEM FOUR for hired or borrowed "autos".	
PHYSICAL DAMAGE TOWING AND LABOR (Not Available in California)		$ for each disablement of a private passenger "auto"	
		PREMIUM FOR ENDORSEMENTS	
		ESTIMATED TOTAL PREMIUM	

added PIP line of the declarations. It provides PIP coverage only for those autos that are required by law to have it.

Symbol 6—Owned Autos Subject to a Compulsory Uninsured Motorists Law

Symbol 6 is normally used only for uninsured motorists coverage. It indicates that coverage is provided only for autos that are required by law to have uninsured motorists coverage.

Symbol 7—Specifically Described Autos

If this symbol is used, coverage applies only to those autos specifically described in the policy and for which a premium is shown in the policy. It also includes, for liability coverage only, any trailer not owned by the insured while it is attached to one of the covered power units.

Symbol 8—Hired Autos Only

Symbol 8 provides coverage only for autos leased, hired, rented, or borrowed by the named insured. It does not cover autos leased, hired, rented, or borrowed from the named insured's employees or members of their families.

Symbol 9—Nonowned Autos Only

Symbol 9 provides coverage only for autos not owned, leased, hired, or borrowed by the named insured while such autos are used in connection with the named insured's business. Symbol 9 includes autos owned by the named insured's employees or members of their households but only while used in the named insured's business or personal affairs. Symbols 8 and 9 are normally used only for liability coverage. A combination of symbols 2, 8, and 9 covers essentially the same vehicles covered by symbol 1.

Exhibit 10-2 summarizes the symbols and their use for business auto coverage.

Coverage for Newly Acquired Autos

If any of symbols 1 through 6 is shown for a coverage, that coverage applies to vehicles of the type indicated by the symbol if such vehicles are acquired during the policy term. Coverage for newly acquired vehicles of the type indicated by the symbol is automatic, without any requirement that the insurer be notified of the acquisition. The insurer typically discovers any newly acquired autos when it audits the insured at the end of the policy period. The insured must then pay an additional premium for any such autos.

Exhibit 10-2
Description of Covered Auto Designation Symbols

SYMBOL	DESCRIPTION

1 = ANY "AUTO".

2 = OWNED "AUTOS" ONLY. Only those "autos" you own (and for Liability Coverage any "trailers" you don't own while attached to power units you own). This includes those "autos" you acquire ownership of after the policy begins.

3 = OWNED PRIVATE PASSENGER "AUTOS" ONLY. Only the private passenger "autos" you own. This includes those private passenger "autos" you acquire ownership of after the policy begins.

4 = OWNED "AUTOS" OTHER THAN PRIVATE PASSENGER "AUTOS" ONLY. Only those "autos" you own that are not of the private passenger type (and for Liability Coverage any "trailers" you don't own while attached to power units you own). This includes those "autos" not of the private passenger type you acquire ownership of after the policy begins.

5 = OWNED "AUTOS" SUBJECT TO NO-FAULT. Only those "autos" you own that are required to have No-Fault benefits in the state where they are licensed or principally garaged. This includes those "autos" you acquire ownership of after the policy begins provided they are required to have No-Fault benefits in the state where they are licensed or principally garaged.

6 = OWNED "AUTOS" SUBJECT TO A COMPULSORY UNINSURED MOTORISTS LAW. Only those "autos" you own that because of the law in the state where they are licensed or principally garaged are required to have and cannot reject Uninsured Motorists Coverage. This includes those "autos" you acquire ownership of after the policy begins provided they are subject to the same uninsured motorists requirement.

7 = SPECIFICALLY DESCRIBED "AUTOS". Only those "autos" described in ITEM THREE of the Declarations for which a premium charge is shown (and for Liability Coverage any "trailers" you don't own while attached to any power unit described in ITEM THREE).

8 = HIRED "AUTOS" ONLY. Only those "autos" you lease, hire, rent or borrow. This does not include any "auto" you lease, hire, rent or borrow from any of your employees or partners or members of their households.

9 = NONOWNED "AUTOS" ONLY. Only those "autos" you do not own, lease, hire, rent or borrow that are used in connection with your business. This includes "autos" owned by your employees or partners or members of their households but only while used in your business or your personal affairs.

If symbol 7 is shown for a coverage, autos acquired during the policy term are covered from the time of acquisition *only* if both of the following conditions are met:

1. The insurer insures all autos owned by the named insured, *or* the newly acquired auto replaces a covered auto.
2. The named insured asks the insurer to cover the newly acquired auto within thirty days after the acquisition.

Other Covered Items

If the coverage form provides *liability* insurance, trailers with a load capacity of 2,000 pounds or less are covered automatically for liability insurance. "Mobile equipment" is automatically covered for liability while being carried or towed by an auto that has liability coverage. Also covered, *for liability insurance only*, is an auto used as a temporary substitute for a covered auto that is out of service because of its breakdown, repair, service, loss, or destruction.

Section II—Liability Coverage

The liability coverage provisions of the business auto coverage form include a coverage agreement, a definition of who is insured, coverage extensions, exclusions, and a limit of insurance clause.

Coverage Agreement

In the liability coverage agreement, the insurer expresses three distinct duties:

1. A duty to pay damages
2. A duty to pay "covered pollution cost or expense"
3. A duty to defend the insured

Each of these duties is described in more detail below.

Duty To Pay Damages

The insurer agrees to pay all sums an "insured" must legally pay as damages because of "bodily injury" or "property damage" to which the insurance applies, caused by an "accident" and resulting from the ownership, maintenance, or use of a covered "auto." The terms in quotation marks impose important restrictions on coverage. Their definitions, from Section V of the coverage form, are as follows:

> "Insured" means any person or organization qualifying as an insured in the Who Is An Insured provision of the applicable coverage.

"Bodily injury" means bodily injury, sickness or disease sustained by a person including death resulting from any of these.

"Property damage" means damage to or loss of use of tangible property.

"Accident" includes continuous or repeated exposure to the same conditions resulting in "bodily injury" or "property damage."

"Auto" means a land motor vehicle, trailer or semitrailer designed for travel on public roads but does not include "mobile equipment."

The insurer's obligation to "pay all sums" is governed not only by these definitions but also by the exclusions, policy limit, and other conditions to be discussed later.

Duty To Pay "Covered Pollution Cost or Expense"

In the event of a pollution incident, damages for bodily injury and property damage are not the only consequences for which the insured can be held liable. The insured can incur various costs and expenses as the result of demands by governmental authorities or private citizens that the insured clean up or otherwise respond to the effects of pollutants.

To address this exposure, the insurer agrees to pay all sums that the insured must legally pay as "covered pollution cost or expense." In order for pollution cost or expense to be covered, it must be caused by an accident and must result from the ownership, maintenance, or use of a covered auto. In addition, the same accident that causes the pollution cost or expense must also result in bodily injury or property damage covered by the policy. The business auto policy is subject to a broad pollution exclusion discussed later in this chapter. Cleanup costs for any incident excluded by the pollution exclusion are not covered.

Duty To Defend

The insurer has the right and the duty to defend any insured against any claim or suit alleging damages that would be covered under the policy. The claim or suit only needs to *allege* damages that would be covered. Hence, the insurer must defend against even false or fraudulent claims or suits as long as they allege covered damages.

The coverage form defines "suit" to include civil proceedings and arbitration proceedings to which the named insured must submit or submits with the insurer's consent. The duty to defend ends when the insurer has paid its applicable policy limit in full or partial settlement of the claim. The costs of defending the claim are payable in addition to the limit of insurance.

Who Is an Insured

Many persons in addition to the named insured may be covered under the liability insuring agreement. Who is insured for liability coverage depends on the circumstances of the accident.

The named insured is an insured for *any covered auto*. If, for example, symbol 1 is shown for liability coverage, the named insured is an insured for any auto. If only symbol 7 is shown for liability coverage, the named insured is an insured only for specifically described autos.

Anyone other than the named insured is an insured while using with the named insured's permission a covered auto owned, hired, or borrowed *by the named insured*. However, the following restrictions apply.

- The owner or anyone else from whom the named insured hires or borrows a covered auto is not an insured, unless the covered auto is a trailer connected to a covered auto owned by the named insured. If, for example, Smith Company hires a car from A-1 Auto Rentals, A-1 will not be an insured under Smith's business auto liability coverage.

- An employee of the named insured is not an insured if the covered auto is owned by the employee or a member of the employee's household. For example, Sue is not an insured under her employer's business auto liability coverage while operating her car on an errand for her employer. (Sue's employer, on the other hand, *is* insured for this use of Sue's car if the policy includes either symbol 1 or symbol 9 for liability coverage.)

- A person using a covered auto while working in the business of selling, servicing, repairing, or parking autos is not an insured unless that business is the named insured's. For example, a mechanic of Bob's Brake Shop is not an insured under Smith's business auto liability coverage while test-driving Smith's car.

- Anyone other than the named insured's employees or partners, or a lessee or borrower of a covered auto or any of their employees, is not an insured while moving property to or from a covered auto. If, for example, employees of Jones Warehouse are unloading Smith Company's truck, the Jones employees are not covered under Smith's business auto liability coverage.

- A partner of the named insured is not an insured for a covered auto owned by that partner or a member of that partner's household.

Also insured is any person or organization (other than those excluded above) liable for the conduct of an "insured." To illustrate the application of this provision, assume that an employee of Jones Corporation operates an auto covered under Smith's business auto insurance. Jones's employee causes an accident, and Jones is held to be liable for its employee's conduct. Because of the provision under discussion, Jones will be an insured under Smith's auto insurance. (Jones's driver will also be an insured because of the earlier provision relating to "anyone else" other than the named insured.)

Coverage Extensions

The business auto liability provisions include coverage extensions for supplementary payments and for increased protection while a covered auto is out of the state where it is licensed.

Supplementary Payments

Business auto liability coverage provides six supplementary payments that are similar in most respects to those provided in the CGL coverage form. As under the CGL coverage form, these supplementary payments are payable in addition to the limit of insurance. Under these supplementary payments the insurer is obligated to pay:

1. All expenses it incurs
2. Up to $250 for the cost of bail bonds required because of a covered accident
3. Premiums on bonds to release attachments in a suit the insurer defends, but only for bond amounts up to the policy limit
4. Reasonable expenses incurred by the insured at the request of the insurer, including up to $100 a day for lost wages
5. All costs taxed to the insured in a suit defended by the insurer
6. All interest accruing after the entry of a judgment, but the insurer's liability for interest ends when it pays or tenders its policy limit in full or partial settlement of the judgment

Out-of-State Extensions

If a covered auto is outside the state where it is licensed, the limit of insurance is, if necessary, increased on that auto to the minimum required by the jurisdiction in which the auto is located. Also, if the other jurisdiction requires a different type of coverage, such coverage is provided automatically.

For example, assume that a business auto policy has a $50,000 limit for liability insurance and that a covered auto is driven out of state through two other states. If the first outside state requires a minimum limit of $100,000, the limit is increased automatically to $100,000 while the auto is in that state. If the second state requires no-fault coverage, the insured's policy will automatically provide no-fault coverage while the auto is in that state.

Exclusions

The exclusions that appear in the liability coverage section impose several limitations on the liability coverage agreement. Some of the exclusions eliminate coverage that insurers prefer to underwrite separately, and others eliminate coverage for exposures that are not deemed to be appropriate for commercial insurance.

Expected or Intended Injury

Bodily injury or property damage expected or intended from the standpoint of the insured is generally not considered to be a legitimate subject of insurance and is therefore excluded.

Contractual Liability

Although liability assumed under any contract or agreement is excluded, the exclusion does not apply to the following:

1. Liability that the insured would have in the absence of the contract.
2. Damages assumed in an "insured contract." The definition of "insured contract" found in Section V of the coverage form lists the types of contracts in which an assumption of liability is covered.

In many ways, this definition resembles the definition of "insured contract" in the CGL coverage form. For example, both definitions include leases of premises. Consequently, the business auto form covers liability assumed under a lease of premises only if the liability being assumed arises out of the ownership, maintenance, or use of an auto, and the CGL form covers liability assumed under a lease of premises if the liability being assumed does *not* arise out of the ownership, maintenance, or use of an auto. The same distinction applies to the other types of insured contracts.

Under the business auto definition, the following are insured contracts:

1. A lease of premises
2. A sidetrack agreement
3. An easement or license agreement except in connection with construction or demolition operations on or within fifty feet of any railroad property
4. An obligation, as required by ordinance, to indemnify a municipality, except in connection with work *for* a municipality
5. That part of any other contract or agreement in which the named insured assumes the tort liability of another to pay damages because of bodily injury or property damage, if the agreement pertains to the named

insured's business and is made before the bodily injury or property damage occurs

6. An auto rental agreement or lease entered into, as part of the named insured's business, by the named insured or any of the named insured's employees

However, an insured contract does not include that part of any contract or agreement that:

1. Indemnifies anyone for injury or damage arising out of construction or demolition operations within fifty feet of any railroad property;

2. Pertains to the loan, lease, or rental of an auto to the named insured if the auto is loaned, leased, or rented *with a driver*;

3. Holds a trucker harmless for the named insured's use of a covered auto over a route or territory the trucker is authorized to serve by public authority; or

4. Obligates the insured to pay for damage to an auto rented or leased to the insured.

Apart from the excluded types of agreements, any other type of auto rental agreement is considered to be an insured contract.

Workers Compensation

Like the CGL coverage form, the business auto coverage form excludes any liability under a workers compensation, disability benefits, or unemployment compensation law.

Employee Indemnification and Employers Liability

This exclusion is also nearly identical to one found in the CGL coverage form. The effect is to eliminate, subject to two exceptions, coverage for bodily injury to employees of the insured that should be covered under workers compensation and employers liability insurance. The two exceptions that allow coverage for employee injury are (1) injury to domestic employees not entitled to workers compensation and (2) liability assumed by the insured under an insured contract.

Fellow Employee

The business auto coverage form excludes bodily injury to any fellow employee of any insured that arises in the course of the fellow employee's employment. If, for example, one of ABC's drivers negligently strikes another ABC employee with a truck while they are at work, ABC's business auto coverage will not protect the driver against any legal action the injured employee might be able to bring against the driver. Insurers are frequently

Severability of Interests Clause

The business auto definition of "insured" contains a sentence commonly known as the severability of interests clause. It reads as follows: "Except with respect to the Limit of Insurance, the coverage afforded applies separately to each insured who is seeking coverage or against whom a claim or 'suit' is brought."

What does this mean? People often can't agree. However, in a number of cases, the severability of interests clause has been crucial in interpreting the exclusion of bodily injury to an employee of the "insured." The effect has been to allow coverage for injury sustained by employees of the *named* insured when the insured against whom the employees made claim was some insured other than the named insured.

To illustrate, say that Sally, an employee of Ray's Hardware Store, is hit by Dan, a friend of Ray's who was driving Ray's delivery truck with Ray's permission. Sally makes claim against Dan, who qualifies as an insured under Ray's business auto policy. Even though Ray's policy excludes bodily injury to an employee of the insured, this exclusion does not eliminate coverage for Sally's claim: Sally is not an employee of the insured *against whom she is making claim* (Dan).

asked to amend or delete this exclusion to allow coverage for fellow employee suits. Such modifications, if allowed, usually require an additional premium.

Care, Custody, or Control

There is no coverage for property owned by the insured or in the care, custody, or control of the insured. Property owned by the insured can be insured under an appropriate form of property insurance. Property of others in the care, custody, or control of the insured is frequently insured under inland marine coverage. For example, motor truck cargo insurance, described in Chapter 7, covers property of others being transported by the insured.

Handling of Property

This exclusion helps to define the scope of coverage for accidents occurring during the loading or unloading of autos. The exclusion eliminates coverage for bodily injury or property damage resulting from the handling of property under *both* of the following conditions:

- *Before* property is moved from the place where it is accepted by the insured for movement into a covered auto

- *After* it has been moved from a covered auto to the place where it is finally delivered by the insured

Consequently, the exclusion does not apply to—and thus there is coverage for—accidents that occur while property is being moved (1) into a covered auto from the place where the insured has accepted the property or (2) from a covered auto to the place where the insured is delivering the property.

If, for example, two employees of an appliance store damage a hallway wall while moving a clothes washer from their delivery truck to a second-floor apartment, the store's business auto insurance will cover the damage to the wall, because the property damage occurred before the washer was moved to the final place of delivery.

As discussed in Chapter 8, the CGL coverage form excludes "loading and unloading" and defines that term in the same manner as set forth above, thus avoiding duplication of business auto coverage. However, the CGL form *covers* the exposures that exist in connection with property before loading begins or after unloading is completed.

Movement of Property by Mechanical Device

The business auto coverage form excludes bodily injury or property damage resulting from movement of property by a mechanical device unless the device is attached to the covered auto or is a hand truck. To illustrate, movement of property by a mechanical hoist attached to a flatbed truck is covered; movement of property by a conveyor belt not attached to the truck is excluded by the business auto form (but covered by the CGL form).

Operations

The definition of "mobile equipment" states that self-propelled vehicles with certain types of permanently attached equipment are "autos" and not "mobile equipment." For example, a truck with a cherry picker (a device for raising and lowering workers) mounted on it qualifies for business auto coverage. The "operations" exclusion clarifies that operating certain types of equipment attached to such autos is *not* covered. (The CGL form covers the excluded exposure.) The types of equipment excluded are:

- Cherry pickers and similar devices mounted on an automobile or truck chassis and used to raise or lower workers

- Air compressors, pumps, and generators, including spraying, welding, building cleaning, geophysical exploration, lighting, or well servicing equipment

To illustrate, assume C&D Electric has a service truck with a cherry picker mounted on it. The driver of the truck causes an accident while driving to a work site. The resulting liability is covered under C&D's business auto insurance. After the truck reaches its work site, a passerby is injured as a result of C&D's operation of the cherry picker. The resulting liability is excluded by C&D's business auto insurance and covered by C&D's CGL insurance.

Completed Operations

This exclusion clarifies that the business auto coverage form provides no insurance for completed operations performed with the insured's autos. For example, injury resulting from allegedly negligent snowplowing performed (and completed) by the insured would not be covered.

Pollution

With few exceptions, the business auto pollution exclusion eliminates coverage for bodily injury or property damage resulting from the discharge of any pollutants being transported or stored in, or moved to or from, a covered auto. The exclusion does *not* eliminate coverage for discharge of pollutants from a vehicle that is not a covered auto (such as an oil tank truck hit by a covered auto) or from other property that is not being handled for movement into or from a covered auto (such as an above-ground storage tank struck by a covered auto).

By a specific exception, the exclusion also does not apply to the escape of fuels, lubricants, fluids, exhaust gases, or other similar pollutants needed for functioning of the covered auto. If, for example, gasoline leaks from the fuel tank of a covered auto after a collision, liability for the spill is covered.

War

Liability assumed under contract for damage caused by war, civil war, insurrection, rebellion, or revolution is excluded, even if the liability is assumed under an "insured contract."

Racing

Much as the CGL policy excludes racing of mobile equipment, the business auto form excludes covered autos while used in organized races or demolition contests. Practice or preparation for such activities is also excluded.

Limit of Insurance

Business auto liability coverage is subject to a combined single limit of insurance applicable to all bodily injury, property damage, and covered pollution cost or expense arising from a single accident. No annual aggregate limit applies. The single limit is the maximum amount the insurer will pay for all claims arising *from a single accident* regardless of the number of vehicles, the number of drivers, or the number of claimants involved.

Repeated exposure to essentially the same circumstances is considered to be a single accident. For example, if a truck is driven across the sidewalk repeatedly over several months, all of the damage it causes to the sidewalk could be considered a single accident.

An endorsement is available to provide split limits of insurance. The endorsement shows a per person limit and a per accident limit for bodily injury and a per accident limit for property damage.

Section III—Physical Damage Coverage

Section III of the business auto coverage form provides **auto physical damage insurance**. The primary purpose of the coverage is to insure loss of or damage to autos owned by the insured. However, coverage can also be arranged to cover autos hired or borrowed by the insured.

Coverages

Four optional physical damage coverages are available:

1. Collision
2. Comprehensive
3. Specified causes of loss
4. Towing

Collision coverage insures "loss" to a covered auto caused by collision with another object or by overturn. ("Loss" is defined in the form to mean direct and accidental loss or damage.)

Comprehensive coverage insures loss to a covered auto by any peril except collision or overturn or a peril specifically excluded. Glass breakage, damage resulting from hitting a bird or an animal, and damage caused by falling objects or missiles, although they might otherwise be considered losses caused by collision, are paid under comprehensive if the auto is insured for comprehensive. This provision usually benefits the insured, since most insureds carry lower deductibles on comprehensive than on collision coverage.

If glass breakage is caused by collision, however, it can be covered by collision (and not under comprehensive) at the option of the insured. In that way, the insured can avoid the application of two deductibles when collision damage to the auto is accompanied by glass breakage.

A somewhat less expensive alternative to comprehensive coverage is **specified causes of loss coverage**. This coverage insures loss to a covered auto caused by any of the following:

1. Fire
2. Lightning
3. Explosion
4. Theft
5. Windstorm
6. Hail
7. Earthquake
8. Flood
9. Mischief
10. Vandalism
11. The sinking, burning, collision, or derailment of a conveyance transporting the insured vehicle

Towing coverage reimburses the insured for necessary towing and labor costs resulting from the disablement of a covered *private passenger* auto. The labor must be performed at the place of disablement. The limit for this coverage, selected by the insured, is the most that the insurer will pay for each disablement.

Coverage Extension

The coverage extension pays for loss of use of a private passenger type auto that has been stolen if it is insured for comprehensive or specified causes of loss. The insurer agrees to pay costs of substitute transportation actually incurred by the named insured, subject to a daily limit of $15 and a total limit of $450. Payments begin forty-eight hours after the theft, and they end when the insured auto is returned to use or when the insurer pays for the auto. Such payments may extend beyond the expiration of the policy.

Because the coverage extension insures loss of use of a covered auto only if the auto is of the private passenger type and is stolen, some insureds want broader coverage for loss of use of covered autos. The broader coverage can be provided through the rental reimbursement coverage endorsement. The endorsement covers the cost of renting a substitute auto for a designated auto of any type that has suffered a covered loss, subject to maximum daily and aggregate limits.

Exclusions

Auto physical damage insurance is subject to few exclusions. Like virtually any other type of property insurance, it excludes nuclear hazards and war or military action. Notably, however, auto physical damage insurance does not exclude earthquake, flood, or other water damage.

Business auto physical damage insurance excludes certain types of losses that are likely to occur as a normal consequence of prolonged use of the vehicle or the owner's neglect. Thus, wear and tear, freezing, mechanical or electrical failure, and road damage to tires are excluded unless they result from other loss insured by the coverage form. For example, an auto with comprehensive coverage may be stolen. If the auto suffers a mechanical breakdown and tire damage resulting from abusive driving by the thief, the mechanical breakdown and tire damage would not be excluded since they were caused by another covered loss (theft).

The business auto form also excludes many types of electronic equipment that might be found in an auto. If the insured wishes to insure such equipment, coverage can usually be added to the business auto form by using special endorsements.

The business auto form does not exclude all types of electronic equipment in a covered auto. In fact, the drafters of the form have gone to great lengths to specify exactly what types of electronic equipment are excluded and which are covered. These exclusions have been redrafted several times in recent years to keep up with technological change.

The insurer will not pay for loss to the following:

1. Tapes, records, discs, or similar devices
2. Radar detectors
3. Any equipment, whether permanently installed or not, that receives or transmits audio, visual, or data signals and that is not designed solely for the reproduction of sound
4. Any accessories used with the equipment described in item 3 above

However, the exclusion contains some detailed exceptions. In summary, these exceptions reinstate coverage for (1) sound-reproducing equipment permanently installed in the auto (or removable from a housing unit that is permanently installed in the auto) and (2) electronic equipment necessary for the normal operation of the auto.

Finally, the business auto form excludes physical damage coverage for autos while used in organized races or demolition contests, including practice or preparation for such activities.

Limit of Insurance

The most the insurer will pay for a physical damage loss is the *smaller* of the following:

1. The actual cash value of the property at the time of loss
2. The cost of repairing or replacing the property with other property of like kind or quality

Deductible

The insurer's payment *for each covered auto* is reduced by any applicable deductible shown in the declarations. However, a deductible applicable to comprehensive coverage does not apply to loss by fire or lightning. This exception can be of considerable value to an owner of a fleet of autos that are garaged at the same location and therefore susceptible to total loss by fire. In the absence of this exemption, the insured would have to bear a portion of the loss equal to the amount of the deductible times the total number of cars destroyed.

Section IV—Business Auto Conditions

Conditions that apply to all coverages under the business auto coverage form are contained in Section IV of the form. Some of the conditions are very similar to those found in the commercial general liability coverage form. Others are designed to meet the specific needs of auto insurance. The first five conditions are loss conditions, and the remaining eight conditions are more general in nature.

Appraisal for Physical Damage Losses

If the named insured and the insurer cannot agree on the amount of loss, either may call for an appraisal. Each will then appoint an appraiser, and the appraisers will appoint a "competent and impartial" umpire. The appraisers then determine actual cash value and the amount of loss payment. Any item on which the appraisers cannot agree is submitted to the umpire, and an award in writing, signed by any two of the three, is binding on both parties. Each party pays its own appraiser, and both parties share the cost of the umpire. This procedure applies only to disagreements about the amount of loss and not to disagreements as to coverage.

Duties in the Event of Accident, Claim, Suit, or Loss

The insured's duties after loss are essentially the same as those imposed by the CGL policy. The named insured must give prompt notice of accident or loss to the insurer or its agent and assist the insurer in obtaining the names of injured persons or witnesses. Also, both the named insured and any other person who seeks liability coverage under the policy (for example, the driver of an insured vehicle) must do the following:

1. Cooperate with the insurer in its investigation and defense of the accident or loss.

2. Immediately send to the insurer copies of any notices or legal papers received in connection with the accident or loss.

3. Submit to physical examinations by physicians selected and paid by the insurer as often as the insurer may reasonably request.

4. Authorize the insurer to obtain medical reports and other medical information.

Moreover, no insured can commit the insurer to make any payment either for damages or expenses.

If the claim is for loss or damage to a covered auto, the named insured must do the following:

1. Promptly notify the police if the insured auto or any of its equipment is stolen.

2. Do what is reasonably necessary to preserve the property from further loss.

3. Permit the insurer to inspect and appraise the damaged vehicle before it is repaired.

4. Agree to be examined under oath at the insurer's request and give a signed statement.

Legal Action Against the Insurer

No legal action can be brought against the insurer under any coverage until the named insured and the insured bringing the action, if different, have complied with all provisions of the coverage form. In addition, under the liability coverage, no action can be brought against the insurer until either a court has determined that the insured is liable for the loss or the insurer has agreed in writing that the insured is liable for the loss.

Loss Payment—Physical Damage Coverages

The insurer has three options with regard to damaged or stolen property:

1. To pay to repair or replace the property

2. To return the property at the expense of the insurer and repair any damage caused by theft

3. To keep all of the property and pay an agreed or appraised value

Transfer of Rights Against Others

The insured may have a right to recover a loss from some other party, usually because the other party caused the loss. If the insurer pays the loss, it is entitled, under this condition, to take over the insured's right of recovery from the other party. The insured must not do anything to impair the insurer's right of recovery and must do everything reasonably necessary to secure and preserve that right.

Bankruptcy

The first of eight general conditions relates to bankruptcy. Bankruptcy or insolvency of the insured does not relieve the insurer of any of its obligations under the policy. If the insured is relieved through bankruptcy of any obligation to pay a liability claim, the insurer is still obligated to make payment just as it would have been if the insured had remained solvent.

Concealment, Misrepresentation, or Fraud

In case of fraud by the named insured relative to business auto coverage, the coverage is void. It is also void if any insured *intentionally* conceals or misrepresents a material fact about the coverage form, any autos covered, the insured's interest in any covered auto, or a claim under the coverage form. A material fact is usually considered one that would have changed the underwriting decision in some way.

Liberalization

If the insurer revises the form to provide more coverage at no increase in premium, the coverage applies to existing coverage as of the date the revision is effective in the insured's state.

No Benefit to Bailee—Physical Damage Insurance Only

Railroads and other transporters of property sometimes try to gain the benefit of the property owner's insurance by inserting a provision in their bill of lading stating that they are not liable for any loss for which the shipper is reimbursed by insurance. This provision in the bill of lading could invalidate the insurer's right of subrogation against the transporting company. Accordingly, the "no benefit to bailee" condition attempts to preserve the insurer's subrogation rights by stating that the insurer does not recognize any assignment of coverage or any other grant of coverage to any person or organization that holds, stores, or transports property for a fee.

Other Insurance

Business auto coverage may be either primary or excess, depending on the circumstances of the accident or loss. For any covered vehicle owned by the named insured, the coverage is primary. For any covered auto not owned by the named insured, the coverage is excess, and the insurance, if any, carried by the owner of the auto is primary.

For purposes of hired auto (symbol 8) physical damage coverage, any auto the named insured leases, hires, rents, or borrows is deemed to be a covered auto owned by the named insured. Such an auto is therefore covered on a primary basis. However, there is no coverage for an auto that is hired or borrowed *with a driver*.

Coverage for trailers follows the autos to which they are attached. Thus, coverage is excess for a trailer attached to an auto not owned by the named insured, and coverage is primary for a trailer attached to an auto owned by the named insured. The coverage is primary for a covered trailer owned by the named insured when it is not attached to any auto.

Regardless of the above provisions, business auto liability coverage is primary for any liability assumed under an insured contract.

If there are two or more policies of the same level (either excess or primary), each contributes to the loss in the proportion that its limit bears to the total limits of all policies of its level. For example, assume there are two primary policies: Policy A with a limit of $100,000 and Policy B with a limit of $300,000. On a $40,000 loss, Policy A, which has one-fourth of the total limits, would pay $10,000, and Policy B would pay $30,000.

Premium Audit

The premium shown on the declarations, which the insured pays at policy inception, is an estimate. The actual premium will be determined by a premium audit and will be based on actual exposures at the end of the policy period. If the final premium is less than the estimate, the named insured gets a refund. If the final premium is greater than the estimate, the named insured gets a bill for the difference.

Policy Period, Coverage Territory

Accidents and losses are covered if they occur (1) during the policy period shown on the declarations and (2) within the coverage territory. Coverage territory includes the United States of America, its territories and possessions, Puerto Rico, and Canada. Losses and accidents involving a covered auto while being transported between the covered territories are also covered.

Two or More Coverage Forms or Policies Issued by the Insurer

A special rule applies when an accident or a loss is covered by two or more policies issued by the same insurer or affiliated insurers. In that case, the maximum amount the insurer or affiliated insurers will be required to pay is the highest limit provided under any one policy. However, this does not apply to any coverage specifically purchased as excess over business auto coverage.

Coverages Added by Endorsement

Apart from the liability and physical damage coverages, all of the coverages listed in the schedule of coverages and covered autos in the business auto declarations must be added by endorsement if they are purchased. The provisions for these coverages are described below.

Medical Payments Insurance

Medical payments insurance covers the reasonable and necessary medical and funeral expenses incurred by a person injured by an accident while entering into, riding in, or alighting from a covered auto. In addition, if the named insured is an individual proprietorship, it covers the named insured and members of his or her family while occupying *any* auto or if struck by an auto while a pedestrian. The expenses must be incurred within three years of the date of the accident, and payments for any one person may not exceed the limit stated in the declarations. This is not a liability coverage; the benefits are payable regardless of liability.

There is no coverage if the injury occurs in the course of employment and is covered under workers compensation. War, nuclear radiation, and radioactive contamination are excluded.

The medical payments limit applies separately to each person, so the insurer may pay several times the limit if several persons are injured.

Personal Injury Protection and Added Personal Injury Protection

If the insured is subject to a no-fault auto law, the required **personal injury protection (PIP)** coverage can be added to the policy by endorsement. Because benefit levels and other features of no-fault laws vary from state to state, a separate PIP endorsement exists for each no-fault state. In some no-fault states, benefit levels can be increased above the minimum required levels by using an *added personal injury protection endorsement*.

The benefits provided by a typical PIP endorsement consist of the following:

1. Medical and rehabilitation expenses
2. Income loss benefit
3. Substitute services benefit
4. Death benefits to survivors

The substitute services benefit pays the cost of purchased services that would have been performed by the injured person if the injury had not occurred. An example is the cost of a housekeeper to do the work usually performed by an injured person.

The limits of the coverage are specified in the applicable state law and are also usually included in the coverage endorsement. The exclusions applicable to the coverage vary with state law.

Property Protection Insurance—Michigan Only

The Michigan no-fault auto insurance law, unlike the laws of other states, applies to property damage as well as bodily injury. The property protection insurance endorsement, available only in Michigan, provides the coverage required by law.

Uninsured Motorists Insurance

Uninsured motorists coverage is a cross between no-fault insurance and liability insurance. It resembles no-fault insurance in that the benefits are paid to the injured person by his or her own insurer. It resembles liability insurance in that no benefits are paid unless the injuries were caused by an uninsured motorist under circumstances that would make the uninsured motorist liable for the injuries. If these conditions are met, the uninsured motorists coverage pays the injured person the amount, subject to policy limits, that the uninsured motorist's liability insurance would have paid if he or she had been insured.

In most states, uninsured motorists coverage is applicable only to bodily injury. In some states, uninsured motorists coverage can be extended to cover property damage as well.

The uninsured motorists insurance covers any person injured by an uninsured motorist while riding in an auto insured under the policy for uninsured motorists coverage. In addition, if the named insured is an individual proprietorship, the policy covers the named insured and members of his or her family while riding in any auto or if struck by an uninsured motorist while a pedestrian. "Uninsured motorist" is defined in the policy to include the following:

1. A driver of a vehicle for which no liability insurance is provided at the time of the accident
2. A driver of a vehicle for which liability insurance is provided, but with limits less than those required by state law
3. A hit-and-run driver

A driver of a governmental vehicle or a vehicle owned by a person or an organization that has qualified as a self-insurer under state law is *not* an uninsured motorist for purposes of this coverage.

An insured can also purchase *underinsured motorists coverage*. Although the details of coverage differ from state to state, the basic purpose of underinsured motorists coverage is to cover injuries caused by motorists who have liability insurance but for an amount less than the insured's limit for underinsured motorists coverage. In some states, underinsured motorists coverage is included in uninsured motorists coverage and does not need to be purchased separately.

Garage Coverage Form

Businesses engaged in selling, servicing, storing, or parking autos have special insurance needs. The **garage coverage form** has been designed to meet those needs. A garage coverage part consists of the garage coverage form, any applicable endorsements, and garage declarations. If the named insured is an auto dealer, a dealers supplementary schedule is attached as well. The garage coverage form contains six sections:

- Section I—Covered Autos
- Section II—Liability Coverage
- Section III—Garagekeepers Coverage
- Section IV—Physical Damage Coverage
- Section V—Garage Conditions
- Section VI—Definitions

Section I—Covered Autos

This section parallels Section I of the business auto coverage form. The symbols for use with the garage form range from 21 through 31.

- Symbols 21 through 29 correspond in most respects to business auto symbols 1 through 9.

- Symbol 30 is used for providing garagekeepers coverage on customers' autos left with the named insured for service, repair, storage, or safekeeping.
- Symbol 31 covers dealers' autos and autos held for sale by nondealers or trailer dealers.

Section II—Liability Coverage

The insurer agrees to pay "all sums the insured legally must pay as damages because of bodily injury or property damage . . . caused by an accident and resulting from *garage operations*." The policy definition of garage operations is as follows:

> The ownership, maintenance or use of locations for garage business and that portion of the roads or other accesses that adjoin these locations. "Garage operations" includes the ownership, maintenance, and use of the autos indicated in Section I of this coverage form as covered "autos." "Garage operations" also includes all operations necessary or incidental to a garage business.

This broad insuring agreement provides bodily injury and property damage liability coverage comparable to that provided by the CGL form (occurrence version) and the business auto coverage form. The insurer also agrees, as in the business auto form, to pay "covered pollution cost or expense" subject to the same limitations in the business auto form.

Despite these similarities to CGL and business auto coverage, garage liability coverage contains some provisions that differ from those of the CGL and business auto coverage forms.

Garage liability coverage is restricted to liability arising out of "garage operations." If the insured opens a new business that is neither a garage nor incidental to the existing garage business, it will not be covered by garage liability coverage. A CGL coverage form, in contrast, automatically covers any additional type of business that the insured may enter into during the policy period.

Garage liability coverage for products is virtually identical to that provided under the CGL coverage form, provided the product was made or sold in a garage business. By endorsement, the named insured can purchase *broad form products coverage*, which eliminates the exclusion of property damage to the named insured's products, subject to a $250 deductible.

Garage liability coverage provides completed operations insurance subject to a $100 deductible. For example, assume that during an oil change, the oil filter is improperly installed, allowing oil to drain from the engine and resulting in engine damage. Costs to repair the engine will be covered subject to a deductible of $100.

Regarding auto liability coverage, the garage liability section contains an exclusion that is not found in the business auto form. The exclusion eliminates liability coverage for any covered auto while leased or rented to others. However, the exclusion does not apply to—and thus there is coverage for—a covered auto the named insured rents to a customer whose auto is being serviced or repaired by the named insured. If the named insured wants liability coverage on autos it rents to other persons, coverage can be arranged by endorsement.

Customers of the named insured qualify as insureds for auto liability coverage only if the named insured's business is an auto dealership. However, a customer who has no other available insurance can only recover the limit required by the state's financial responsibility law, even if that is less than the garage liability limit. For an additional premium, customers can be covered for the full limit of insurance.

Garage liability coverage does not provide the following coverages contained in the CGL coverage form: personal injury, advertising injury, host liquor, fire damage, incidental medical malpractice, and nonowned watercraft. However, these coverages can be added as a package to garage liability coverage by the *broadened coverage—garages endorsement*.

Coverage for garage operations *other than auto* is subject to an annual aggregate limit. An "each accident" limit applies to both auto claims and other-than-auto claims.

Section III—Garagekeepers Coverage

Garagekeepers insurance covers the insured's liability for damage by a covered cause of loss to autos left in the insured's care while the insured is attending, servicing, repairing, parking, or storing the autos in the garage operation. Garagekeepers coverage is desirable because liability for such damage is excluded under the garage liability section by the care, custody, or control exclusion. The causes of loss that may be insured against are collision, comprehensive, and specified causes of loss. The specified causes of loss are fire, explosion, theft, and mischief or vandalism. Like other types of liability insurance, garagekeepers coverage also pays the cost of defending the insured against suits alleging covered losses.

For an additional premium, garagekeepers coverage can be modified by a "direct coverage" endorsement to pay for losses to customers' cars without the usual requirement that the insured be legally liable. This is sometimes referred to as "goodwill" coverage because it can preserve good customer relations when a customer expects to be paid for a loss even though the garage is not legally obligated to do so.

Some restaurants, hospitals, or other organizations have incidental valet parking operations that pose the same loss exposure faced by garages. Although these types of organizations are not eligible for the garage coverage form, they can obtain coverage under a separate form that provides garagekeepers coverage only.

Section IV—Physical Damage Coverage

Garage physical damage insurance provides the collision, comprehensive, and specified causes-of-loss coverages available under the business auto coverage form. Towing coverage is provided only for nondealers. In most ways, garage physical damage insurance is subject to the same provisions as business auto physical damage insurance. Notable differences are described below.

Dealers' Autos

Autos held for sale by a dealer are not listed individually in the policy but are insured in the aggregate. A designation on the auto dealers' supplementary schedule indicates both the type of auto (new, used, demonstrator) and the interests covered (owned, financed, consignment, and so forth). A reporting form, which requires the dealer to report the value of such vehicles either monthly or quarterly, is available for dealerships when the value of such vehicles on hand fluctuates widely from month to month. Under a reporting form, the annual premium is calculated on the basis of the insured's reports of values.

Exclusions

Garage physical damage insurance contains several exclusions that are not found in the business auto coverage form.

The false pretense exclusion eliminates coverage for loss to a covered auto resulting from someone's causing the named insured to *voluntarily* part with the auto by trick, scheme, or other false pretense. The exclusion also eliminates coverage for an auto the insured has acquired from a seller who did not have legal title. If, for example, the rightful owner repossesses the auto, the insured cannot recover for the loss under garage physical damage insurance. Coverage for false pretense losses can be arranged by adding the *false pretense coverage endorsement* for an additional premium.

Another exclusion eliminates collision coverage for any covered auto while being driven or transported from the point of purchase or distribution to its destination if such points are more than fifty road miles apart. Because the "driveaway" exposure can be significant, insurers do not want to cover it without being able to assess the risk and charge an appropriate additional premium. The coverage is added by attaching the *dealers driveaway collision coverage endorsement*.

Other exclusions eliminate coverage for the named insured's expected profit and for loss to any auto stored at a location not shown in the declarations if the loss occurs more than forty-five days after the named insured begins using the location.

Section V—Garage Conditions

The general conditions of the garage coverage form are virtually identical to those of the business auto coverage form.

Section VI—Definitions

The garage form includes all of the definitions included in the business auto coverage form except the definitions of "auto" and "mobile equipment." "Mobile equipment" is not defined in the garage coverage form because that term is not used in the policy. "Auto" is defined, but the definition differs substantially from that in the business auto coverage form. The garage coverage form defines "auto" as a "land motor vehicle, trailer or semitrailer." This definition includes all of the equipment included within the definition of "mobile equipment" in the business auto coverage form. Consequently, such equipment is covered under the garage form if it is used in operations necessary or incidental to garage operations.

Motor Carrier Coverage Form

ISO has developed two forms for insuring firms that use trucks to transport property of others. The truckers coverage form was introduced in the late 1970s for insuring the auto exposures of any person or organization in the business of transporting goods, materials, or commodities for others.

Because of the deregulation of the trucking industry since the truckers form was introduced, the truckers form is no longer as useful as it once was. Accordingly, ISO introduced the **motor carrier coverage form** in 1994 to serve as a more flexible alternative to the truckers coverage form. Because the truckers form may eventually be withdrawn, the discussion that follows focuses on the motor carrier coverage form. (In most respects, the truckers form and the motor carrier form are very similar.)

Eligibility

Under ISO *Commercial Lines Manual* rules, any "motor carrier" is generally eligible for the motor carrier form. The manual defines "motor carrier" to include any person or organization providing transportation by auto in the furtherance of a commercial enterprise. This definition is broad enough to encompass any of the three basic types of carriers:

1. Common carriers, who offer their transportation services indiscriminately to the general public
2. Contract carriers, who transport property only for those with whom they have chosen to enter into contracts of carriage
3. Private carriers, who transport their own property

The lines between these three types of carriers are often blurred. For example, a private carrier may occasionally operate as a common carrier or contract carrier in order to keep its trucks working to capacity. Thus, the broad definition of "motor carrier" allows the motor carrier form to be used for any organization that might need it.

Contrast With Business Auto Form

The motor carrier form is similar in most respects to the business auto coverage form but contains some provisions that address specific characteristics of the trucking business. These differences from the business auto form are described below.

Coverage for Owner-Operators

Motor carriers commonly hire independent contractors known as **owner-operators**. These owner-operators use their own trucks to haul property for the motor carriers that hire them. The terms of hire are spelled out in a lease, which may apply to a single trip, to several trips, or for a specified period. The motor carrier customarily provides liability insurance for owner-operators while they are operating under lease for the motor carrier.

Accordingly, the motor carrier coverage form provides insured status to the lessor of a covered auto that is leased to the named insured under a written lease agreement. However, the lessor (that is, the owner-operator) is an insured only while the auto is being used in the named insured's business as a motor carrier. In addition, the written agreement must not contain an agreement requiring the lessor to hold the named insured harmless.

The owner-operator's liability coverage under the motor carrier's insurance ends as soon as the owner-operator has completed his or her obligations under the lease. For example, the lease may only apply until a trailer load of goods is delivered in a distant city. While driving home or to another job, the owner-operator will not have liability insurance unless he or she has a separate policy.

An owner-operator's own coverage is often provided under a business auto policy that has been modified with the *truckers—insurance for non-trucking use endorsement*. This endorsement excludes liability coverage for the covered auto while it is used to carry property in any business or in the business of anyone to whom the auto is rented. Thus, the policy covers the owner-operator while he or she is not insured under a motor carrier's policy. This type of coverage is often called **bobtail and deadhead coverage**, because bobtailing (operating a power unit without a trailer) and deadheading (operating with an empty trailer) are the most common situations in which an owner-operator is not covered under the motor carrier's policy.

Owner-operators may also need or want physical damage insurance, uninsured motorists insurance, personal injury protection, or medical payments coverage under their own auto policies.

Trailer Interchange Coverage

In addition to the use of owner-operators, another unique feature of the trucking business is the common use of trailer interchange agreements. A **trailer interchange agreement** is a contract under which a motor carrier agrees to swap trailers with another carrier. Normally, each carrier agrees to indemnify the other for any damage that occurs to the other's trailer while in the borrowing carrier's possession. Thus, trailer interchange agreements create liability exposures for the parties to these agreements.

A motor carrier can cover its liability for damage to trailers in its possession under written trailer interchange agreements by purchasing **trailer interchange coverage** under the motor carrier form. The insurer also agrees to defend the insured against claims or suits alleging covered damages. The provisions for trailer interchange coverage are contained in the motor carrier coverage form. These provisions can be activated by placing the appropriate coverage symbol (69) beside whichever of the following are desired:

- Trailer interchange comprehensive coverage
- Trailer interchange specified causes-of-loss coverage
- Trailer interchange collision coverage

Physical Damage Exclusion

Another difference between the business auto and motor carrier forms is that physical damage coverage under the motor carrier form excludes loss to a covered auto while in someone else's possession under a trailer interchange agreement. If the insured wants its own physical damage coverage to apply to its trailers while in another carrier's possession under a trailer interchange agreement, this exclusion can be eliminated by showing the appropriate coverage symbol (70) for physical damage insurance.

Rating Commercial Auto Insurance

Commercial autos can be rated using rules found in the automobile division of the ISO *Commercial Lines Manual*. Under these rules, the rating procedure to be used for a particular insured depends on which of five classification subsections the insured's autos fall into. Separate rating procedures apply to (1) trucks, tractors, and trailers, (2) private passenger vehicles, (3) public transportation vehicles, (4) garages, and (5) special types of vehicles. The procedures for trucks, tractors, and trailers and private passenger vehicles are described below.

Trucks, Tractors, and Trailers

A large part of the loss experience for any trucking operation depends directly on the area in which the insured's trucks are operated. The exposures faced by a local delivery truck are different from those encountered by a large tractor-semitrailer used for cross-country hauling. Except for light trucks (one of the truck weight classifications discussed below), any vehicle in the truck, tractor, or trailer category that is regularly operated over a route that takes it more than 200 miles from its principal garaging location must be zone rated to account for the different hazards facing local and long-distance driving.

Primary Factor

The first step in rating a vehicle (whether zone rated or not) is to determine the vehicle's *primary factor*. The primary factor depends on the vehicle's *size class*, its *business use*, and its *radius class*.

Size Class

There are four size classes for trucks (light, medium, heavy, and extra-heavy) determined by the vehicle's gross vehicle weight (GVW). GVW is the vehicle's maximum loaded weight specified by the manufacturer. In addition, there are two size classes for truck-tractors (heavy and extra-heavy) determined by the vehicle's gross combination weight (GCW). GCW is the maximum loaded weight for a truck-tractor and its semitrailer or trailer together.

Business Use

Business use for trucks, tractors, and trailers is categorized as service, retail, or commercial. Service use describes the use of vehicles to carry workers, equipment, supplies, and so forth to or from job sites at which the vehicle generally remains parked for most of the workday. Retail use principally involves pickup and delivery of property to or from individual households. Commercial use is the category into which vehicles are put if they do not qualify for the service or retail use categories.

Radius Class

Primary factors are also governed by the radius of the area within which the vehicle is operated—within 50 miles of the principal garaging location (local), between 51 and 200 miles (intermediate), and beyond 200 miles (long distance). **Zone rated vehicles** are medium and larger trucks in the long-distance class.

Premium Computation

After the primary factor has been determined, premium computation methods differ depending on whether the vehicle is zone rated or not.

Non-Zone Rated Vehicles

A truck, tractor, or trailer is not zone rated if it is a light truck operating over any distance or a larger truck operating predominantly within 200 miles of its principal garaging location. When a commercial auto is not zone rated, the primary factor (already discussed) is added to a secondary factor associated with the nature of the insured's business operations. The sum of the primary factor and the secondary factor is called the combined factor.

Secondary factors correspond to a number of industry classifications. Depending on the degree of hazard that is characteristic of the particular industry, these factors either increase or decrease the primary factor.

The base premiums for liability and physical damage coverage are multiplied by the combined factor. Base *liability* premiums are determined on the basis of the policy limit and the territory in which the auto is principally garaged. Base *physical damage* premiums are determined on the basis of the vehicle's age and its cost new.

Zone Rated Vehicles

After the primary factor has been determined for a zone rated vehicle, its physical damage and liability premiums are calculated by applying the primary factor to base premiums. Secondary factors are not used for zone rated autos.

Base premiums for zone rated autos are affected by the various geographical zones in which the vehicles are operated, since liability and collision losses are much more likely in metropolitan areas than on the open road. Moreover, the probability of some comprehensive physical damage losses, such as theft or windstorm, varies from one region of the country to another. Base physical damage premiums also depend on the vehicle's cost new, the current age of the vehicle, the type of vehicle (with respect to collision coverage), and the chosen deductible.

Private Passenger Vehicles

Premiums for private passenger autos insured under a business auto coverage form are obtained directly from private passenger premium tables. Liability premium tables list premiums by rating territory and policy limit. Physical damage tables list comprehensive and collision premiums by rating territory, original cost new of the vehicle, and deductible amount chosen. These premiums are not multiplied by rating factors.

Summary

The business auto coverage form, garage coverage form, and motor carrier coverage form are available to cover loss exposures that are excluded under commercial property and commercial general liability coverage forms.

Auto property loss exposures exist for any organization that owns one or more autos. Physical damage to or loss of an auto from many different causes of loss can reduce the auto's value or reduce business income until the vehicle can be repaired or replaced.

The auto liability exposure is the possibility that the organization may have to defend itself against, and perhaps pay damages as a result of, suits alleging negligent ownership, maintenance, or use of autos. Liability can arise from owned autos, hired or borrowed autos, or employees' autos operated on behalf of the organization. In addition, one organization may assume by contract the auto liability of another organization. Some auto businesses, such as dealers and repair shops, have a bailee liability exposure for customers' autos.

The business auto coverage form, together with business auto declarations and any applicable endorsements, can be included in a commercial package policy or issued in a monoline policy. The business auto coverage form contains five sections.

Section I contains nine descriptions of covered auto symbols. These symbols are entered in a schedule in the declarations to indicate which autos are covered for each coverage selected.

Section II contains the provisions for auto liability insurance, including an insuring agreement, a definition of who is an insured, supplementary payments, out-of-state extensions, exclusions, and a limit of insurance clause.

Section III contains four optional insuring agreements for auto physical damage insurance: collision, comprehensive, specified causes of loss, and towing. Other provisions of Section III include a coverage extension for loss of use following theft of a covered auto, exclusions, a limit of insurance clause, and a deductible clause.

Section IV contains business auto conditions, and Section V contains policy definitions. Among the coverages that can be added by endorsement are personal injury protection, added personal injury protection, auto medical payments, uninsured motorists, and rental reimbursement.

Because the auto exposures of a garage are difficult to separate from its general liability exposures, the garage coverage form combines auto liability and commercial general liability coverage. Garage physical damage coverage can be extended to cover an auto dealer's inventory of autos on a reporting basis.

The garage coverage form also includes optional provisions for garagekeepers insurance, which covers damage to customers' autos in the insured's care, custody, or control. Garagekeepers insurance applies on a legal liability basis unless the insured pays an extra premium for direct ("goodwill") coverage.

The motor carrier coverage form resembles business auto coverage in most ways. However, because of frequent leasing arrangements within the trucking industry, the motor carrier form provides coverage for the owner-operators who lease their trucks to the named insured. The motor carrier form also includes provisions for trailer interchange insurance, which covers the insured's liability for damage to trailers of others while in the insured's care, custody, or control.

An owner-operator who hauls under lease with a trucker can cover its liability for "deadheading" or "bobtailing" by purchasing a business auto policy with the "insurance for non-trucking use" endorsement.

The methodology for rating trucks, tractors, and trailers depends on whether the vehicle must be zone rated or not. A vehicle is zone rated if it is a "medium" or "large" truck operating more than 200 miles from its principal garaging location. The premiums for zone rated vehicles reflect the various zones in which they are operated.

Chapter 11

The Businessowners Policy

The **businessowners policy (BOP)** is a property and liability insurance package designed for small to medium-sized businesses. Although the BOP does not have the potential breadth of various coverages available under the commercial package policy (CPP) program, it is broad enough to meet the property and liability insurance needs of many businesses eligible for the BOP.

Because it is easy to use, the BOP is usually preferred over the CPP by insurers and producers for insureds that qualify. Insureds also prefer the BOP, since it is frequently substantially less expensive than a CPP with comparable coverages. The BOP has become the dominant policy in the small business market.

The forms and rules described in this chapter are primarily those filed by Insurance Services Office (ISO) on behalf of its member insurance companies. Although these forms and rules are widely used, a considerable number of insurers use independently filed businessowners programs that differ from the ISO businessowners program in terms of coverage and eligibility rules.

Eligibility for BOP

Eligibility rules for the ISO businessowners program are contained in the multiple line division of the ISO *Commercial Lines Manual*. Subject to size criteria, apartment buildings, office buildings, and various types of occupancies are eligible for the BOP.

Apartment Buildings and Office Buildings

Apartment buildings and office buildings, including residential condominium associations, are eligible for businessowners coverage. An apartment building must contain no more than sixty units, and an office building must not exceed 100,000 square feet in total floor area. An eligible building may contain certain incidental occupancies (such as apartments in part of an office building) that do not exceed 15,000 square feet in total.

Other Buildings

In addition to apartment buildings and office buildings, buildings with the following occupancies are also eligible for the BOP:

- Mercantile occupancies (essentially, retailers)
- Specified types of wholesaler occupancies
- Specified types of service and processing occupancies

Because the lists of eligible wholesalers and service and processing risks are long, they are not included here. However, some notable examples of occupancies that are *not* eligible for the BOP are contractors, auto dealers and repair shops, and bars, grills, and restaurants.

Size limitations apply to mercantile occupancies and eligible wholesalers, service businesses, and processing occupancies. Total floor area in an eligible building cannot exceed 15,000 square feet, and annual gross sales cannot exceed $2 million. Incidental storage space of up to 15,000 square feet in an additional building is permitted.

Personal Property

Personal property eligible for the BOP includes the following:

- Building owners' personal property in eligible apartment buildings
- Personal property in offices that do not occupy more than 15,000 square feet in any one building
- Personal property in mercantile, service, or processing operations that do not exceed 15,000 square feet and $2 million in annual gross sales at any insured location, including separate incidental storage facilities not exceeding 15,000 square feet
- Personal property in condominium units used for eligible wholesaler, mercantile, service, processing, or office occupancies

Ineligible Risks

The *Commercial Lines Manual* specifically excludes the following from BOP eligibility:

- Automobile businesses, such as garages, auto dealers, and parking lots
- Bars, grills, and restaurants
- Condominium associations other than office or residential condominiums
- Contractors
- Places of amusement
- Banks and similar financial institutions

ISO Filing Broader Businessowners Eligibility Rules

When this text went to press in early 1996, ISO was in the process of filing new, broader eligibility criteria for its BOP program. The proposed effective date for these changes was January 1, 1997. In those states in which the new filing is approved, eligibility for the ISO businessowners program will be expanded in the following ways:

- The maximum area for mercantile, service, office, and wholesale risks will be increased from 15,000 square feet to 25,000 square feet.
- The gross sales limit for existing eligible classes will be increased from $2 million to $3 million.
- The following new classes of eligible risks will be added:

Contractors

- Risks up to 25,000 square feet in area
- Gross sales limit of $3 million

Restaurants

- Limited to specified classes
- Limited to specified classes of limited cooking and fast-food restaurants
- Gross sales limit of $1 million

Convenience Stores With Gasoline Pumping

- Risks up to 25,000 square feet
- Gross sales limit of $3 million
- Gasoline sales not exceeding 50 percent of gross sales

Laundries and Dry Cleaners

- Risks up to 25,000 square feet
- Gross sales limit of $3 million

Eligibility for Independently Developed BOPs

Many insurers offer independently developed BOPs or have adopted policy forms filed by the American Association of Insurance Services (AAIS). Those insurers frequently use broader eligibility rules than those of ISO. The building height and size limits are often larger, and in some cases, no limits apply at all. Moreover, coverage is frequently available for classes of business ineligible for the ISO businessowners program. For example, the AAIS Artisans Program uses a businessowners-type policy tailored to meet the coverage needs of small contractors.

Overview of ISO Businessowners Policy Forms

The documents used to make up an ISO businessowners policy are as follows:

1. Policy declarations, containing the same types of information as included in the declarations for a commercial package policy (CPP)

2. Businessowners common policy conditions, containing various provisions drawn from the CPP common policy conditions, the commercial property conditions, and the commercial general liability (CGL) coverage form

3. Businessowners property coverage form, comparable in many respects to the building and personal property coverage form

4. Businessowners liability coverage form, which closely resembles the CGL coverage form

5. Endorsements, which meet various coverage needs

Businessowners Property Coverage

There are two versions of the businessowners property coverage form, designated "standard" and "special," which differ principally with respect to covered causes of loss. Each version of the form insures buildings, business personal property, business income, and extra expense. In addition, each version contains provisions for several optional coverages that can be activated by making appropriate entries on the businessowners declarations page.

In most respects, the BOP property coverages are similar to provisions of coverage forms discussed in earlier chapters of this text. For that reason, the following sections describe the BOP standard and special forms in terms of their *differences* from the comparable commercial property coverage forms.

Thus, the material in this chapter assumes an understanding of previous course material.

Covered Property

The description of covered building property and business personal property in the BOP property forms is only slightly different from that in the building and personal property coverage form.

Covered building property in the BOP includes the named insured's personal property in apartments or rooms furnished by the named insured as landlord, which is not included under building coverage in the building and personal property coverage form. For example, an apartment building owner with no personal property to insure other than apartment furnishings can cover building and furnishings for a single amount of building insurance. In the building and personal property form, landlords' personal property in furnished units is insurable as business personal property only.

The principal difference between the BOP and the building and personal property coverage form with respect to covered personal property is that the BOP automatically includes legal liability for personal property of others under the same limit that applies to business personal property owned by the named insured. In the building and personal property coverage form, coverage must be specifically included in order for property of others to be covered, and it is full coverage, not just legal liability coverage.

Property Not Covered

The list of property not covered by the BOP is considerably shorter than the comparable list of property not covered in the building and personal property coverage form. For example, the following are *not* excluded under the BOP:

1. Animals
2. Cost of excavations
3. Underground pipes
4. Foundations below the lowest floor
5. Retaining walls
6. Wharves or docks

Covered Causes of Loss

The **BOP standard property coverage form** covers the same causes of loss as the causes of loss—basic form (fire, lightning, explosion, windstorm, hail, smoke, aircraft, vehicles, riot, civil commotion, vandalism, sprinkler leakage, sinkhole collapse, and volcanic action). In addition, the BOP standard form covers **transportation**, which is defined to mean loss to covered property caused by any of the following:

1.   Collision, derailment, or overturn of a vehicle

2.   Stranding or sinking of vessels

3.   Collapse of bridges, culverts, piers, wharves, or docks

The **BOP special property coverage form** covers against risks of direct physical loss unless the loss is subject to policy exclusions and limitations. This is the same coverage approach provided by the causes of loss—special form. However, the BOP special form is potentially broader in that it does not contain certain restrictions present in the special causes-of-loss form, such as the following:

1.   The exclusion of damage to the interior of any building or structure caused by or resulting from rain, snow, sleet, ice, sand, or dust, unless the building or structure first sustains damage by a covered cause of loss to its roof or walls through which the rain (etc.) enters. For example, the BOP special form covers water damage that results from rain entering the building through an open window or door.

2.   The exclusion of theft of building materials and supplies not attached as part of the building or structure.

3.   The exclusion of damage to gutters and downspouts caused by or resulting from the weight of snow, ice, or sleet.

Additional Coverages

The BOP provides several additional coverages. Four of the BOP additional coverages, listed below, are the same as those provided by the building and personal property coverage form (see Chapter 2 for details).

*   Debris removal

*   Preservation of property

*   Fire department service charge

*   Pollutant cleanup and removal

The BOP special property form also provides the following additional coverages, which are the same as those provided under the causes of loss—special form, as described in Chapter 3.

*   Collapse

*   Water damage, other liquids, powder, or molten material damage

The BOP forms provide some further additional coverages, as described below.

Business Income, Extra Expense, and Civil Authority

Three of the BOP additional coverages provide insurance similar to the separate business income (and extra expense) coverage (BIC) form discussed in Chapter 4, with a few differences that could be significant for some insureds.

First, business income and extra expense coverage under the BOP is not subject to coinsurance, monthly limitation, or even a total dollar limit. However, the BOP applies two limitations that are not present in the BIC form:

1. Under the BOP, business income loss and extra expenses are payable for only twelve consecutive months following the occurrence of the direct physical damage.
2. The BOP covers ordinary payroll expense for only sixty days after the occurrence of the direct physical damage.

"Ordinary payroll" is defined in the BOP as the payroll of all employees other than officers, executives, department managers, and employees under contract. Coverage can be provided for payroll of other classifications or specific employees by listing them in the declarations. Any other employee can be included subject to rates set by the insurer. For a firm with specialized employees who would be hard to replace, such as a skilled designer or a highly successful salesperson, full payroll coverage could be important.

Like the business income coverage form, BOP business income coverage does not cover loss during the first seventy-two hours following the occurrence of physical damage. ISO rules do not allow the insured to reduce this time deductible by paying an additional premium. However, the seventy-two-hour limitation does not apply to extra expense coverage.

Although the 1995 edition of the BOP includes "extended business income" coverage identical to that provided by the BIC form, other business income coverage enhancements are not available in the BOP. For example, the BOP has no provision for business income losses involving the following:

1. Dependent properties
2. Delay caused by compliance with building ordinances or laws
3. Loss of utility services

The BOP civil authority coverage is the same as that provided by the BIC form.

Crime Coverages

The 1995 BOP revision added the following additional coverages:

*   Forgery and alteration ($2,500 limit)
*   Money orders and counterfeit paper currency ($1,000 limit)

These additional coverages provide essentially the same protection as crime coverage forms B and R, described in Chapter 5.

Coverage Extensions

Businessowners property coverage, like the building and personal property coverage form, provides for certain coverage extensions. Apart from the few differences described below, the BOP extensions are the same as those of the building and personal property coverage form.

The BOP extension for newly acquired premises applies only to personal property at those premises, with a limit of $10,000 at each location. The comparable extension in the building and personal property form applies to both newly acquired buildings (not to exceed $250,000) and personal property at newly acquired locations (not to exceed $100,000 per building).

The personal property off-premises extension in the BOP is limited to $5,000, as opposed to a $10,000 limit for the property off-premises extension in the building and personal property coverage form. However, the BOP extension is broader in that it applies to property while it is in the course of transit or temporarily at premises not owned, leased, or operated by the named insured. The comparable extension in the building and personal property form does not cover property in or on a vehicle, in the care of the insured's salespersons, or at a fair or exhibition. These limitations are not present in the BOP version.

Limits of Insurance

Businessowners property coverage differs in one important way from the limits of insurance provision in the building and personal property coverage form. The BOP contains a **seasonal increase provision**, which automatically increases the limit of insurance for business personal property by 25 percent if actual values exceed the limit of insurance. However, the increase applies only if the limit of insurance shown in the declarations is at least 100 percent of the insured's average monthly values during the twelve months immediately preceding the loss. The seasonal increase provision might be needed, for example, by a store that experiences a property loss when its inventory is at a higher-than-normal level during the holiday shopping season.

The BOP limits of insurance clause also includes the building "inflation guard" provision that is an optional coverage under the building and personal property coverage form. Under either form, a percentage must be entered in the declarations to activate the inflation guard feature.

Loss Conditions

The businessowners property loss conditions are comparable in most respects to the loss conditions of the building and personal property form. These conditions relate to abandonment, appraisal, duties in the event of loss, recovered property, loss payment, and so on.

A significant difference between the two forms concerns insurance-to-value provisions. The building and personal property coverage form is subject to a coinsurance clause, as explained in Chapter 2. Originally, the ISO businessowners policy had no coinsurance clause or other insurance-to-value provision. However, ISO added an 80 percent insurance-to-value requirement to its businessowners property forms in the 1995 BOP revision. The 80 percent insurance-to-value provision is intended to work as follows:

- If the limit of insurance on lost or damaged property is 80 percent or more of the full replacement cost of the covered property, the insurer will pay the loss on a full replacement cost basis, subject to the limit of insurance.

- If the limit of insurance is *less* than 80 percent of the covered property's replacement cost, the insurer will pay an amount that is less than full replacement cost, in accordance with the terms of the insurance-to-value provision. In no event, however, will the insurer pay less than the actual cash value of the lost or damaged property, subject to the policy limit.

Apart from the 80 percent insurance-to-value provision, the replacement cost coverage in the BOP is comparable to the optional replacement cost coverage under the building and personal property coverage form. Even when replacement cost coverage applies, the BOP covers the following types of property for actual cash value:

- Used or secondhand merchandise held in storage or for sale
- Property of others
- Household contents, other than landlords' furnishings
- Manuscripts
- Works of art, antiques, or rare articles

Deductibles

Under ISO rules, a basic deductible of $250 applies to all businessowners property coverages other than the additional coverages for business income, extra expense, civil authority, and fire department service charges. The $250 deductible also applies to all of the optional coverages described below.

Optional deductibles of $500, $1,000, and $2,500 are also available. However, even if one of these higher deductibles is chosen, it does not apply to any of the BOP optional coverages except breakdown coverage. The maximum deductible that applies to all other optional coverages is $250.

A windstorm and hail percentage deductible is also available. The deductible can be set at 1 percent, 2 percent, or 5 percent of the limit of insurance applicable to the loss.

Optional Coverages

Each of the businessowners property coverage forms contains provisions for six optional coverages. Any or all of these coverages can be activated by making appropriate entries on the businessowners declarations page. The insured must pay an additional premium for each optional coverage that is activated. The optional coverages are as follows:

1. Outdoor signs
2. Exterior glass
3. Interior glass
4. Employee dishonesty
5. Mechanical breakdown
6. Burglary and robbery (BOP standard form only)
    Money and securities (BOP special form only)

Outdoor Signs

When no optional coverages apply, the BOP covers outdoor signs not attached to the building against only five named perils (fire, lightning, explosion, riot or civil commotion, and aircraft). Moreover, coverage on any outdoor sign (whether attached to a building or not) is limited to $1,000. The **outdoor signs optional coverage** allows an insured to purchase a larger amount of insurance on outdoor signs. The coverage is on an "all-risks" basis subject to very few exclusions.

Exterior Glass

The BOP *standard* property coverage form covers glass breakage only if it is caused by a covered cause of loss (other than vandalism). The BOP *special* property form covers glass breakage by those same specified causes of loss. In addition, the special form covers glass breakage resulting from any other unexcluded causes of loss (including vandalism), but when glass breakage results from such causes, the insured can recover no more than $100 per pane or plate and $500 per occurrence.

The **exterior glass optional coverage** allows an insured to purchase "all-risks" coverage, without the dollar limitations of the BOP special form, on all exterior glass at the described premises, including lettering and ornamentation. The insured has the option to cover only "exterior grade floor glass" or to cover "exterior glass, all floors."

- "Exterior grade floor glass" refers to glass at the ground level ("grade floor") or basement that is part of the exterior of the building.
- "Exterior glass, all floors" refers to glass at all levels that is part of the exterior of the building.

Interior Glass

The **interior glass optional coverage** applies to all items of glass that are permanently affixed to the interior walls, floor, or ceilings of the covered building. As with exterior glass, the insured may cover (1) glass located in the basement and ground-floor levels only or (2) all interior glass. Interior glass coverage does not apply to ornamentation or lettering. Otherwise, the coverage and exclusions are similar to those applicable to exterior glass.

Employee Dishonesty

Employee dishonesty is not a named peril under the BOP standard form and is excluded under the BOP special form. When the **employee dishonesty optional coverage** is purchased, the insured is covered for direct loss or damage to business personal property, including money and securities, that results from dishonest acts of any of the insured's employees, whether acting alone or in collusion with others (except the named insured or his or her partners). The coverage is essentially the same as that provided by Form A (blanket) of the commercial crime program, as described in Chapter 5.

Mechanical Breakdown

The BOP, like the commercial property causes-of-loss forms, excludes loss caused by electrical breakdown, mechanical breakdown, or explosion of steam boilers or steam pipes. An insured with a CPP can insure against the excluded perils by purchasing a boiler and machinery coverage part. A BOP insured can purchase comparable coverage under the **mechanical breakdown optional coverage**.

The BOP mechanical breakdown coverage is similar to what is provided by the boiler and machinery coverage form, covering direct damage to covered buildings and personal property caused by an accident to an insured object. However, the types of objects insured under the mechanical breakdown option are limited to the following:

- Boiler and pressure vessels used for maintenance or service of the insured premises but not for processing or manufacturing

- Air conditioning units with a capacity of 60,000 Btu (British thermal units) or more

The boiler and machinery coverage form can be used to insure a much broader variety of objects.

Burglary and Robbery

The **burglary and robbery optional coverage** under the BOP standard form provides coverage like that provided by crime forms D, E, and Q, as described in Chapter 5. Personal property other than money and securities is covered for up to 25 percent of the limit applying to business personal property. The limits applicable to money and securities are shown on the businessowners declarations page.

Money and Securities

An insured with the BOP special form has no need for optional burglary and robbery coverage on personal property other than money and securities, since such coverage is included in the broad scope of the special covered causes of loss. However, even the special form excludes money and securities. Accordingly, the **money and securities optional coverage** allows the BOP insured to buy coverage like that provided under Form C of the crime program.

The optional coverage insures money and securities used in the insured's business against theft, disappearance, or destruction, subject to policy exclusions and limitations. The limits applicable to money and securities are shown on the declarations page. Separate limits apply inside and outside the premises.

Businessowners Property Endorsements

In addition to the optional coverages discussed above, other property coverages can be added to a BOP by endorsement. Some of the notable businessowners property endorsements are as follows:

- Computer coverage (standard or special form)
- Accounts receivable coverage
- Valuable papers and records coverage
- Earthquake and volcanic eruption coverage
- Condominium association coverage
- Condominium commercial unit-owners coverage
- Condominium commercial unit-owners optional coverages (loss assessments and miscellaneous real property)

Businessowners Liability Coverage

The **businessowners liability coverage form** is similar in most ways to the occurrence version of the commercial general liability (CGL) coverage form. The significant differences are described below.

Druggists Liability Included

Businessowners liability coverage is subject to a lengthy exclusion designed to eliminate coverage for bodily injury or property damage due to the rendering of or failure to render any professional service. (Professional liability will be discussed in Chapter 13.) However, there is a specific exception to the exclusion that allows professional liability coverage for an insured whose operations include those of a retail druggist or drugstore.

Limits of Insurance

In the BOP, the general aggregate limit is fixed at two times the applicable each occurrence limit, and the products-completed operations aggregate limit is fixed at the same amount as the each occurrence limit. Under the CGL form, both aggregate limits can be arranged at various multiples of the each occurrence limit.

In addition, payment of fire legal liability losses does not reduce the BOP aggregate limit. Under the CGL form, payment of fire legal liability losses reduces the general aggregate limit.

Hired and Nonowned Autos Coverage

Hired and nonowned autos liability coverage, like that provided through symbols 8 and 9 of the business auto coverage form, can be added to a businessowners policy by endorsement. For an insured without any owned automobiles, the availability of hired and nonowned autos coverage under the BOP eliminates the need to obtain separate business auto coverage.

Proposed 1997 Changes to the ISO Businessowners Policy

As noted earlier in this chapter, ISO filed changes to its businessowners program in 1996 for a proposed effective date of January 1, 1997. In addition to broadening businessowners eligibility requirements, the 1997 amendments would modify coverage in several ways. Some of the proposed changes are listed below.

1. The limit for newly acquired personal property is increased from $10,000 to $100,000 per location.

2. Accounts receivable coverage and valuable papers coverage are included, subject to a $5,000 limit. Higher limits are available by endorsement.

3. Coverage for increased cost of construction because of ordinance or law is included, subject to a limit of $5,000 or 5 percent of the building limit.

4. A provision allowing the insured to purchase optional dependent property business income coverage is added to the policy.

5. A provision is added that allows the insured to purchase optional coverage for loss caused by failure of utility service equipment.

6. The insured can purchase increased limits for forgery coverage.

7. An amendatory endorsement for eligible contractors adds $5,000 coverage for portable tools and $5,000 coverage for contractors' equipment.

8. The basic deductible on property coverage is increased to $500.

9. Professional liability endorsements are being offered for funeral directors, hearing aid stores, opticians, beauticians, barbers, printers, and small-animal veterinarians.

Non-ISO Businessowners Policies

Numerous insurers, including some with the largest volumes of businessowners insurance in force, do not use the ISO businessowners program. Many use forms that they have developed; others use the programs developed by the American Association of Insurance Services (AAIS). These other forms, although generally similar to ISO forms, may have a name other than "businessowners" and frequently differ from the ISO forms in ways that can be important in specific instances.

The broader eligibility rules for some non-ISO businessowners programs were discussed earlier in this chapter. In addition, many independent BOPs include coverages that are either optional or unavailable under the ISO businessowners program. Conversely, non-ISO businessowners policies sometimes contain provisions that are more restrictive than those of the ISO forms.

Because of these differences, policy forms should be carefully compared when one policy is being replaced with another—even if both policies are titled "businessowners." In one case, Company A's businessowners policy was replaced with Company B's. Until an employee dishonesty loss occurred, no one noticed that in Company B's policy, employee dishonesty was an optional coverage that had not been activated. The old policy covered employee dishonesty automatically.

Rating Businessowners Coverage

Rating a BOP is considerably less complicated than rating comparable coverages provided under a CPP. Under ISO rating procedures, businessowners building and personal property rates include "loadings" (built-in charges) for business income, extra expense, and liability coverage. Thus, the rater does not have to compute separate premiums for those coverages.

Some companies use a separate rating procedure for liability coverage, especially in the case of contractor insureds. Under the proposed 1997 ISO businessowners changes, liability coverage for eligible contractors is rated separately from the property coverages by applying a separate liability rate to the insured's payroll.

Businessowners policies are class rated; specific rates are not used. The rater ordinarily looks up the applicable building and personal property rates in simple rate tables that take into consideration the following variables:

1. Territory
2. Construction of the building
3. Public fire protection
4. Occupancy of the building
5. Whether the building is sprinklered or nonsprinklered

The listed rates are increased by appropriate factors if the policy uses the special property form or if the insured wants increased limits for liability insurance. If the insured has purchased optional coverages, the policy premium is increased, either by adding a flat premium for each optional coverage requested or by applying a rate to the insured values.

Summary

The businessowners policy is designed for small to medium-sized businesses. In its package approach and simplified rating procedures, it meets the needs of both insurers and policyholders.

The insured can choose from two businessowners property coverage forms: the standard form and the special form. Both forms cover buildings and business personal property on a replacement cost basis.

- The businessowners *standard* property coverage form covers the same perils as the commercial property causes of loss—basic form plus the additional peril of transportation.

- The businessowners *special* property coverage form covers on an "all-risks" basis like the commercial property causes of loss—special form, but without several restrictions present in the causes of loss—special form.

Both forms provide business income and extra expense coverage without any monetary limit; however, loss is only payable for up to one year after the date the physical damage occurred. Both forms also provide $2,500 forgery and alteration coverage and $1,000 money orders and counterfeit paper currency coverage.

A seasonal increase provision provides for an automatic 25 percent increase in the amount of insurance on business personal property if the applicable limit is at least equal to the monthly average of the insured's personal property values during the past year. Another provision automatically increases building coverage by a selected annual percentage.

Both businessowners property forms contain five optional coverages in common:

1. Outdoor signs
2. Exterior glass
3. Interior glass
4. Employee dishonesty
5. Mechanical breakdown

In addition, the standard form contains a burglary and robbery coverage option, and the special form contains a money and securities coverage option. By endorsement, coverage can be added for several other exposures.

The businessowners liability coverage form is similar in most respects to the occurrence version of the CGL coverage form.

Many insurers develop their own businessowners policies or use those of AAIS. These policies may provide either broader or narrower coverage than the ISO program. Thus, forms should be compared carefully when an insured is switching from one insurer's businessowners program to another's.

For most insureds, a single rate is used to calculate the premium for a businessowners policy. In the case of eligible contractors, some independent programs (and the proposed 1997 ISO program) rate the property and liability coverages separately. If the insured buys optional coverages, additional charges are added to the base premium.

Chapter 12

Workers Compensation and Employers Liability Insurance

Workers compensation and employers liability insurance responds to two basic loss exposures:

1. An employer's legal responsibility to pay required workers compensation benefits to employees
2. The possibility of an employee or some other person or organization making a liability claim against the employer for bodily injury to an employee

This chapter examines the common characteristics of workers compensation statutes, the provisions of the standard workers compensation and employers liability insurance policy, and the rating of workers compensation and employers liability insurance.

Workers Compensation Statutes

Before the enactment of workers compensation statutes, beginning with the Wisconsin statute in 1911, workers injured in industrial accidents could, under the common law, sue their employers for damages resulting from the injury. It was up to the employee to establish that the employer was at fault for the injury. The following defenses were usually offered by employers:

- The employee contributed to the accident.
- Risk of injury was assumed when the employee took the job.
- Fellow workers were responsible.

Successful lawsuits were few, and the majority of injured workers received nothing. Court delays placed a financial strain on families, and the system created antagonism between employers and employees.

Because of these problems, each of the United States (including several U.S. territories) and each of the Canadian provinces have enacted **workers compensation statutes**. These laws provide "no-fault" protection by removing the right of employees to sue their employers while obligating employers to compensate injured employees even if negligence is not involved. In return for definite payment, the employer's liability is limited (but not eliminated) by statute. The system has the effect of guaranteeing injured workers some payment while reducing costs and court workloads arising out of litigation.

Requirements for Benefits

Workers compensation statutes provide benefits for expenses and wage loss resulting from either occupational injury or occupational disease.

Although workers compensation laws originally had no specific provisions for occupational diseases (diseases thought to be caused by work or the work environment), the workers compensation laws of all states now include benefits for occupational diseases. Most occupational diseases become evident during employment or soon after the exposure to injurious conditions, although for some exposures the disease may be latent for a long time. Consequently, many states provide extended periods of time for the discovery of these slowly developing diseases. Although some states cover only occupational diseases that are specifically named in the law, the majority of states provide coverage for all occupational diseases.

Not all diseases contracted in the course of an occupation can be attributed to the work or occupational exposure. For example, the common cold is generally not a covered disease. In general, there must be a cause and effect relationship between the occupation and the disease.

To be covered under a workers compensation statute, an injury or disease must (in most states) arise out of *and* in the course of employment. In other words, the injury or disease must be causally related to the employment and occur while the employee is engaged in work-related activities. Generally, the employee is covered for any work-related injury sustained while the employee is at the place of employment or traveling for the employer. Injuries occurring while the employee is on his or her way to or from work at a fixed location are generally not covered.

Benefits Provided

A typical workers compensation statute imposes absolute liability on employers for the benefits provided under the statute. The intent is that an employee be at least partially compensated for expenses and loss of earnings incurred as a result of an occupational injury or disease. The benefits prescribed by the various state workers compensation laws generally include medical benefits, disability income benefits, rehabilitation benefits, and death benefits.

Medical Benefits

In most instances, the workers compensation law provides full and unlimited medical expense benefits for a covered injury or disease. These benefits include medical, hospital, surgical, and other related medical-care costs, including physical therapy and prosthetic devices.

Disability Income Benefits

Workers compensation statutes typically classify disabilities as follows:

- **Temporary partial disability**, meaning that the injured worker is unable to perform all duties of a job for a definite period of time, such as thirty or sixty days. After that period, the worker will be able to resume all job duties.

- **Temporary total disability**, meaning that the injured worker is unable to perform any job duties for a specific period of time but will ultimately recover and be able to resume all job duties.

- **Permanent partial disability**, meaning that the injured worker suffers an irreversible injury, such as the loss of sight in one eye. However, the worker will be able to resume some job functions.

- **Permanent total disability**, meaning that the worker suffers catastrophic injuries and will never be able to perform any job functions.

Disability income benefits are intended to compensate an injured employee for wage loss in any of the above categories. Unlike medical benefits, income benefits are payable subject to a deductible in the form of a waiting period. Disability benefits do not begin until the waiting period has expired. The waiting period varies from three to seven days, depending on the state. If disability continues beyond a specified number of days, most laws provide for payment of benefits retroactive to the date of injury.

The benefit is payable weekly and is expressed as a percentage of the employee's average weekly wage at the time of disability. In addition, maximum and minimum amounts that vary widely from state to state are placed on the weekly benefit.

State laws also require compensation for a specific number of weeks for the loss (or loss of use) of specific body parts such as fingers. These injuries are referred to as "scheduled" injuries because the injuries and corresponding benefits are listed in a document called a schedule. Scheduled injuries do not generally create permanent total disability, but the resulting permanent impairment is assumed to produce long-term loss of wages. As a result, the benefits for scheduled injuries are payable without regard to actual wage loss. In most states, the compensation for scheduled injuries is in addition to any other temporary disability benefits payable.

Rehabilitation Benefits

Rehabilitation of injured workers is a goal of the workers compensation system, and most state laws include some rehabilitation benefits. The primary rehabilitation benefit prescribed is the payment of expenses for complete medical treatment and medical rehabilitation. Vocational rehabilitation may also be required by law. Most workers compensation laws provide a mainte- nance allowance to injured workers during rehabilitation in addition to other compensation benefits. Many insurers provide rehabilitation services extend- ing beyond the requirements of the law. Often, rehabilitation can cut the cost of a workers compensation claim by shortening the length of time that the injured employee is disabled.

Death Benefits

Death benefits include a flat amount for burial expense and partial replace- ment of the worker's former weekly wage. The burial expense allowance varies among the states. The percentage of wage loss payable also varies by state and depends primarily on the number and types of dependents. Some states provide a maximum benefit expressed as either a total amount or time period.

Benefit Administration

Most states have a workers compensation board or industrial commission with responsibility for administering the workers compensation law. A few states employ the courts to administer claims instead of a specific administrative agency.

To initiate a claim, the injured worker notifies the employer of the injury. The employer submits the injury report to the insurer, which then transmits the report to the administrative agency. If the claim is not contested by the employer, it is usually settled by agreement. The injured employee and the employer's insurer agree on a settlement. The agreement must be in compli-

Second-Injury Funds

An injured worker who has sustained a partial yet permanent impairment that precludes returning to the prior job will frequently seek other types of employment—perhaps less strenuous or of a type that will enable the worker to use other skills he or she possesses. All too often the prospective employer is reluctant to hire an impaired or disabled worker, fearing the new job responsibilities will aggravate or otherwise magnify an already existing injury or occupational illness.

Second-injury funds have been established in most states to encourage employers to hire partially impaired workers and to encourage these workers to seek gainful employment. Should additional injury occur to an already impaired worker that results in a total or near total impairment, the applicable fund will pay a portion of the claim. Although the precise method of sharing the losses varies among the states, the basic idea is to limit the second employer's share of the loss to what would have been payable for the second injury if the first injury had not occurred.

For example, if an employee lost one eye in the first injury and the other eye in the second injury, total disability benefits would be payable after the second injury. However, the second employer would be required to pay only the benefit for the loss of one eye. The second-injury fund would pay the difference between the benefit for the loss of one eye and the benefit for permanent total disability.

This arrangement is attractive to employers, who do not want to be assessed, unfairly, for the amount of benefits payable for a total impairment. Usually, second-injury funds are established by assessing both workers compensation insurers and self-insurers in the particular state.

ance with the workers compensation law and is subject to review by the workers compensation agency. Some states use a direct payment system that does not require an agreement before benefits begin. Under this system, benefits are paid immediately, and the administrative agency reviews the amounts paid to determine compliance with the law.

If the claim is contested by the employer, most states require a hearing by an officer of the administrative agency. The decision of the hearing officer may be appealed to the workers compensation board or commission and then to the appropriate court.

Persons and Employments Covered

One objective of workers compensation statutes is that the number of employees subject to state workers compensation law should be as large as possible. However, for a variety of reasons, workers compensation laws do not cover all employments.

Workers compensation statutes apply to virtually all industrial workers and most other kinds of private employment. The statutes of some states exempt employers with fewer than a stipulated number of employees, and many statutes specifically exclude certain employments such as farm labor, domestic workers, and casual employees. (A casual employee is one hired for a short period only, usually to accomplish a particular task.)

Many states provide workers compensation protection for all or certain classes of public employees. However, some employees are excluded because alternate plans are provided for them. For example, federal statutes govern the rights of various classes of employees for recovery of benefits or damages from their employers for occupational injury or disease. Examples of such classes of employees are federal government workers, maritime workers, and interstate railroad workers.

Employee Status

Entitlement to benefits under a workers compensation law depends on whether a person qualifies as an employee according to the law. An **employee** is a person hired to perform services for another under the direction and control of the other party, called the employer.

Sometimes it is hard to determine whether an individual is an employee or an independent contractor. Unlike employees, **independent contractors** are not subject to direction and control regarding the details of the work. They agree to perform a task meeting the specifications stipulated in the contract but are free to use their own judgment and methods in performing the task. They may also employ others to perform the task, but they remain responsible under the contract for its completion.

Employment status is a question of fact, not of law. If doubt arises concerning whether an individual is an employee or an independent contractor, a court or an administrative body decides the issue on the basis of the facts. Courts have interpreted the definition of an employee broadly in workers compensation cases in order to provide legal protection to those who need it.

Out-of-State Application of Laws

When a worker is required to travel into another state and is injured in the other state, questions arise as to which workers compensation law applies. Most state laws have **extraterritorial provisions** dealing with this issue. The determination of which law applies depends on the provisions of the laws in question. Typical considerations include the following:

1. Place and nature of employment
2. The place where the employee was hired
3. The employee's place of residence
4. The state in which the employer is domiciled

The problem is complicated by different coverage and benefit provisions in the various states. For example, a truck driver might live in Massachusetts, work for a trucking firm in Texas, and drive through many states as part of the employment. According to the laws of about half of the states, if the driver is injured, a compensation claim conceivably could be filed in the state where the injury occurred, where the employment was principally located, or where the employee was hired. Because benefit levels vary from state to state, the employee, when permitted to choose which law will apply, can select the workers compensation law with the most generous benefits.

Federal Jurisdiction

As noted earlier, occupational injuries of most maritime workers, employees of interstate railroads, and certain other workers are under the jurisdiction of federal law. Federal jurisdiction over these workers' injuries arises either as a result of specific federal statutes or because the work location comes within the jurisdiction of admiralty (maritime) law.

The **United States Longshore and Harbor Workers' Compensation Act (LHWCA)** provides an exclusive remedy to injured maritime workers (workers engaged in longshoring or shipbuildling) subject to the act. Like state workers compensation statutes, the LHWCA eliminates the right of injured workers to sue their employers but prescribes compensation for work-related injuries without regard to fault. Congress has also extended the LHWCA to cover some government-related employment.

Officers and crew members of vessels are not covered by the LHWCA. However, they have various legal remedies they can pursue for job-related injuries. One of the remedies is provided by the United States Merchant Marine Act of 1920, more commonly known as the **Jones Act**, which permits an injured crew member (or his or her survivors, in the case of death) to sue the employer for damages resulting from the employer's negligence. Admiralty law, the branch of federal law that governs most maritime matters, provides additional remedies to injured crew members, including the following:

- A lawsuit against the employer for injury resulting from unseaworthiness of the vessel
- An injured crew member's right to "maintenance" (food and shelter) and "cure" (medical attention), regardless of whether the employer was at fault

Interstate railroad workers, like the officers and crew of vessels, can sue their employers for injuries resulting from employer negligence. This remedy is provided by the **Federal Employers' Liability Act.**

Methods for Meeting the Employer's Obligation

Most workers compensation statutes require employers to demonstrate financial ability to pay any claims that may arise. Possible methods of meeting this obligation include the following:

- Private insurance
- Insurance through assigned risk plans
- Insurance through state funds
- Qualified "self-insurance" plans
- Excess insurance

However, every state does not allow all of these methods.

Private Insurance

An employer can meet its workers compensation obligation by purchasing insurance from a private insurer licensed to write workers compensation coverage in the state. In return for the premium, the insurance company promises to pay the benefits and assume most administrative duties required by law for work-related injuries.

Assigned Risk Plans

Some businesses cannot obtain private insurance because they do not meet insurers' underwriting criteria. Because of the compulsory nature of workers compensation, a firm without insurance could be forced out of business because of the penalties imposed. For this reason, assigned risk plans exist to make insurance available. An employer rejected by private insurers can apply to the plan in the appropriate state to obtain coverage.

State Funds

In eighteen states, state funds provide workers compensation insurance. Territorial funds are in effect in Puerto Rico and the U.S. Virgin Islands. Although controlled by the state government, these state and territorial funds operate in essentially the same manner as private insurance companies. The most significant difference is that they accept any good faith applicant for insurance in the state, and no assigned risk plan is necessary. In most jurisdictions, the fund competes with private insurers. In a few other jurisdictions, only the state fund may provide workers compensation coverage.

Competitive State Funds

In twelve states, state funds sell workers compensation insurance in competition with private insurance companies and are thus called **competitive state funds**. An employer in these states can purchase insurance from either a private insurer or the state fund.

Monopolistic State Funds

Six states plus Puerto Rico and the U.S. Virgin Islands require all workers compensation insurance to be placed with the state or territorial fund. Because no private insurer is licensed to write workers compensation coverage in these jurisdictions, the state or territorial funds have no competition and are thus known as **monopolistic state funds**. Workers compensation coverage, but not necessarily employers liability coverage, is available from these funds.

Self-Insurance

Almost all states allow employers to retain the risk of workers compensation losses if they demonstrate the financial capacity to do so by meeting certain requirements.

To qualify as a "self-insurer," an employer must post a surety bond with the workers compensation administrative agency of the state to guarantee the security of benefit payments. In addition, most states require evidence of an ability to administer the benefit payments and services mandated by the law. Self-insurance is usually practical only for large employers.

Excess Insurance

An employer that qualifies for self-insurance may still decide to purchase excess insurance to cover catastrophic losses. Excess workers compensation insurance includes the following types:

1. Aggregate excess
2. Specific excess

Aggregate excess (also called "stop loss excess") requires the employer to retain a specific amount of loss from the first dollar during a specified period of time, usually one year. For example, if the insurance required a retention of $200,000, the employer would pay losses up to an aggregate amount of $200,000. The insurer would pay any losses above $200,000 up to some stated limit such as $1 million. The amounts of the retention and the insurer's maximum limit are negotiated.

Specific excess also requires a retention limit, but the limit is for one loss or all losses from one occurrence. If covered losses exceed the retained limit, the insurer would pay any additional losses up to policy limits. Examples of aggregate and specific excess insurance are shown in Exhibit 12-1.

Exhibit 12-1
Aggregate Excess Versus Specific Excess

Aggregate Excess Policy

$100,000 aggregate retention $1,000,000 maximum limit

Losses from separate occurrences	$ 25,000
	75,000
	90,000
	35,000
Total losses	$225,000
Aggregate retention	100,000
Excess insurance will pay	$125,000

Specific Excess Policy

$100,000 per occurrence retention $1,000,000 maximum limit

Losses from separate occurrences	$ 25,000
	75,000
	90,000
	35,000
	$225,000

Since none of the losses exceeds the $100,000 per occurrence retention, the insured must retain all losses.

The Workers Compensation and Employers Liability Policy

In the United States, workers compensation insurance is provided under a standard form known as the "workers compensation and employers liability insurance policy." This form is maintained and filed in most states by the National Council on Compensation Insurance, an organization that will be described in more detail later in this chapter in connection with workers compensation rating.

The **workers compensation and employers liability (WC&EL)** policy combines coverage for both of the following:

1. Obligations imposed by workers compensation statutes
2. Employee injury claims that are not covered by workers compensation statutes

The policy contains uniform provisions even though workers compensation benefits vary by state. It is possible to use the same policy in various states because the applicable workers compensation laws are incorporated by reference in the policy. Thus, the covered workers compensation benefits are not itemized in the policy. The benefits specified in the applicable statute govern the types and amounts of benefits payable by the insurer.

A complete WC&EL policy consists of the following documents:

1. Information page
2. Policy form
3. Endorsements (if any apply)

These documents are not designed to be included in the ISO commercial package policy format.

Information Page

The information page is equivalent to the declarations page of other policies. The WC&EL information page is divided into four major parts or items, as shown in Exhibit 12-2.

Item 1 gives essential information about the insured, including the insured's name and mailing address, the type of legal entity, and workplaces other than the insured's mailing address.

Item 2 shows the coverage period. Coverage begins and ends at 12:01 A.M. at the address of the insured given in item 1.

Exhibit 12-2
WC&EL Information Page

WORKERS COMPENSATION AND EMPLOYERS LIABILITY INSURANCE POLICY

INFORMATION PAGE

Insurer:

P O L I C Y   N O.

1. **The Insured:**   AMR Corporation   ___ Individual   ___ Partnership
   Mailing address: 2000 Industrial Highway   X Corporation or _____
                    Workingtown, PA 19000

   Other workplaces not shown above:

2. The policy period is from   10/1/96   to   10/1/97   at the insured's mailing address.

3. A. Workers Compensation Insurance: Part One of the policy applies to the Workers Compensation Law of the states listed here: PA

   B. Employers Liability Insurance: Part Two of the policy applies to work in each state listed in Item 3.A. The limits of our liability under Part Two are:

Bodily Injury by Accident	$ 100,000	each accident
Bodily Injury by Disease	$ 500,000	policy limit
Bodily Injury by Disease	$ 100,000	each employee

   C. Other States Insurance: Part Three of the policy applies to the states, if any, listed here:

   All except those listed in Item 3A and ME, NV, ND, OH, WA, WV, WY and OR

   D. This policy includes these endorsements and schedules:

   See Schedule

4. The premium for this policy will be determined by our Manuals of Rules, Classifications, Rates and Rating Plans. All information required below is subject to verification and change by audit.

Classifications	Code No.	Premium Basis Total estimated Annual Remuneration	Rate Per $100 of Remuneration	Estimated Annual Premium
Sheet Metal Shop	0454	300,000	11.53	34,590
Clerical Office	0953	275,000	.49	1,348
		Experience Modification of 1.382 Applied		13,728
		Estimated Premium Discount		(4,869)
		Total Estimated Annual Premium $		44,797

   Minimum Premium $ 1,273   **Expense Constant $**   140

   Countersigned by _____

WC 00 00 01 A
© 1987 National Council on Compensation Insurance.

Item 3 summarizes the coverage provided by the policy. Benefits required by the workers compensation law of the state or states listed in item 3(A) will be paid in the event of an injury to an employee. This space should normally list all states in which the insured has operations and the insurer is licensed to provide coverage. Item 3(B) shows the limits of liability under the employers liability coverage for bodily injury by accident and by disease. An entry in item 3(C) indicates that workers compensation coverage will be extended automatically to additional states if the insured expands operations. In addition, all endorsements and schedules attached to the policy at inception are listed on the information page or in a schedule attached to the policy.

The information necessary to calculate the estimated policy premium appears in item 4. It includes a description of the classification(s) (explained later) assigned to the insured's business. This description and the corresponding code number are taken from the appropriate workers compensation manual. Another column contains the insured's estimate of what the remuneration (payroll) will be for the period covered by the policy. The estimated payroll is shown beside each classification.

The next column shows the rate applicable to each classification. Usually the rate is expressed in dollars of premium per $100 of payroll. The last column shows the estimated premium determined by multiplying the estimated payroll by the rate for each classification.

Policy Form

The standard WC&EL policy form includes a general section and six parts, as follows:

- Part One—Workers Compensation Insurance
- Part Two—Employers Liability Insurance
- Part Three—Other States Insurance
- Part Four—Your Duties If Injury Occurs
- Part Five—Premium
- Part Six—Conditions

General Section

The general section explains the nature of the policy and defines important terms. The first paragraph explains that the policy is a contract and that the parties are "you" (the insured) and "we" (the insurer). The insured is the employer named in item 1 of the information page. The policy states that if that employer is a partnership, coverage applies to the partners only in their capacity as employer of that partnership's employees. If one of the partners is also involved in an enterprise other than the entity named in the policy, and that enterprise also has employees, there must be a separate workers compensation policy or self-insurance plan.

Paragraph C of the general section defines "workers compensation law" to mean "the workers or workmen's compensation law and occupational disease law of each state or territory named in item 3(A) of the Information Page." Any amendments in effect during the policy period are included, but any provisions of a statute that relate to nonoccupational disability benefits are not included within this definition. Moreover, the definition is limited to *state* laws. The United States Longshore and Harbor Workers' Compensation Act and other federal laws are not included.

According to Paragraph D, the term "state" means any of the fifty states or the District of Columbia. Coverage for the workers compensation law of a United States territory applies only when item 3(A) of the information page explicitly names that territory.

Covered locations are defined to include all workplaces listed on the information page and all of the insured's workplaces in states listed in item 3(A) unless other insurance or self-insurance applies.

Part One—Workers Compensation Insurance

The coverage provided by Part One obligates the insurer to pay all compensation and other benefits required of the insured by the workers compensation law or occupational disease law of any state listed in item 3(A) of the information page. The employer automatically receives coverage for all benefits required by that state's workers compensation law for all locations, operations, and employees as designated by the law. The policy applies to all operations of the employer except those otherwise insured or specifically excluded by endorsement.

The coverage applies to bodily injury by accident and by disease. The accident must occur during the policy period, and the last exposure to disease in the employment of the insured must occur during the policy period.

According to the policy, the insurer will pay the benefits required by the workers compensation law. The policy shows no dollar limit for these benefits. Any applicable limits would be those found within the law itself. Part One of the policy contains no exclusions.

The policy establishes the insurer's right and duty to defend claims covered by the policy, and it disclaims any duty to defend a claim not covered. The insurer also agrees to pay additional costs, such as the expense of investigating a claim and litigation costs.

The policy provides that the insured will reimburse the insurer for any penalties required under a workers compensation law because of (1) willful misconduct, (2) illegal employment, (3) failure to comply with health and safety laws and regulations, and (4) discrimination against employees who claim workers compensation benefits.

Subrogation rights of the insurer are reaffirmed in the policy. When the insurer pays compensation or employers liability benefits on behalf of an insured, any right of recovery the insured or the injured employee may have against a third party becomes the right of the insurer.

The policy also recognizes the legal requirements that directly obligate the insurance company to pay workers compensation benefits to any injured employee or, in the event of death, to the employee's dependents. Since the contract is made primarily for the benefit of employees and their dependents, they have a direct right of action against the insurance company.

For the protection of the employee, the policy provides that the obligations of the insurance company will not be affected by the failure of the employer to comply with the policy requirements.

All workers compensation laws covered by the policy become a part of the insurance contract just as if they were written into the policy, and employees have the rights to compensation defined by those laws. If the policy and the applicable workers compensation law conflict, the policy agrees to conform to the law. The policy is automatically amended when there are changes in the law.

Part Two—Employers Liability Insurance

Part Two of the policy, which provides employers liability coverage, is structured like a traditional liability policy, containing an insuring agreement and exclusions.

Employers Liability Insuring Agreement

The insurer agrees to pay damages that the insured becomes legally obligated to pay because of bodily injury by accident or disease to an employee. The bodily injury must arise out of and in the course of the employee's employment and not be covered under a state or federal workers compensation or disability benefits law. The insurer also agrees to defend the insured against claims or suits seeking covered damages.

Although the coverage provided by workers compensation laws is extensive, there are numerous ways in which an employer can be held liable under the common law as the result of employee injuries. The following are examples:

- An employee of the insured sues a third party (such as a machine manufacturer) for an occupational injury, and the third party makes a "third-party-over action" against the employer. The third party's suit might allege, for example, that the employer was negligent in maintaining the defective machine and that the employer must therefore indemnify the manufacturer for all damages the manufacturer had to pay to the employee.

- The spouse or a family member of an injured employee sues the employer for loss of companionship or services (such as housekeeping or yard work that the employee would otherwise have performed) resulting from the injury.

Another requirement of Part B is that the employment out of which the injury arises must be necessary or incidental to the insured's work in a state or territory listed in Item 3A of the information page. This provision is not a requirement that the injury must *occur* in one of the states or territories listed. For example, an employee might be injured after driving into an unlisted state to buy supplies for work being performed in a listed state. Even though the injury occurred outside the listed state, the injury still arose out of employment that was necessary or incidental to the insured's work in a listed state.

Employers liability coverage is subject to the following coverage triggers:

- For bodily injury *by accident,* the policy that is in effect when the *injury occurs* is the policy that applies.

- For bodily injury *by disease,* the policy that is in effect on the employee's *last day of last exposure* to the conditions causing or aggravating the injury is the policy that applies.

Employers Liability Exclusions

Like most other liability policies, employers liability coverage is subject to many exclusions, which prevent overlapping coverage with other forms of insurance and eliminate coverage not intended by the insurer.

Statutory Obligations   In keeping with the basic purpose of employers liability coverage, several exclusions are aimed at eliminating coverage for claims that would be covered under various statutes, including the following:

- Any workers compensation, occupational disease, unemployment compensation, or disability benefits law

- The Longshore and Harbor Workers' Compensation Act (LHWCA)
- The Federal Employers' Liability Act (which gives workers on interstate railroads the right to sue their employers for injuries resulting to any degree from the employer's negligence)
- Any other federal workers compensation or occupational disease law

Also excluded is bodily injury to a master or member of the crew of any vessel. Masters and crew members of vessels are not eligible for LHWCA benefits but can pursue remedies described earlier in this chapter.

Various endorsements are available for deleting or modifying most of the exclusions listed above in order to extend the policy to cover those liabilities. The endorsement for covering LHWCA obligations is discussed later in this chapter. A shipowner's liability for crew injuries, although insurable by endorsement to the WC&EL policy, is usually covered under the shipowner's protection and indemnity policy (see Chapter 7).

Injury Outside the United States or Canada   Employers liability coverage does not apply to bodily injury that occurs outside the United States, its territories or possessions, and Canada. However, this exclusion does not apply to injury to a resident or citizen of the United States or Canada who is *temporarily* outside the places listed above.

Liability Assumed Under Contract   Employers liability coverage does not apply to liability assumed under contract—even if the insured has assumed another party's liability for injury to the insured's own employee. (Recall from Chapter 8 that the CGL policy covers liability assumed under an "insured contract," even if the liability assumed is for injury to an employee of the insured.)

Other Exclusions   Employers liability insurance also does not apply to any of the following:

1. Punitive damages for injury or death of any illegally employed person
2. Bodily injury to employees employed in violation of the law with the knowledge of the insured or any executive officers of the insured
3. Bodily injury intentionally caused by the insured
4. Damages arising out of employment practices, including (but not limited to) demotion, evaluation, harassment, discrimination, and termination
5. Fines or penalties imposed for violation of federal or state law
6. Damages payable under the Migrant and Seasonal Agricultural Worker Protection Act

Limits of Liability

Unlike workers compensation coverage, employers liability coverage is subject to limits of liability stated in the policy. The three limits that apply to employers liability coverage are as follows:

1. The "bodily injury by accident" limit is the most that the insurer will pay for bodily injury resulting from any one accident, regardless of the number of employees injured.

2. The "bodily injury by disease—policy limit" is the most that the insurer will pay for bodily injury by disease, regardless of the number of employees who sustain disease.

3. The "bodily injury by disease—each employee" limit is the most that the insurer will pay for bodily injury by disease to any one employee.

Defense costs, as well as supplementary payments similar to those covered under the CGL coverage form, are covered in addition to the limits of liability. However, the insurer has no duty to pay defense costs or supplementary payments after it has paid the applicable limit of insurance.

Part Three—Other States Insurance

Employers need workers compensation coverage if they expand their operations into states not listed on the information page when the policy is issued or last renewed. This coverage, called **other states insurance**, is incorporated within the policy form as Part Three. It extends workers compensation and employees liability coverage to operations in any state listed in item 3(C) of the information page. If coverage applies to a state designated in item 3(C), and the insured begins operations in that state, the policy provides the same coverage as if that state were listed in item 3(A). The policy requires the insured to "Tell us at once if you begin work in any state listed in Item 3(C) of the Information Page."

If the insured has operations in a particular state on the effective date of the policy but that state is not listed in item 3(A), the insured must notify the insurer within thirty days or else no coverage will apply for that state. Thus, when operations are *known* to exist in a particular state, that state should be listed in item 3(A). When operations do not currently take place in additional states but *could* be extended into those states, those states should be listed in item 3(C). Naturally, states in which the insurer is not licensed to write workers compensation insurance (including those that have monopolistic state funds) should not be listed in either item.

If the insured anticipates operating in a state with a monopolistic workers compensation fund, the insured should obtain workers compensation insurance from the state fund. Because the workers compensation policies issued by state funds do not include employers liability insurance, many employers buy a type of employers liability insurance called **stop gap coverage**. This coverage is often provided by the same insurer that provides the insured's general liability insurance.

Part Four—Your Duties If Injury Occurs

Part Four explains the duties of the insured when a loss occurs. The insured must promptly notify the insurer of injury, claims, or suit. The insured must also cooperate with the insurer, attend hearings and trials at the request of the insurer, and help secure witnesses. The insured cannot, except at his or her own expense, voluntarily make any payment, assume any obligation, or incur any expenses except for immediate medical and other services at the time of injury as required by the workers compensation law.

Part Five—Premium

Workers compensation premiums are based on the insured's payroll, which cannot be precisely determined until after the policy expires. Part Five explains premium determination procedures, establishing the role of insurance company manuals in determining premium and stipulating that the manuals and the premium may change during the policy period. The policy tells the insured that the classifications and rates shown on the information page may change if they do not accurately describe the work covered by the policy.

Part Five also defines payroll as the premium base and stresses that it includes the remuneration of executive officers and the payroll of employees of uninsured contractors and subcontractors. The audit provision explains the insurer's right to examine and audit the insured's books and records at any time during the policy period and within three years after expiration insofar as such books and records relate to the policy. It explains why the final premium may be different from the estimated premium and shows how the premium will be determined on cancellation of the policy. The insured must keep records of information needed to compute the policy premium and provide such records to the insurer when requested.

Part Six—Conditions

The policy conditions limit or define the rights and obligations of the parties to the insurance contract. The conditions address insurer inspections, policy years, assignment, cancellation, and who represents the insured.

Inspection

One condition gives the insurer permission to inspect a policyholder's workplaces and operations. These inspections allow the insurer to determine that safe practices are employed and proper precautions taken for the safety of employees.

Although this condition states that the insurer is permitted to inspect workplaces, the policy does not require the insurer to perform inspections. When such services are performed, however, the policy indicates that this does not constitute an undertaking to warrant that any workplaces, operations, machinery, or equipment inspected are safe or healthful.

Long-Term Policy

If the policy period is longer than one year, each year is considered separate as far as policy provisions are concerned, and premium is computed in accordance with the manual rules and rates in effect for that year. An exception is a three-year fixed-rate policy that would carry an endorsement modifying this provision. Such three-year policies are rarely issued.

Assignment

With the written consent of the insurer, the insured can transfer or assign the policy to cover a new interest. For example, if the insured business is sold, the workers compensation policy can be transferred to the new owner if the current insurer agrees. However, it is generally preferable that a new policy be issued and the old policy canceled.

Cancellation

Cancellation of the policy is generally permitted by law. However, some laws restrict the insurer's right of cancellation. This condition outlines the cancellation right of the insurer and insured and is subject in all cases to any requirements of the workers compensation law. In essence, it is possible for the insured to cancel the policy virtually without notice. The insurer, however, must provide at least ten days' notice before cancellation becomes effective.

Sole Representative

The first named insured acts on behalf of all insureds for premium payment, refund, cancellation, and other rights and duties under the policy.

Endorsements

Despite the flexibility offered by the standard workers compensation policy, a number of situations require modification of standard policy provisions by adding an appropriate endorsement to the policy. Two of the more important endorsements are examined below.

Voluntary Compensation Endorsement

The workers compensation laws of most states exempt some types of employment from statutory workers compensation benefits. The most commonly exempted occupations are farm labor, domestic employment, and casual labor. In some cases, the law does not apply to employers with fewer than a certain minimum number of employees. The workers compensation laws of some states do not apply to partners, sole proprietors, or executive officers. Even when exempt persons are not entitled to workers compensation benefits by law, the same benefits may be extended to them by voluntary action.

The **voluntary compensation endorsement** amends the standard policy to include an additional coverage called "voluntary compensation." The additional coverage does not make employees subject to the workers compensation law, but it obligates the insurance company to pay, on behalf of the insured, an amount equal to the compensation benefits that would be payable to such employees if they were subject to the workers compensation law designated in the endorsement.

The voluntary compensation endorsement states that if an employee entitled to payment under the endorsement brings a suit under the common law, the coverage provided by the endorsement reverts to employers liability insurance. The insurer will defend the insured against the employee's suit and pay any settlement awarded, subject to the stipulated limits of liability.

LHWCA Coverage Endorsement

The United States Longshore and Harbor Workers' Compensation Act follows the same principles as the state workers compensation laws. In some circumstances, an employer may be subject to both the LHWCA and the state workers compensation law at the same time. Although both of these exposures may be insured, they must be covered and rated separately.

Coverage can be provided by adding the **United States Longshore and Harbor Workers' Compensation Act endorsement** to the workers compensation policy. The endorsement amends the definition of "workers compensation law" to include the LHWCA with respect to operations in any state designated in the endorsement's schedule. (In practice, many WC&EL insurers are unwilling to add LHWCA coverage because of the unfavorable loss experience associated with the LHWCA.)

Rating Workers Compensation Insurance

Most states require insurers to belong to a single approved rating organization in order to write workers compensation and employers liability insurance. This bureau is the statistics-gathering organization for workers compensation in those states. Different bureaus may exist for different states. The bureau files with the supervisory authority the manuals for classifications, rules, rates (or loss costs, depending on the state), rating plans, and policy forms on behalf of its members.

The **National Council on Compensation Insurance (NCCI)** serves as the filing agency for insurers in most states and prepares standard forms and endorsements. Several states have independent rating bureaus for workers compensation insurance. Some of these use the services of NCCI. Other states make their own rates and issue their own rules and manuals. However, the procedures generally resemble those of NCCI.

Workers compensation insurance protects employers from losses resulting from the work-related injuries or diseases of employees as determined by statute. The premium for that protection should reflect the exposure to such losses. The exposure varies considerably according to the size of the employer's work force and the degree of hazard in the work performed. Workers compensation premiums reflect these two factors because the premium depends on the amount of the employer's payroll (the basis of premium) and the type of business (classification) involved.

Basis of Premium

With only a few exceptions, the premium base for workers compensation insurance is remuneration (that is, payroll). Payroll serves as an effective premium base because it varies directly with the exposure covered by the insurance, it is relatively easy to determine and verify from available records, and it is not readily subject to manipulation by the insured.

A business obtaining workers compensation insurance may not know how many employees it will have during the coming year. The policy, however, bases the premium on the manual rate for the applicable classification per $100 of payroll for the year. At the inception of the policy, the insured pays an estimated premium based on an estimate of the annual payroll, and a premium auditor may examine the insured's records at the end of the policy period (or at shorter intervals during the policy period) to determine the actual payroll. The insurer then calculates the actual earned premium. If it is greater than the deposit premium, the insured receives a bill for the additional premium due. If it is less, the insured receives a refund.

Classifications

Rates for workers compensation insurance vary considerably according to the classification of workers. The class rating system serves to identify groups of similar employments whose experience is then combined for the purpose of establishing rates. To achieve this result, however, it is necessary for both premiums and losses to be accurately and consistently assigned to the proper classes. Any business may involve many different operations in widely varying combinations. Some of these operations may be extremely hazardous, while others are not. The classification rules attempt to delineate classification procedures that are both equitable and simple to apply.

The classification section of the workers compensation manual alphabetically lists several hundred classifications. Other than the so-called standard exception classifications (such as clerical employees and drivers), each one describes a particular business. For each employer, it is necessary to determine the basic classification that best describes the business of the employer within the state so that the employer's exposure base and loss experience can be pooled with all similar businesses.

Merit Rating Plans

Some rating techniques reward the insured for successful loss control measures. The most common of such techniques are experience rating and retrospective rating. Both are used frequently with workers compensation insurance.

Experience Rating

Under an **experience rating plan,** the premium applicable to a particular insured is increased or decreased for a future period based on that insured's loss experience for a period in the recent past. For example, an insured's premium for 1997 might be adjusted based on that insured's loss experience for the years 1993, 1994, and 1995. Premiums would be reduced if the insured's losses were less than the average for the class and increased if the insured's losses were higher.

Retrospective Rating

Under a **retrospective rating plan**, an insured's premium for a given period is reduced or increased based on that insured's losses during the same period. The insured pays an estimated premium at the beginning of the period and receives either a refund or a bill for an additional premium after the end of the period, depending on the losses during the period. A formula for calculating the retrospective premium adjustment is written into the policy at its inception. Underwriters sometimes require retrospective rating plans as a condition of providing insurance for marginal accounts that may generate high losses. Conversely, insureds that expect lower than average losses may find retrospective rating attractive, particularly when combined with an effective loss control program.

Summary

Workers compensation laws were adopted in each of the United States and the Canadian provinces in order to assure workers and their families of prompt payment for occupational injuries and diseases and resulting disabilities or deaths. For an injury or disease to be covered under a typical workers compensation law, the injury or disease must arise out of and in the course of employment.

The benefits provided by workers compensation laws include medical benefits, disability income benefits, death benefits, and rehabilitation benefits. The amounts collectible for these benefits are defined in the applicable law. Workers compensation laws apply to most employees. Some of the workers that are not covered by state workers compensation laws include federal government employees, maritime workers, and employees of interstate railroads.

Employers can meet their workers compensation obligations by buying workers compensation insurance from private insurers, assigned risk plans, or state workers compensation insurance funds. Alternatively, larger employers can self-insure (retain) their workers compensation exposure if they meet certain tests specified in the applicable workers compensation law. A combined approach is to self-insure up to a certain point and purchase excess insurance above that point.

In the United States, workers compensation insurance is mainly provided under a standard form called the workers compensation and employers liability insurance (WC&EL) policy. The policy not only covers the insured's obligations under workers compensation laws but also provides employers liability coverage. Employers liability coverage protects the insured against claims for employee injuries that are not subject to workers compensation.

The workers compensation part of the policy obligates the insurer to pay all compensation and other benefits required of the insured by the workers compensation law of any state listed in Item 3(A) of the policy's information page (declarations). Coverage for federal compensation laws, such as the Longshore and Harbor Workers' Compensation Act, is excluded unless coverage is extended by endorsement.

The employers liability part of the policy obligates the insurer to pay damages that the insured becomes legally obligated to pay because of bodily injury by accident or disease to an employee. The bodily injury must arise out of and in the course of the employee's employment and not be covered under a workers compensation law. The insurer also agrees to defend the insured. Several exclusions apply to employers liability coverage.

A policy feature called "other states insurance" extends the policy to cover obligations under workers compensation laws of states in addition to those listed in Item 3(A) of the information page. Such additional states, however, must be listed in Item 3(C) of the information page.

Common endorsements to the WC&EL policy include voluntary compensation coverage (providing workers compensation benefits for employees not subject to a workers compensation law) and Longshore and Harbor Workers' Compensation Act coverage (covering an employer's obligations under the LHWCA).

The premium base for WC&EL insurance is ordinarily the insured's payroll. The premium base is multiplied by a rate that depends on the insured's classification. An estimated premium is usually charged at the beginning of the policy period. At the end of the policy period, the insured's actual payroll figures are used to determine the final premium. The difference between the two is reconciled between the insured and the insurer. Experience rating plans and retrospective rating plans are often used for WC&EL policies.

Chapter 13

Miscellaneous Coverages

The types of insurance described in preceding chapters of this text cover the common property and liability exposures of most organizations. Many other forms of commercial insurance are available to cover specialized or unusual exposures. This chapter surveys several commercial insurance coverages that fill gaps left by the more basic policies.

Five of the coverages described in this chapter are liability coverages designed to treat the following specific exposures:

- Professional liability—liability for errors or omissions made in the course of rendering professional services.

- Directors and officers liability—liability of corporate directors and officers for their wrongful acts.

- Employment practices liability—liability for various offenses against the insured's employees or co-workers, such as discrimination, sexual harassment, and wrongful termination.

- Employee benefits liability—liability for the negligent administration of employee benefit plans.

- Fiduciary liability—liability for negligence of employee benefit plan fiduciaries in making discretionary decisions that adversely affect the plan's funds.

Other topics covered by this chapter are aircraft insurance, excess and umbrella liability insurance, and surety bonds.

- Aircraft insurance, which resembles auto insurance, covers both property and liability exposures arising out of the ownership, maintenance, or use of airplanes.

- Excess or umbrella liability insurance provides additional amounts of insurance above one or more "primary" liability policies.

- Surety bonds, although provided by commercial insurers, are neither property insurance nor liability insurance but unique types of guarantee contracts that are vital to the construction business and many other occupations and professions.

Professional Liability Insurance

The word "profession" was associated historically with the occupations known as the learned professions—law, medicine, education, and the clergy. However, as society has become more complex and specialized, the number of occupations requiring extensive technical knowledge or training has increased dramatically. "Professional liability," therefore, is not restricted to the traditional professions; rather, **professional liability** can be defined as liability for the failure to use the degree of skill expected of a person in a particular field.[1] The list of occupations that have a professional liability exposure is expanding, including such recent additions as computer programmers and management consultants.

In part because of this expansion in the number of occupations exposed to professional liability, this exposure is also known as "malpractice" or "errors and omissions." "Malpractice liability" is commonly used to describe liability in connection with professions that involve contact with the human body, ranging from physicians to beauticians. "Errors and omissions liability" is more likely to be used to describe professional liability for occupations such as attorneys, insurance agents, and engineers. However, there is no consistent use of the terms, and in some cases, they are used interchangeably. Professional liability, however, is generally understood to include all of these exposures, and that is how it is used in this chapter.

Professional Liability Exposures

A practitioner of any profession has a legal obligation to perform the duties of that profession according to the standards of the profession, as measured by the knowledge, skill, and performance of his or her peers. Failure to do so may bring liability for any resulting injury or damage. Space does not permit a detailed discussion here of the liability exposures of all occupations classified as professions. The exposures of two groups—physicians and insurance producers—will be used for illustrative purposes.

Physicians

A physician's professional liability usually arises from improper performance in the practice of the profession that results in injury. A few of the medical errors that cause injury and can result in liability are as follows:

- Failure to properly diagnose a disease, resulting in more serious illness, disability, or even death
- Improper performance of a surgical procedure, causing injury to a patient
- Failure to warn a patient of the hazards involved in a course of treatment
- Leaving a surgical instrument or other foreign object in a patient following surgery

In addition to purely medical errors such as those cited, physicians may be held liable for administrative errors or omissions connected with their medical practice. For example, a physician who serves on a hospital's accreditation committee may be held liable for injury resulting from improperly refusing hospital staff privileges to another physician (or even granting staff privileges to a physician who is careless or incompetent).

Insurance Producers

Insurance agents and brokers have recently achieved increasing recognition as professionals. A part of the price they pay for the rise toward professionalism is an increase in their professional liability exposure—that is, they are held to a higher standard of care in responding to their clients' insurance needs. When an uninsured or underinsured loss occurs, the insurance agent or broker is more likely than in the past to be held accountable to the client. A few of the errors or omissions for which insurance agents or brokers have been held liable to their clients include the following:

- Failure to properly advise the client regarding his or her insurance needs
- Failure to obtain insurance for a client in a timely manner after agreeing to do so
- Failure to renew a policy at expiration without giving prior notice to the client
- Failure to properly advise the client regarding appropriate limits

In addition to incurring possible liability to clients, insurance producers can become liable to the insurance companies they represent. For example, an agency that binds coverage that the insurance company has not authorized the agency to bind can be held liable to the insurer if any claims are made under the coverage. Similarly, a producer who fails to cancel a policy when directed to do so by the insurer can be held liable for any claims that the insurer is required to pay as a result of the failure to cancel.

Coverage Under CGL Policies

The liability of some types of professionals would be covered under a commercial general liability (CGL) policy unless an endorsement excluding professional liability was added. For example, the injury caused by a sponge left in a patient's abdominal cavity is certainly "bodily injury" as that term is used in the CGL policy. Insurers generally do not want to cover such professional liability exposures under their CGL policies. (Insurers want to evaluate the professional liability exposure, charge an appropriate premium for coverage, and provide the coverage under a policy that contains appropriate provisions.) Consequently, when insuring persons or organizations that render certain professional services, insurers routinely endorse their CGL policies to exclude professional liability. The ISO *Commercial Lines Manual* requires the use of a professional liability exclusion for numerous occupations. (See the list in Exhibit 13-1.) Each of these occupations may have a need for professional liability insurance.

However, even in the absence of the professional liability exclusion, the CGL policy would not cover many professional liability losses because they would not come within the CGL definitions of "bodily injury," "property damage," "personal injury," or "advertising injury." For example, a lawyer representing a client in a contract dispute might negligently fail to file a suit within the time period allowed by the applicable state law. If the failure to file suit caused a financial loss to the client, the lawyer would probably be liable for the loss. The lawyer's liability would not be covered under the lawyer's CGL policy even if a professional liability exclusion had not been attached to the policy, because the type of injury incurred was not bodily injury, property damage, advertising injury, or personal injury.

Liability Insurance for Professionals

Because the liability exposures of one profession (such as medicine) may differ considerably from the liability exposures of another profession (such as engineering), insurers use different policies to insure each. In most cases, only a few insurers who specialize in a particular type of professional liability insurance

Exhibit 13-1
Some Classifications Requiring Professional Liability Exclusions
on Their CGL Policies

Ambulance services	Hearing aid stores*
Analytical chemists	Inspection or appraisal
Barber shops	companies
Beauty parlors	Insurance agents
Blood banks	Insurance companies
Cemeteries	Laboratories—research,
Computer manufacturers	development, or testing
Cosmetic, hair, or skin	Marine appraisers or
preparation stores	surveyors
Crematories	Medical offices
Drugstores*	Medical or x-ray laboratories
Electronic data processing	Optical goods stores*
operations	Penal institutions
Engineers or architects	Saunas and baths
Fire departments	Tanning salons
Funeral homes or chapels	Tattoo parlors
Health-care facilities	Veterinarians or veterinary hospitals
Health or exercise clubs	

* Professional services exclusion is not required for drugstores, hearing
  aid stores, and optical goods stores if products liability coverage is
  included.

write that type of insurance. Specialization is necessary to develop the skills required to successfully underwrite risks and adjust claims that differ from the usual bodily injury or property damage exposures faced by most insureds.

Although ISO has developed professional liability forms for physicians, surgeons, and dentists, as well as some other professionals, most professional liability insurance is written on forms developed by individual insurers. The sections that follow describe typical provisions used in independently developed forms for two occupations: physicians and insurance agents and brokers.

Physicians Professional Liability Coverage

The insuring agreement in a typical **physicians professional liability policy** covers damages resulting from "providing or withholding professional services" by the insured or anyone else for whose acts the insured is legally responsible. The insuring agreement also covers liability arising out of the insured's service on a formal accreditation board. For example, assume that Dr. Smith applies for staff privileges at the hospital where the insured, Dr. Jones, serves on the accreditation committee. If Dr. Smith is denied staff privileges and sues Dr. Jones, the insurer will defend the suit and pay any resulting damages.

The damages that the insurer will pay on behalf of the insured are not restricted to those for bodily injury or property damage. Damages for libel, slander, defamation, invasion of privacy, and similar offenses are generally covered by professional liability policies unless otherwise excluded. Some insurers, however, specifically exclude damages caused by libel, slander, or defamation in their professional liability policies.

Insurance Agents and Brokers Errors and Omissions Coverage

For some professions, professional liability usually results from loss or damage to *intangible* property, that is, a purely economic loss. For example, an insurance agent or broker might issue an insurance policy improperly, depriving the insured of the right to collect for a loss that would have been covered under a properly issued policy. In fact, professional liability policies issued to lawyers, accountants, and insurance producers specifically exclude coverage for liability resulting from bodily injury or damage to tangible property.

Although there is no standard **errors and omissions liability policy** for insurance agents and brokers, the policies issued by various insurers are similar. A typical policy agrees "to pay on behalf of the insured all sums that the insured shall become legally obligated to pay as damages . . . arising out of any negligent act, error or omission . . . in the conduct of the insured's business [as an insurance agent or broker]."

As noted above, an exclusion makes it clear that the policy does not cover damages for bodily injury or damage to tangible property. The policy may, however, pay damages indirectly related to either. For example, an insurance agent's client might be sued for bodily injury, property damage, or both arising from an auto accident. If, because of negligence on the part of the agent, the client does not have insurance to cover the damages, the agent's errors and omissions policy would pay them unless some other exclusion applied. The damages that the insurance agent would become legally obligated to pay would have resulted from the agent's negligent failure to procure insurance rather than from bodily injury or property damage.

Exclusions

Professional liability policies, like other policies, contain exclusions. Certain exclusions are common to most professional liability policies, while others pertain only to specific professions.

Most professional liability policies exclude claims arising from the insured's dishonest, criminal, or malicious acts. Policies written to cover "errors or omissions" usually exclude bodily injury or damage to tangible property. Contractual liability is frequently excluded, and so are punitive damages.

Professional liability policies for some professions contain specialized exclusions. For example, professional liability policies for lawyers and accountants may exclude liability arising from practice before the Securities and Exchange Commission. Insurance agents and brokers errors and omissions policies may exclude liability for failure to remit premium refunds or policy dividend payments to insureds.

Conflicts and Overlaps Between CGL and Professional Liability Policies

As noted above, ISO manual rules require that CGL policies issued to certain professionals contain a professional liability exclusion endorsement. Moreover, some professional liability policies exclude bodily injury and property damage. Nevertheless, coverage conflicts sometimes arise between CGL and professional liability insurers.

For example, if a patient falls off the examining table in a physician's office, is the cause of the accident defective maintenance of the examining table (probably covered by the physician's CGL policy)? Or is the cause of the accident the failure of the physician to monitor a patient suffering from vertigo (probably covered by the physician's professional liability policy)? In one such case, the court ordered both insurers to share the loss.[2]

The standard recommendation for avoiding such disputes is to obtain professional liability insurance and CGL coverage from the same insurer. However, that is often not possible, given the limited number of insurers writing professional liability insurance. When coverage has been placed with separate insurers, any claim with a possible overlap in coverage should be reported to both insurers. Investigation of the claim by the insurers may clarify whether it is a general liability or a professional liability claim.

Claims-Made Versus Occurrence Coverage Triggers

Many professional liability coverages develop "long-tail" claims—that is, claims that are presented long after the policy has expired. A classic case involves professional liability of obstetricians. In most states, a statute of limitations provides that claims are barred unless a lawsuit is filed within a specific period. For negligence claims, this period is often two years. In such states, most negligence claims are unenforceable unless suit is begun within two years after the date of the injury. However, in cases involving injury to newborn babies, the time limit does not begin to run until an infant has reached majority (eighteen years in most states).

Thus, it is not unusual for an obstetrician who is alleged to have negligently inflicted an injury on a newborn infant to be faced with a claim many years later, after the infant has reached majority. The same pattern exists for other professions. For example, a building may collapse many years after the architect prepared the allegedly deficient plans. Consequently, insurers prefer to use claims-made professional liability policies in order to avoid liability for such long-tail claims.

The claims-made approach was discussed in Chapter 9 in connection with the CGL policy. The primary difference between independently developed claims-made forms and the ISO claims-made CGL form is in the extended reporting period provisions. The ISO form automatically includes a basic extended reporting period, and a supplemental extended reporting period can be added for an additional premium. If the insured purchases the supplemental extended reporting period, there is an unlimited time period to report claims that occurred during the policy period.

In contrast, the claims-made provisions found in independently developed professional liability policies generally do not contain an automatic extended reporting period. Any extended reporting period must usually be specifically requested and paid for, and few (if any) offer an *unlimited* extended reporting period; one to three years is more usual.

Directors and Officers Liability Insurance

The directors of a computer manufacturing company were sued by a shareholder who alleged mismanagement when a new disk drive failed to achieve any substantial sales volume, resulting in a drop in the stock price. The claim was settled for $16 million. A major oil company and two of its senior executives were hit with a $69 million jury verdict in a wrongful termination lawsuit brought by two former officers.[3]

As these and dozens of other cases show, the individuals who serve as the directors and officers of a corporation can be sued, as individuals, for breach of their corporate duties. Frequently, the plaintiffs are stockholders of the corporation, who may feel that they have been harmed financially by negligent management of the corporation. In other cases, the suit may be brought by employees of the corporation or by outsiders, such as customers or clients.

In recognition of the potentially devastating liability exposure faced by individual directors and officers, many corporations agree to indemnify their directors and officers for the costs resulting from suits against them. The laws of several states permit or even require corporations to provide such indemnification to their directors and officers.

Thus, the directors and officers liability exposure affects both the individual directors and officers and the corporation itself. Many corporations protect themselves and their directors and officers against this exposure by purchasing **directors and officers (D&O) liability insurance**. There is no standard form for D&O liability insurance. Each insurer offering the coverage develops its own policy.

Because stockholders are the largest class of claimants, it is sometimes assumed that directors and officers liability insurance is not needed by corporations with no public stockholders (known as "closely held" corporations). However, recent surveys have shown that more than half of all D&O claimants are not stockholders.[4]

Insuring Agreements

A D&O policy ordinarily contains two insuring agreements:

1. The first agreement covers the directors and officers of the insured corporation for their personal liability as directors or officers that results from a "wrongful act." "Wrongful act" is usually defined to include any breach of duty, neglect, error, misstatement, misleading statement, omission, or other act done or wrongfully attempted by the directors or officers.

2. The second insuring agreement, often referred to as company reimbursement coverage, covers the sums that the insured corporation is required or permitted by law to pay to the directors and officers as indemnification.

D&O insurance is written on a claims-made basis. The availability and terms of extended reporting periods vary among policies but generally are not as favorable as those of the ISO claims-made CGL policy. For example, a D&O policy might allow the insured to purchase an extended reporting period (or "discovery period") only if the policy is canceled or not renewed by the insurer. Moreover, the discovery period may be limited to a relatively short period, such as one year.

Exclusions

Virtually all D&O policies exclude bodily injury and damage to tangible property. (As explained in Chapter 9, CGL insurance covers the directors and officers of the insured corporation against liability resulting from bodily injury or damage to tangible property.) D&O policies ordinarily exclude liability for pollution and nuclear hazards as well.

Other exclusions commonly found in D&O policies eliminate coverage for claims made against directors or officers because of the following:

1. Libel or slander
2. Gaining any personal profit to which they were not legally entitled
3. Return of salaries or bonuses received without the stockholders' prior approval
4. Failure to effect or maintain adequate insurance for the corporation
5. Certain violations of the Securities Exchange Act
6. Acts of deliberate dishonesty
7. Liability under the Employee Retirement Income Security Act (ERISA)

Some of these exclusions can be eliminated or modified by negotiation with the insurer.

Other Provisions

The costs of defending against D&O suits are notoriously high. Although D&O policies usually cover the costs of defending against claims alleging loss covered by the policy, these costs are typically subject to policy limits instead of being outside policy limits as in most other liability policies.

D&O policies are usually subject to both a flat deductible amount and a specified percentage of participation by the insured in all losses exceeding the retention. To illustrate, assume that KRE Corporation has a D&O liability policy with a $1 million limit, a $25,000 deductible, and a 5 percent participation. If KRE's insurer settles a covered D&O claim for $100,000, KRE and its insurer will pay the amounts shown below:

KRE will pay the deductible	=	$25,000
KRE will pay 5% of the remaining $75,000	=	$3,750
The insurer will pay 95% of $75,000	=	$71,250

Although the D&O policy is written in the name of the corporation, the corporation is usually not an insured. The D&O policy's reimbursement coverage will pay the corporation for payments it makes to indemnify its directors and officers. However, if the corporation itself is named as a defendant in a covered suit, as occurred in the oil company case mentioned above, the insurer will not defend the corporation or make any payment to settle claims against the corporation.

D&O Coverage for Nonprofit Corporations

D&O coverage was originally developed to meet the needs of the largest corporations. However, the growth of claims against all corporations has created a need for this coverage by entities of all sizes, including even small nonprofit organizations. Smaller corporations and nonprofit organizations often find that outside directors will not serve on their boards unless such coverage is provided. Policies written for smaller entities are similar to D&O policies written for large corporations except that, in the case of nonprofit organizations, policies are often written to include the organization as an insured.

Employment Practices Liability Insurance

The growth of federal and state legislation dealing with employment discrimination and sexual harassment, the changing legal views on wrongful termination, and the increasing tendency of aggrieved parties to turn to the courts for settlement of such disputes have caused insurers to specifically exclude coverage for such employment-related claims from CGL policies. To fill this gap in coverage, a number of insurers offer **employment practices liability (EPL) insurance.** Since EPL policies are independently developed, there is no standard form; however, most policies are similar in their terms and conditions.[5]

Coverage under EPL policies does not apply to all employment practices; rather, the policies specify the exact types of claims that are covered. Claims by employees alleging discrimination, sexual harassment, and wrongful termination are usually included as covered events. Some policies also cover breach of employment contract, failure to employ or promote, and wrongful discipline.

EPL policies are usually written on a claims-made basis. Extended reporting periods of from one to three years are usually provided with an additional premium required to activate them.

In addition to damages paid for judgments or settlements, the cost of defense is covered, but it is usually paid *within* (not in addition to) the limit of insurance. Most EPL policies specifically cover "back pay." Back pay—the wages and salary lost by a discharged employee—is commonly awarded to successful claimants in discrimination and wrongful termination actions.

Typically, the definition of "insured" in an EPL policy includes the corporation, its directors and officers, its employees, and, in most policies, its former employees. In some policies, coverage for employees applies only to managerial or supervisory employees.

All policies carry a deductible, which might range from $1,000 to $250,000, depending on various factors. Like D&O policies, most EPL policies also require the insured to participate in losses exceeding the deductible. The insured's participation rate is usually 5 to 10 percent but could be as high as 25 percent.

Employee Benefits Liability and Fiduciary Liability Insurance

Virtually all employers provide some noncash benefits as a part of the total compensation of their full-time employees. These employee benefits include privately sponsored retirement plans, 401(k) plans, group life insurance, group nonoccupational disability insurance, educational assistance plans, and others.

Providing employee benefits exposes the employer to liability under the common law and state and federal statutes. Under the common law, the employer (or professional adviser) has a duty to provide competent advice to employees regarding their choices among employee benefits. A person or an organization that breaches that duty can become liable for resulting damages.

The most comprehensive statute regarding employee benefits is the Employee Retirement Income Security Act (ERISA) of 1974. Among other things, ERISA imposes specific duties on all employee benefit plan "fiduciaries." ERISA defines as a fiduciary practically anyone whose role in employee benefits involves discretionary control or judgment in the design, administration, funding, or management of a benefit plan. (In a general sense, "fiduciary" is defined as someone who is bound by an agreement to act primarily for someone else's benefit.[6]) A fiduciary who causes a loss to the plan by breaching the statutory duties can be held personally liable for the full amount of the loss. Moreover, the employer of the fiduciary can become vicariously liable for the loss.

Two types of insurance—employee benefits liability insurance and fiduciary liability insurance—are the principal means of covering the liability exposures arising out of employee benefit plans.

Employee Benefits Liability Insurance

Employee benefits liability insurance covers an employer (and, in some policies, its employees who act on its behalf) against liability claims alleging improper advice or other errors or omissions in the *administration* of the employer's employee benefit plans. The coverage is provided either in an endorsement to the employer's CGL policy or in a separate policy. Examples of administrative errors include the following:

- Providing negligent advice on the selection of employee benefit programs

- Failing to enroll an employee in the employer's group health insurance program, with the result that the employee has no health insurance for a condition that would have been covered by the health insurance

- Improperly calculating a retiree's pension benefits, resulting in wrongful reduction of the retiree's retirement income

Fiduciary Liability Insurance

In addition to facing claims for errors or omissions in carrying out their *administrative* duties (covered by employee benefits liability insurance), fiduciaries can be sued if they breach fiduciary duties involving *discretionary* judgments. An example of a duty involving discretionary judgments is using due care in investing funds accumulated for an employee retirement income plan. If the plan's fiduciaries make negligent investment decisions and thus cause financial harm to the plan's participants, the participants can sue the fiduciaries. Employee benefits liability insurance does not cover liability for such discretionary judgments. **Fiduciary liability insurance** covers the exposure.

Fiduciary liability policies also usually include coverage for administrative errors in the same manner as employee benefits liability coverage. However, many fiduciary liability policies do not include the corporation as an insured; coverage is restricted to the individual fiduciaries themselves. The corporation can sometimes be added as an insured to the fiduciary liability policy, in which case the employee benefits liability insurance coverage is duplicate insurance. Since the cost of employee benefits liability coverage is usually quite reasonable, some insureds maintain the duplicate coverage in order to obtain higher limits.

Aircraft Insurance

Aircraft insurance is purchased by a broad spectrum of insureds, ranging from the individuals who own and operate small planes for pleasure to the major airline companies that own and operate large fleets of aircraft. The purpose-of-use categories that insurers use to classify aircraft risks, shown in Exhibit 13-2, demonstrate the diverse risks covered by aircraft insurance.

Comparable to Auto Insurance

Aircraft insurance in many ways resembles auto insurance. Like auto insurance, aircraft insurance policies are divided into physical damage and liability sections. Aircraft physical damage insurance is also referred to as "hull insurance," reflecting the marine insurance origins of aircraft insurance.

A fundamental difference between auto insurance and aircraft insurance is that pilots of insured aircraft must meet strict qualifications. In addition to holding both the appropriate license and current medical certification from the Federal Aviation Administration (FAA), the pilot is often required to have at least a specified number of hours of experience flying the type of aircraft insured.

In addition, except for policies covering airlines, aircraft policies cover only the plane or planes specifically described in the policy. Aircraft insurance policies written for general aviation risks (all classes of aircraft shown in Exhibit 13-2 other than airliners and military aircraft) usually have no counterpart to the "any auto" coverage provided by symbol 1 of the business auto policy.

Aircraft Hull Coverage

The two most common aircraft hull coverages are (1) "all risks—ground and flight" and (2) "all risks—not in motion."

All risks—ground and flight, the broader of the two, covers most causes of loss whether the plane is in flight or on the ground at the time of the loss.

All risks—not in motion covers the plane only when it is on the ground and not moving *under its own power*. Thus, coverage applies while the plane is being towed, because it is not moving under its own power. Coverage does not apply, however, while the plane is taxiing, since the plane is moving under its own power.

The principal exclusions that apply to "all-risks" aircraft hull coverage are as follows:

Exhibit 13-2
Purpose-of-Use Categories

Category	Description
Airline	International, national, and regional air carriers.
Business and Pleasure	Individually owned aircraft used for owner's personal purposes. No charge is made or direct profit derived from use.
Industrial Aid	Corporate-owned aircraft that are (1) used for transporting employees, associates, and executives and (2) flown by full-time professional pilots.
Commercial Use	Charter operators, air taxi operators, and other profit-seeking operators.
Special Use	Crop dusting, banner towing, law enforcement, pipeline patrol, hunting, etc.

- Wear and tear
- Tire damage unless caused by theft, vandalism, or other physical damage covered by the policy
- Embezzlement or conversion by someone legally in possession of the aircraft (a lessee, for example)
- War

Some aircraft policies exclude losses on any aircraft whose FAA Airworthiness Certificate has become void or has been restricted.

Hull insurance on smaller aircraft is usually subject to a dollar deductible, either for a flat amount (such as $1,000) or for a stated percentage (such as 10 percent) of the plane's value. Some policies are written with a specified dollar deductible for ground coverage and a percentage deductible when the aircraft is in flight. Larger multi-engine aircraft are sometimes insured with no deductible since a deductible would not eliminate many claims; the cost to repair even minor damage to such planes can be thousands of dollars.

Aircraft Liability Insurance

Aircraft liability insurance protects the insured against third-party claims for bodily injury and property damage resulting from the ownership, maintenance, or use of insured aircraft. Separate limits of insurance usually apply to (1) bodily injury excluding passengers, (2) passenger bodily injury, and (3) property damage. For example, the limits might be expressed as follows:

- Bodily injury excluding passengers $250,000 each person
                                               $500,000 each occurrence

- Passenger bodily injury $250,000 each person
                                               $750,000 each occurrence

- Property damage $500,000 each occurrence

Most insureds purchase all three coverages, but some insureds, such as cargo carriers, may not need *passenger* bodily injury coverage. Aircraft liability insurance can also be written with a single limit applying to all coverages.

Aircraft liability coverage typically excludes the following:

- Intentional injury, except to prevent interference with safe operations.
- Liability assumed under contract. However, some policies cover liability assumed under incidental contracts, such as a contract for use of an airport.
- Bodily injury to an employee of the insured.
- Obligations under workers compensation or similar laws.
- Damage to property owned, leased, occupied, controlled, or under the care of the insured. However, some policies provide basic limits of coverage for passengers' baggage or for damage to hangars leased by the insured.

Various provisions are included in, or can be added to, aircraft policies to cover the insured's potential liability arising out of aircraft not specifically described in the policy. Such provisions can cover newly acquired aircraft, temporary substitute aircraft, and other aircraft not owned, leased, or regularly used by the insured.

Other Aircraft Coverages

Aircraft liability insurance is often supplemented by medical payments coverage and passenger voluntary settlement coverage. These coverages provide a way to make prompt payments to injured persons and perhaps avoid liability claims that could be more costly.

Aircraft medical payments coverage is similar to the medical payments coverage available in auto policies. The coverage pays, regardless of the insured's legal liability, for reasonable medical or funeral expenses incurred by occupants of the insured aircraft.

Passenger voluntary settlement coverage, also commonly known as *admitted liability coverage*, is unique to aircraft insurance. It is normally available to industrial aid aircraft (see Exhibit 13-2). The coverage provides scheduled benefits if a passenger suffers death, dismemberment, or loss of sight. In order for benefits to become payable, both of the following actions must be taken:

1. The insured must ask the insurer to pay.
2. The claimant must release the insured from liability for all bodily injury caused by the accident.

Excess and Umbrella Liability Insurance

Excess liability insurance and umbrella liability insurance are two similar types of coverage that organizations buy mainly to extend the limits of their CGL, commercial auto, and other "primary" liability policies.

Need for Excess or Umbrella Liability Coverage

To understand why excess or umbrella insurance is needed for liability exposures, it is helpful to review three basic characteristics of liability insurance that are not shared by property insurance.

1. Difficulty in estimating maximum possible loss for liability exposures
2. Layering of liability coverages
3. Effect of aggregate limits

Maximum Possible Loss

Most *property* loss exposures have a reasonably clear maximum possible loss (MPL). For example, the maximum possible building loss for a building that would cost $2 million to rebuild is, simply, $2 million. There is no comparable way to estimate MPL for most liability exposures. Awards to injured persons can, in severe cases, reach staggering totals. A Coca-Cola distributor paid more than $145 million to settle claims growing out of the collision of one of its delivery trucks with a school bus. Even property damage claims can involve enormous settlements; the cleanup costs alone for the *Exxon Valdez* oil spill in Prince William Sound on the Alaskan coast exceeded $2.5 billion.

Moreover, million-dollar verdicts have become increasingly frequent. There were no million-dollar verdicts in the U.S. before 1962, but from January 1990 through July 1993, over 2,000 were recorded—an average of more than 550 a year. In that period, every state in the nation reported at least one million-dollar verdict.[7]

Although most organizations are not likely to experience million-dollar liability losses, the possibility of a large liability loss exists for virtually any business, regardless of the size of the business and the type of service or product the business offers.

Layering of Coverage

Another difference between property and liability coverage is the way in which insurers provide high limits of coverage. Most property exposures are covered entirely by one insurer. If several insurers participate on the risk, they generally do so on a pro-rata basis: each insurer shares proportionately in all losses.

In contrast, high-limit liability insurance is generally arranged in "layers." That is, the coverage provided by the first (or "primary" insurer) must be totally exhausted before the next layer of insurance makes any payment. (Highly valued properties are also sometimes insured in layers, but that is the exception.) The primary layer of liability insurance seldom exceeds $1,000,000 per occurrence.

Effect of Aggregate Limits

Unlike property insurance, liability insurance is usually subject to an aggregate limit for the policy period. Thus, even if a business is never faced with a verdict that exceeds the *each occurrence* limit of one of its primary liability policies, the business could have several liability losses during one policy year that could reduce its *aggregate* limit, leaving a subsequent loss underinsured or uninsured.

For example, assume that an insured has CGL coverage with a $1,000,000 each occurrence limit, a $2,000,000 general aggregate limit, and a $2,000,000 aggregate limit for products and completed operations. If the insured has four products liability losses for $500,000 each during the policy period, the policy will pay nothing for other products liability losses that occur during the same policy period, even if no claim exceeds the each occurrence limit. ($500,000 x 4 = $2,000,000—the aggregate limit.)

Insurance Treatment

The large liability loss exposures described above can be insured with additional policies known as excess liability policies and umbrella liability policies. These policies provide limits of insurance in excess of the limits of an "underlying" primary policy or policies, or in excess of a significant dollar amount (such as $500,000) to be retained by an insured that is financially able to retain large losses.

Excess or umbrella liability coverage comes into play when the amount of damages exceeds the each occurrence limit of an underlying policy or when the aggregate limit of an underlying policy has become depleted by prior claims during the policy period. Umbrella liability policies may also cover some claims that are not covered at all by the underlying policy or policies.

Excess Liability Insurance

Excess liability policies may take any of three basic forms:

1. A "following form" subject to the same terms as the underlying policy
2. A self-contained policy subject to its own terms only
3. A combination of the two types above

A following-form excess policy covers a liability loss that exceeds the underlying limits *only if the loss is covered by the underlying insurance.* To illustrate, assume that an insured has an underlying liability policy with an each occurrence limit of $1,000,000 and a following-form excess policy with an each occurrence limit of $1,000,000. If a claimant obtains a judgment of $1,250,000 against the insured for bodily injury covered by the underlying policy, the underlying policy will pay the each occurrence limit of $1,000,000, and the excess policy will pay the remaining $250,000. The application of the primary and excess policies to the claim is illustrated in Exhibit 13-3.

Exhibit 13-3
Application of Primary and Excess Liability Policies

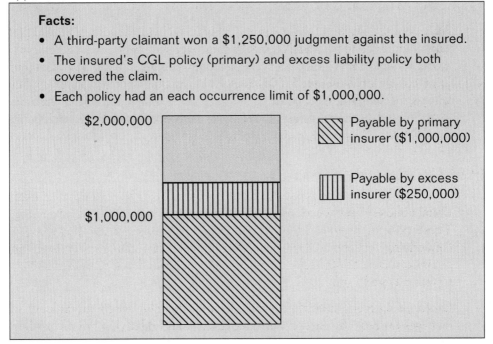

Facts:
- A third-party claimant won a $1,250,000 judgment against the insured.
- The insured's CGL policy (primary) and excess liability policy both covered the claim.
- Each policy had an each occurrence limit of $1,000,000.

$2,000,000

$1,000,000

Payable by primary insurer ($1,000,000)

Payable by excess insurer ($250,000)

A self-contained excess policy applies to a loss that exceeds the underlying limits *only if the loss is also covered under the terms of the excess policy.* For example, the excess policy may not cover injury within the products-completed operations hazard, even though the underlying policy does. In that case, the excess policy will not pay for a products liability claim, even though the claim was covered by the underlying policy and exceeded the each occurrence limit of the underlying policy.

Alternatively, an excess policy may combine both of the above approaches by incorporating the provisions of the underlying policy and then modifying those provisions with additional conditions or exclusions in the excess policy.

Umbrella Liability Insurance

The term "umbrella liability" is generally used to describe a type of excess insurance that is broader than ordinary excess liability policies. Although ordinary excess policies may apply in excess of only one underlying policy, an **umbrella liability policy** provides excess coverage over several primary policies, such as CGL, auto liability, and employers liability. The distinguishing feature of umbrella liability policies is coverage that is broader in some respects than that of the underlying policies, thus providing primary coverage for certain occurrences that would not be covered by any of the underlying policies. In contrast, ordinary excess liability policies tend to be on the same terms as the underlying coverage or even on narrower terms than the underlying.

An umbrella liability policy thus performs three functions. Like an ordinary excess liability policy, it (1) provides additional limits above the each occurrence limits of the insured's primary policies and (2) takes the place of the primary insurance when primary aggregate limits are reduced or exhausted. In addition, it (3) covers some claims that are not covered by the insured's primary policies, subject to a retention (an amount of loss retained by the insured).

Drop-Down Coverage

The latter two functions—providing primary coverage when either the underlying aggregate limits are exhausted or the underlying policy simply does not cover the type of loss that has occurred—are often referred to as **drop-down coverage**.

To illustrate the first function of drop-down coverage (which may also be performed by an ordinary excess policy), assume that a manufacturer has the following policies:

1. A CGL policy with an each occurrence limit of $1,000,000 and a products-completed operations aggregate limit of $2,000,000

2. An umbrella policy with an each occurrence limit of $5,000,000 and an aggregate limit of $10,000,000

During one policy period, the primary CGL insurer pays products liability claims totaling $1,800,000, leaving only $200,000 under the CGL policy for additional products claims during that policy period. If the insured is held liable for an additional judgment of $300,000, the CGL insurer will pay $200,000 and the umbrella policy will "drop down" to pay the additional $100,000 that would have been payable by the CGL insurer if the aggregate limit had not been reduced. Furthermore, since the exhaustion of the underlying policy's limit ends that insurer's duty to defend, the excess or umbrella policy will defend all other claims during the period unless its limit is also exhausted.

As an example of the second aspect of drop-down coverage, assume that a manufacturer has a CGL policy and an umbrella liability policy. A products liability suit is brought against the manufacturer in a country not included in the CGL coverage territory. The CGL policy covers products liability worldwide but only if the suit is first made in the United States or Canada. Thus, in this case, the CGL policy does not apply. However, if the umbrella policy does not contain the same territorial restriction on products suits, it will "drop down" and pay the claim as though it were the primary policy.

When a claim covered by the umbrella policy is not covered at all by any primary policy, the drop-down coverage is subject to a retention (also known as a **self-insured retention** or **SIR**). If the retention shown in the umbrella is $25,000, for example, the umbrella will pay that part of the claim that exceeds $25,000, subject to the applicable limits of insurance under the umbrella policy. (See Exhibit 13-4.) Retentions vary in amount, from as low as $500 for a very small business to $1,000,000 or more for the largest businesses. In many policies, particularly those issued to small businesses, the retention does not apply to defense costs. Coverage for these costs is provided in full, often referred to as "first-dollar defense coverage."

The retention does *not* apply when the umbrella is (1) paying in excess of a claim covered by the primary policy or (2) dropping down to pay a claim because the primary policy's aggregate limit has been exhausted.

Required Underlying Limits

Each insurer writing umbrella liability policies has its own requirements for the types and amounts of underlying insurance that the insured must have. For

Exhibit 13-4
Application of Umbrella Policy to Claim Not Covered by Primary Policy

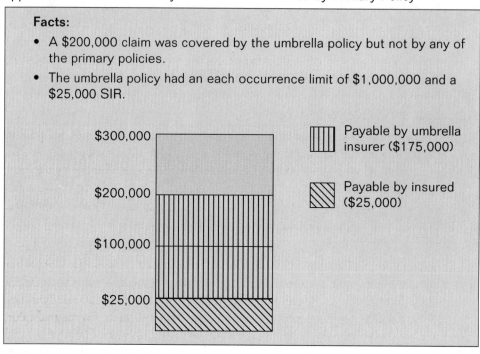

Facts:

- A $200,000 claim was covered by the umbrella policy but not by any of the primary policies.

- The umbrella policy had an each occurrence limit of $1,000,000 and a $25,000 SIR.

$300,000
$200,000
$100,000
$25,000

Payable by umbrella insurer ($175,000)

Payable by insured ($25,000)

example, an umbrella insurer might require the insured to have the following primary coverages and limits:

Commercial General Liability

- $1,000,000 each occurrence
- $2,000,000 general aggregate
- $2,000,000 completed operations aggregate

Business Auto Liability

- $1,000,000 combined single limit

Employers Liability

- $100,000 bodily injury each accident
- $100,000 bodily injury by disease each employee
- $500,000 disease aggregate

The umbrella limits apply in full in excess of each of the underlying coverages. Thus, if an insured with the underlying limits shown above also carried a

$10,000,000 umbrella policy, the total coverage available for one occurrence covered by the CGL policy and the umbrella would be $11,000,000 ($1,000,000 primary plus $10,000,000 umbrella), but the total coverage for one employers liability claim would be only $10,100,000 ($100,000 primary plus $10,000,000 umbrella). If the umbrella policy included a $25,000 retention for coverages it provided on exposures not covered in the primary policies, the $10,000,000 coverage would apply above the $25,000 retention.

Aggregate Umbrella Limits

The previous example ignores any aggregate limit in the umbrella policy. Almost all umbrella policies now contain aggregate limits that operate like the aggregate limits in the primary insurance. In some cases, the aggregate limit applies to all claims under the umbrella; in other cases, the aggregate limit applies only to coverages that are subject to an aggregate in the underlying policies.

If the umbrella policy in the previous example included an aggregate limit, then the total available insurance would be reduced by payments on other claims covered by the umbrella policy. For example, assume that the umbrella policy described in the example had a $10,000,000 each occurrence limit *and a $10,000,000 aggregate limit.* Assuming also that no other claims had been paid by either policy, if a $3,000,000 premises liability claim was paid ($1,000,000 by the primary policy and $2,000,000 by the umbrella), only $9,000,000 would be available for the next covered claim—$1,000,000 (the balance of the underlying aggregate) from the primary policy and $8,000,000 (the balance of the umbrella aggregate) from the umbrella.

Broad Insuring Agreement

Many umbrella liability policies contain one comprehensive insuring agreement instead of several specific ones. A common approach is for the insurer to promise to pay "ultimate net loss" in excess of the "underlying limit" that the insured becomes legally obligated to pay as damages for bodily injury, property damage, personal injury, or advertising injury arising out of an occurrence to which the policy applies.

"Ultimate net loss" is typically defined as the total amount that the insured is legally obligated to pay as damages for a covered claim. It may or may not include defense costs related to the claim. Often, defense costs are payable in addition to the umbrella limits, in which case defense costs would not be included in "ultimate net loss."

"Underlying limit" is usually defined to mean either (1) the limit of the applicable coverage listed in the umbrella policy's schedule of underlying insurance or (2) if the underlying insurance does not apply, the self-insured retention shown in the umbrella declarations. If, for example, ultimate net loss of $2,500,000 is covered by underlying insurance totaling $1,000,000, the umbrella insurer will pay the difference between those amounts, $1,500,000.

The definitions of bodily injury, property damage, personal injury, and advertising injury in an umbrella policy may differ from those in the underlying policies. For example, personal injury could be defined to include an offense, such as discrimination, that is not covered by the underlying insurance.

Some umbrella policies have broader, or additional, insuring agreements to cover exposures such as employee benefits liability or professional liability. However, these coverages are not always available under umbrella liability policies. If an insured wants higher limits for its more unusual types of liability insurance, the coverage must usually be arranged under a separate excess liability policy covering only that specific type of liability.

Occurrence and Claims-Made Coverage Triggers

Umbrella policies are usually occurrence forms. However, the underlying primary policies sometimes include both occurrence and claims-made coverages (such as a claims-made CGL policy and an occurrence-basis auto liability policy). In addition, some insurers will provide only claims-made umbrellas even when the primary coverage is written on an occurrence basis.

Gaps in coverage can occur when the umbrella or excess policy has a different coverage trigger than the underlying coverage. To avoid this problem, some insurers provide both occurrence and claims-made triggers in their umbrella policies. These policies provide that the trigger for the umbrella coverage will be the same as that used for the underlying coverage.

Exclusions

Like a CGL or an auto liability policy, an umbrella liability policy contains exclusions that restrict the broad coverage granted by the insuring agreement. Although the exclusions of umbrella policies resemble those found in underlying policies, there is usually some variation. In fact, much of the broadened coverage provided by umbrella liability policies is achieved by using exclusions in the umbrella policy that have narrower application than the exclusions of the underlying policies.

To illustrate, an umbrella policy might contain a watercraft exclusion that is stated not to apply to any watercraft, owned or nonowned, less than *fifty* feet long. In contrast, the watercraft exclusion of the underlying CGL coverage form is stated not to apply to nonowned watercraft less than *twenty-six* feet long. Consequently, the umbrella policy will provide drop-down coverage for owned boats less than fifty feet long and for nonowned boats between twenty-six and fifty feet long.

Sometimes, an umbrella policy may not contain any equivalent to an exclusion in the underlying policies. For example, some umbrella policies do not contain any watercraft exclusion. With such a policy, claims arising out of incidental ownership, maintenance, or use of watercraft would be covered. (However, if the policy application shows that the insured owns watercraft at the policy inception, underlying watercraft liability coverage would most likely be required.)

Another possibility is that the umbrella policy will contain an exclusion that does not exist in any of the underlying policies. Although an umbrella policy ordinarily provides broader coverage than the underlying policies in some ways, it may provide narrower coverage than the underlying insurance in other ways.

Conditions

The principal differences between the general conditions of primary liability policies and umbrella policies concern maintenance of underlying insurance and the coverage territory.

Maintenance of Underlying Insurance

The **maintenance of underlying insurance condition** expresses the insured's agreement to maintain all required underlying coverages in full force and effect during the policy period, except to the extent that their aggregate limits become reduced by payment of claims. The insured further agrees to notify the insurer promptly if any underlying policy is changed or replaced by a policy issued by another insurer.

If the underlying insurance is not maintained, the umbrella policy will apply as though the underlying insurance *had* been maintained. That is, a claim that would have been covered by an underlying policy, had it been kept in force, will only be covered for the amount that exceeds the limit of the underlying policy. The umbrella policy will not drop down to pay claims that would have been covered by the required underlying policy.

Because of a clause usually included in the "maintenance of underlying" provision, it is extremely important to make sure that the inception and expiration dates of all underlying policies are the same as those of the umbrella policy. Failure to maintain concurrent inception and expiration dates can result in situations in which the umbrella policy will not drop down to pay claims when aggregate limits in a primary policy are exhausted.

Coverage Territory

Most umbrella policies provide worldwide coverage, in contrast with the more limited coverage territories ordinarily found in primary policies. However, some umbrella policies require that suit be brought in the United States or Canada.

Surety Bonds

In its most fundamental form, suretyship represents the promise of one person (called the surety) to answer for the failure of another person (called the principal) to do something as promised. Suretyship, in this sense, has been used since the beginnings of civilization. Suretyship today is usually conducted by insurance companies and is evidenced by a written contract called a **surety bond**. Surety bonds are used to provide a wide range of guarantees.

Surety Bonds Contrasted With Insurance

Although there are many different types of surety bonds, they share four qualities that distinguish them from most property and liability insurance policies:

1. There are three parties to the contract.
2. The principal is liable to the surety for losses paid by the surety.
3. The surety expects no losses on the surety contracts.
4. The coverage period is indefinite.

Three Parties

A surety bond is a contract that involves three parties—the **surety**, the **obligee**, and the **principal**. The surety (usually an insurance company) guarantees to the obligee that the principal will fulfill an obligation or perform as promised. For example, a surety could guarantee that a construction contractor (principal) will complete a building for a property owner (obligee) in accordance with the construction contract.

Principal Liable to Surety

If the principal fails to fulfill the obligation, the surety must either fulfill the obligation or indemnify the obligee. However, the principal becomes liable to the surety to the extent of the surety's expenditures. The surety bond, in other words, pays the obligee's loss, not the principal's, even though the principal pays the premium.

Surety Expects No Losses

Before issuing a surety bond, a surety examines the prospective principal's qualifications. A principal's qualifications are sometimes summed up as the "three Cs"—capital, capacity, and character:

1. Capital. Does the principal have sufficient funds and credit to finance the project and all other ongoing work?

2. Capacity. Does the principal have the skill, experience, staff, and equipment to successfully execute the work?

3. Character. Does the principal have a reputation for honoring agreements even when there are adverse developments?

At least in theory, no surety bond is issued unless the surety is satisfied that the principal is capable of performing the obligation that is the subject of the surety bond. In issuing a surety bond, the surety is attesting to the principal's ability to perform. In some cases, the surety will require that the principal post collateral to make sure that the principal will be able to repay the surety if the surety has to perform on behalf of the principal.

Indefinite Coverage Period

Surety bonds ordinarily do not terminate until the principal has fulfilled its obligations, which may take only a few days or as long as many years. Consequently, surety bonds are not issued as year-to-year contracts, and they normally do not allow either the surety or the principal to cancel them.

However, some types of surety bonds may be cancelable. Typically, bonds allowing cancellation require the surety to give notice of cancellation to the obligee. Cancellation becomes effective a certain number of days thereafter as stipulated in the bond itself or provided by law or regulation.

Other Characteristics of Surety Bonds

Other characteristics of surety bonds (which do not necessarily represent a contrast with property and liability insurance contracts) include the statutory nature of some surety bonds and the use of a limit.

Statutory Nature of Bonds

Many bonds are required by municipal ordinance or federal or state regulations or statutes. The provisions of statutory bonds, and therefore the obligations of the three parties to the bond, are spelled out in the law. Other bonds are not required by statute. The need for a nonstatutory bond is usually established in the contract between the obligee and the principal. For example, a construction contract between a private owner and a contractor may require the contractor to obtain certain types of contract bonds.

Bond Limit

A bond is written for a set limit, sometimes called the "penalty." If the principal's obligation exceeds the limit, the surety will be liable only for the amount of the limit. However, like liability insurance policies, some bonds pay court costs and interest on judgments in addition to the stated limit. If the obligee's actual loss is less than the limit, most surety bonds provide only for the payment of the actual loss. Some surety bonds are issued on a forfeiture basis, meaning that the entire amount of the bond is paid if the principal defaults.

Types of Surety Bonds

There is no single form of bond suitable for the many circumstances that may require bonding. The many different types of surety bonds can be grouped into the following five broad categories:

1. Contract bonds
2. License and permit bonds
3. Public official bonds
4. Judicial bonds
5. Federal noncontract surety bonds

Contract Bonds

Contract bonds guarantee the fulfillment of contract obligations. In many cases, contract bonds relate to construction contracts. However, some contract bonds cover other types of contracts, such as a supplier's obligation to furnish supplies and materials for a certain period at an agreed price. The most common types of contract bonds are bid bonds, performance bonds, payment bonds, and maintenance bonds.

Bid Bonds

Before awarding a supply or construction contract, the obligee may require a bid bond from each bidder. A **bid bond** guarantees that the bidder will actually enter into the contract at the price bid. If the principal fails to fulfill this obligation, the surety will pay the obligee the difference between the amount of the principal's bid and the bid finally accepted, plus any additional expenses incurred because of the contractor's default.

Performance Bonds

If awarded the contract, the principal must usually provide a performance bond. The **performance bond** guarantees the obligee that work will be completed in accordance with the contract. If the contractor defaults, the surety will be responsible for completing the work or paying damages to the obligee.

In some cases, a surety will find that its principal is in danger of defaulting before work actually comes to a standstill. Depending on the circumstances, the surety may take steps to help the contractor complete the work, such as lending money to the contractor, guaranteeing bank credit, or providing consultation services.

Payment Bonds

Also called a labor and material bond, a **payment bond** guarantees that the contractor/principal will pay when due all of the labor and material bills arising out of the work that the contractor is obligated to perform. This guarantee is important to the owner because if subcontractors and suppliers are not paid, they may file liens against the owner's property, impairing the owner's title to the property. The payment guarantee is usually included in the contractor's performance bond but may be issued in a separate bond.

Maintenance Bonds

A **maintenance bond** guarantees the principal's work against defects in workmanship or materials for a specified period after the project is completed. Some performance bonds automatically include this coverage without an additional charge for one year.

License and Permit Bonds

Cities, states, and other political subdivisions often require persons or organizations wishing to engage in a particular business or trade to obtain a *license*. Similarly, a person or an organization wishing to exercise a particular privilege in connection with its business may be required to obtain a *permit*.

Before a license or permit is granted, the applicant is commonly required to obtain a license bond or a permit bond. A **license bond** provides payment to the obligee (the state, city, or other public entity) for loss or damage resulting from violations by the licensee of the duties and obligations imposed on the licensee. A **permit bond** serves the same purpose with respect to the duties and obligations imposed on a permit holder. For example, an operator of a liquor store may have to post a bond guaranteeing that it will not sell liquor in violation of alcoholic beverage control laws.

Public Official Bonds

Certain types of public officials are required by law to have bonds that protect the public against the official's failure to perform his or her duties faithfully and honestly. Officials generally required to obtain such **public official bonds** are those whose duties involve the handling of public funds, the seizure and disposition of property, the arrest or detention of persons, or any other duties that could result in violation of the rights of others. Among the public officials required to be bonded are treasurers, tax collectors, sheriffs and deputies, police officers, judges and court clerks, notaries public, insurance commissioners, and bank examiners.

Judicial Bonds

A **judicial bond** is a statutory bond guaranteeing that a person or an organization will fulfill all obligations that the court or the law imposes on the person or organization. Judicial bonds are either fiduciary bonds or court bonds.

Fiduciary Bonds

Fiduciary bonds are commonly required of persons selected or approved by courts to perform certain duties that involve holding property in trust for the benefit of others. For example, probate courts frequently appoint administrators to settle estates of deceased persons who died without wills, to appoint guardians of minors, and to appoint conservators of estates of incompetent persons. A person who is appointed to any of these positions by a court is required to post a fiduciary bond with the court. The bond guarantees that the principal will faithfully perform all duties as prescribed by law or as specified by the court.

Court Bonds

Court bonds are often required by courts in connection with lawsuits. For example, if a defendant wishes to appeal an adverse court decision, he or she must provide an appeal bond guaranteeing that the judgment will be paid if the appeal is unsuccessful.

Court bonds are also required in connection with disputes over the ownership of personal property. As an illustration, A might ask the court to compel B to return property that A claims belongs to A. The court will likely require both A and B to post court bonds until the case is decided. A's bond will guarantee that A will pay B any damages resulting from this action if it is decided in B's favor. B's bond will guarantee that B will turn the property over to A if the case is decided in A's favor.

Federal Surety Bonds

Federal surety bonds include bonds required by federal agencies that regulate activities such as immigration, the manufacture or distribution of alcohol and tobacco products, and importing and exporting. Because these bonds pose special risks, sureties often require the principal to post cash collateral in connection with the bond.

Summary

Various policies are available for covering special exposures not insured under the more common forms of commercial insurance.

Professional liability policies cover liability for the failure to use the degree of skill expected of a person in a particular field. These policies are needed by physicians, lawyers, architects, engineers, insurance agents and brokers, and persons engaged in many other occupations.

Directors and officers liability policies cover corporate directors and officers against their personal liability for wrongful acts in the scope of their corporate duties. D&O liability insurance also covers the corporation for all sums it is required or permitted by law to pay as indemnification of its directors and officers.

Employment practices liability insurance covers an employer and its employees against claims alleging various employment-related offenses such as wrongful termination, sexual harassment, and discrimination.

Two types of liability insurance are available for covering liabilities arising out of duties imposed by the common law and the Employee Retirement Income Security Act (ERISA) on fiduciaries of employee benefit plans:

- Employee benefits liability insurance covers the employer (and in some cases the employees acting on its behalf) against liability for *administrative* errors and omissions (such as failing to enroll an employee in a plan).
- Fiduciary liability insurance covers plan fiduciaries against liability for doing harm to employee benefit plans through *discretionary* errors and omissions (such as investing plan assets unwisely).

An aircraft insurance policy can include the following coverages:

- Hull (physical damage) insurance, covering the insured aircraft on an "all-risks" basis for either "ground and flight" or "not in motion."
- Liability insurance, covering liability for bodily injury and property damage resulting from the ownership, maintenance, or use of the insured aircraft.

- Aircraft medical payments insurance, covering medical or funeral expenses incurred by occupants of the insured aircraft.

- Passenger voluntary settlement coverage, providing scheduled benefits if a passenger suffers death, dismemberment, or loss of sight.

Most organizations need higher limits of liability insurance than those provided by their CGL, commercial auto, and other primary liability policies. The higher limits can be provided by an excess liability policy or an umbrella liability policy. Both types of policies pay damages that exceed the per occurrence or aggregate limits of underlying policies. An umbrella policy may also cover, subject to a self-insured retention, claims that are not covered under any of the insured's primary policies.

In a surety bond, the surety (which is usually an insurance company) guarantees to the obligee that the principal will fulfill an obligation or perform as promised. If the principal does not perform as promised, the surety must fulfill the obligation or indemnify the obligee. The major categories of surety bonds include (1) contract bonds, (2) license and permit bonds, (3) public official bonds, (4) judicial bonds, and (5) federal surety bonds.

Chapter Notes

1. "Professional Liability and Claims Made Coverage" (St. Paul, MN: St. Paul Fire and Marine Ins. Co., Rev. 6-94), p. 1.

2. American Casualty Company v. Hartford Insurance Company, 479 So.2d 577 (1985), cited by Westchester Chapter CPCU Research Committee, Jerome Trupin, chairman, in "Problems with Personal Injury Liability Insurance for Professionals" (Malvern, PA: CPCU Society, 1990), p. 11.

3. "CNA: The D&O Market," *Viewpoint* (Chicago, IL: CNA Insurance Companies, Fourth Quarter, 1992), p. 10.

4. 1993 and 1994 editions of the *Wyatt D&O Liability Survey Summary* (Chicago, IL: The Wyatt Co.), p. 6.

5. Derived from an unpublished study on employment practices liability insurance, prepared by Betterly Risk Consultants, Inc., Worcester, MA.

6. *Black's Law Dictionary*, 6th ed., s.v. "fiduciary."

7. Marie Reubi and Jill Foster, "Current Award Trends," *Personal Injury Valuation Handbook* (Horsham, PA: LRP Publications, Inc., 1994), p. 56.

Bibliography

Betterly Risk Consultants, Inc. Unpublished study on employment practices liability insurance. Worcester, MA.

"CNA: The D&O Market." *Viewpoint.* Chicago, IL: CNA Insurance Companies, Fourth Quarter, 1992.

O'Reilly, Brian. "J&J is on a Roll." *Fortune Magazine.* December 26, 1994, pp. 178-192.

"Professional Liability and Claims Made Coverage." St. Paul, MN: St. Paul Fire and Marine Ins. Co., Rev. 6-94.

Reubi, Marie, and Jill Foster. "Current Award Trends." *Personal Injury Valuation Handbook.* Horsham, PA: LRP Publications, Inc., 1994.

Trieschmann, James S., et al. *Commercial Property Insurance and Risk Management.* 4th ed. Malvern, PA: American Institute for CPCU, 1994.

Westchester Chapter CPCU Research Committee. "Problems with Personal Injury Liability Insurance for Professionals." Malvern, PA: CPCU Society, 1990.

Wyatt D&O Liability Survey Summary. Chicago, IL: The Wyatt Co., 1993 and 1994 editions.

Index

D

G

H

I

J

L

M

T

U